WRITTEN BY THE BODY

Indigenous Americas

Robert Warrior, Series Editor

WRITTEN BY THE BODY

Gender Expansiveness and Indigenous Non-Cis Masculinities

LISA TATONETTI

Indigenous Americas

University of Minnesota Press | Minneapolis | London

Portions of chapter 1 are adapted from "The Indigenous Erotics of Riding Bareback, or, the West Has Always Been Queer," *WLA 50th Anniversary*, special issue edited by Susan Bernardin and Krista Comer, *Western American Literature* 53, no. 1 (2018): 1–10. Portions of chapter 5 were originally published as "Carole laFavor's Indigenous Feminism and Early HIV/AIDS Activism: Health Sovereignty in the 1980s and 1990s," in *Global Indigenous Health: Reconciliation, Engaging, Decolonizing*, edited by Robert Henry, Amanda LaVallee, Nancy Van Styvendale, and Robert Alexander Innes, 275–94 (Tucson: University of Arizona Press, 2018). Portions of chapter 5 were originally published as "Detecting Two-Spirit Erotics: The Fiction of Carole laFavor," in *Native American Men–Women, Lesbians, Two-Spirits: Contemporary and Historical Perspectives*, special issue edited by Sabine Lang, *Journal of Lesbian Studies* 20, no. 3–4 (2016): 372–87. Portions of chapter 6 were originally published as "Affect, Female Masculinity, and the Embodied Space Between: Two-Spirit Traces in Thirza Cuthand's Experimental Film," in *Sexual Rhetorics: Methods, Identities, Publics*, edited by Jonathan Alexander and Jacqueline Rhodes, 211–33 (New York: Routledge, 2016); reprinted with permission of The Licensor through PLSclear. Portions of chapter 6 were published as "Two-Spirit, Not Trans: Joshua Whitehead's Erotic Sovereignty," in *Male Femininities*, edited by Dana Berkowitz, Elroi J. Windsor, and Chong-suk Han (New York: New York University Press, forthcoming).

Excerpts from Carrie House's poetry are reprinted with permission of the author.

Cover art, *Sisters of War*, used by permission of artist, Jolene Nenibah Yazzie.

Published by the University of Minnesota Press
111 Third Avenue South, Suite 290
Minneapolis, MN 55401-2520
http://www.upress.umn.edu

ISBN 978-1-5179-0603-0 (hc)
IBSN 978-1-5179-0604-7 (pb)
Library of Congress record available at https://lccn.loc.gov/2021022966.

Printed in the United States of America on acid-free paper

The University of Minnesota is an equal-opportunity educator and employer.

28 27 26 25 24 23 22 21   10 9 8 7 6 5 4 3 2 1

For my mom, Edna May Tatonetti,
who taught me bravery and kindness, in equal measure

CONTENTS

ACKNOWLEDGMENTS

Thanks to Kansas State University and the National Humanities Center for their support of the project.

I'd like to warmly acknowledge the many friends and colleagues who have supported this work, whether by reading and commenting on parts of the manuscript, by writing letters of support, or by writing and talking with me, including Kirby Brown, Val Padilla Carroll, Jim Cox, Qwo-Li Driskill, Rebecca Goetz, Audrey Goodman, Michele Janette, Meta DuEwa Jones, Daniel Heath Justice, Abby Knoblauch, Cameron Leader-Picone, Rachel Levitt, Anuja Madan, Sam McKegney, Dian Million (an initial reader for the manuscript proposal and theoretical mind-blower), Tara Pauliny, Julie Velasquez Runk, Honor Sachs, Tom Sarmiento, Katie Walkiewicz, and Harlan Weaver.

To my academic family—Chad Allen, Susan Bernardin, and Joanna Hearne—you hold me up, read all the things, and make me smarter. I love you peeps.

Heartfelt appreciation to Theresa LaFavor for multiple interviews about her mother, Carole laFavor, and likewise to Sharon Day and Irene Vernon for interviews, to Jolene Nenibah Yazzie for her incredible art for the book cover, and to Carrie House and Kai Minosh Pyle for poetry permissions.

Thanks and love, as well, to my superfriends for fierce support, baked goods, and laughter: Jenn Anthony, Tanya González, Val Padilla Carroll, and Krista Walton.

Much appreciation to my coconspirators in the Indigenous Faculty and Staff Alliance: LaVerne Bitsie-Baldwin, Debra Bolton, Brandon Haddock, Alex Red Corn, and Audrey Swartz.

Special love to my sisters, Nancy and Judy, and to Dan, Cam, Rob, and Deb. We made it through the difficult year of mom's illness and death together. She wasn't perfect, but she was so loved, and, in the end, she gave us each other.

TEXT, ARCHIVE, AND ACTION
The Body in Motion

> This, I think, is where kinship is of particular importance, especially for Indigenous peoples. The "I" in *I am one* stands in meaningful relation to the "we" in *we exist*. Together they're an affirmation not only of individual survival, but of a community connected beyond the self. Relationships require bodies; bodies connect; connections make good relations possible and meaningful.
>
> —Daniel Heath Justice, *Why Indigenous Literatures Matter*

On November 30, 2018, Kansas representative-elect Sharice Davids did a series of "good luck" push-ups on the floor of the Rayburn House Office Building in Washington, D.C., as she waited for the member-elect lottery draw that determines office locations. Pictures of her smiling black-clad figure made the rounds of Twitter and filled the daily news rotation. Davids, a member of the Ho-Chunk Nation, an attorney, and a Cornell graduate, was the first openly queer person elected to represent Kansas in Congress. As a settler resident of Kansas who teaches queer Indigenous literatures on the ancestral lands of the Kaw, Osage, and Pawnee and regularly allies with Indigenous partners to make change here, I supported Davids's campaign, shed tears when she won her seat, and cheered these photographs. In the media coverage of the event, which was fairly widespread, I found out that only five years earlier, in November 2013, Davids had logged another victory—that time in her first professional mixed martial arts fight. The story of her previous career came up repeatedly in the short period in which the media made much of Davids's athletic performance. That publicity spectacularized the freshman House member's athleticism and humor—she did, as undoubtedly intended, make "an impact," to use her words.

There was much to love about that impact and this coverage, just as there had been in Davids's campaign. Key among them were not only the circulation of the striking images that she purposefully disseminated but also the ways in which this performance highlighted the affective power of the body, a key concern of *Written by the Body: Gender Expansiveness and Indigenous Non-Cis Masculinities.* In these interactions, Davids's body had weight beyond its physical mass. At the most basic level, her image, her body bespoke anomaly—a newly elected representative doing calisthenics on the plush carpets of Capitol Hill? Davids's lean horizontal plane—fitted black pants, knee-length boots, arms supporting her frame in well-practiced form—juxtaposed a line of seated men and women in suits to her left and the tall, long wooden podium to her right where senior members sat with microphones. The pictures spoke of strength, of beauty, of the unexpected. The anomaly wasn't limited to setting or action, however. Davids's very presence as an Indigenous woman broke with the still very white, very male traditions of the U.S. Congress. Davids and Deb Haaland (Laguna Pueblo), a Democratic representative for New Mexico, are, as most readers likely know, the first two Native American women ever elected to the House of Representatives. (There has yet to be an Indigenous woman in the Senate.) Davids is, as well, the first queer woman of color elected to Congress. In this case, then, the somatic intervention of Davids's body on the floor of the Capitol explodes, not just with the pictured kinetic activity, but also with possibility.

The photographs, whether of Davids on the floor or of her standing—arms raised, biceps flexed, in the classic position of body builders—evoked exuberance and confidence. For her supporters there would be laughter mixed with hope and likely, as in my case, a little elation. Yet not all responses to Davids's person have been laudatory. In her 2018 campaign, for instance, the Kansas right categorized Davids as "radical," "risky," and "dangerous," as did the attack ads disseminated by their funding super PACs. Though denied by the party, there were charges from the Kansas Democratic Committee that Republican ad campaigns used "lighting techniques . . . to darken [Davids's] skin in some . . . ads."[1] Kansas Democratic Committee member Chris Reeves stated: "There's a lot of dog whistle going on . . . there's no denying they're trying to say, 'Hey, she's not white.'"[2] Each of these moments—Davids's own purposeful image dissemination and the campaign ads that purportedly used and manipulated such images for their own ends—speaks to the body's affective resonance, of its ability to persuade, to influence, to function as both text and canvas.

The use of images of the Indigenous body for hegemonic ends has been a recurring reality for Native peoples across the globe. For centuries, Indigenous people have been portrayed as by turns dangerous and exotic, debased and desirable, so the fact that such settler resonances arose in the battlefield of Davids's hard-won victory should come as no surprise. Eminently more interesting than the marking of Davids's body as other by the opposing political party is her deployment of her image and athleticism to bolster her political capital. In the pictures, Davids's body is palimpsestic—it indexes physical strength and purposely invokes her history as a professional fighter. It speaks of humor on one hand, inviting audiences in, and tenacity on the other, suggesting notable strength, both corporeal and psychological. As well, given the historic nature of this moment and of her election more broadly, these photos and the resonance of Davids's presence in the highest offices of the settler state carry traces of the powerful Indigenous women and the other queer and gender-variant Indigenous folks who came before her.

WRITTEN BY THE BODY turns on these rich intersections in which the body serves as text, archive, and action, considering stories and spaces where the body holds a deep affective resonance. Looking across the historical record and the literary canon as well as into the realms of documentary film and activism, this book asks how we read the affective power of the body as deployed by Indigenous peoples. In what contexts do bodies become intelligible? How do they become intelligible, and for whom? And within these realms, how do Indigenous gender knowledges serve as embodied narratives of survivance, or what Anishinaabe theorist Gerald Vizenor terms stories that "are renunciations of dominance, tragedy, and victimry"?[3]

Such questions have a deep history that entwines with the way settler-colonial structures have tried—and repeatedly failed—to control and discipline Indigenous bodies and, simultaneously, to enclose and restrict the rich array of Indigenous gender knowledges. If we think here, then, of Sharice Davids's push-ups as signaling bodily strength and power and, in the process, as invoking a symbolic long associated with men in mainstream cultural norms, we can see her as, at the very least, bringing into visibility dominant expectations of gender. In this light, Davids can arguably be read within the long history of Indigenous women, Two-Spirit, and gender-variant peoples who exceed limited and limiting understandings of the body.

Indigenous peoples' destabilization of Spanish, French, and English norms are part of such a history. The historical record offers numerous instances of such disjunctions in which the expansiveness of Indigenous gender traditions came up against the limited understandings of settler-invaders. Tiya Miles observes in *Ties That Bind* that "in the view of federal officials, [Cherokee] lifestyle was backwards and wasteful. They felt that Cherokee men were embarrassingly feminized, that Cherokee women were improperly masculinized."[4] Qwo-Li Driskill makes similar observations in *Asegi Stories*, commenting that the "trope of Cherokee women as 'Amazons'" circulated regularly in narratives of colonization and conquest, "signaling to [the] audience the sexual and gender nonconformity of Cherokee women."[5] Considering the like genealogy in terms of men, masculinities, and settler expectations, Brendan Hokowhitu (Ngāti Pūkenga) notes that "the colonial power complex established invader masculinity through its claim that the invading heterosexual male embodied the power of human reason" and, as a result, that "colonial discourses often aligned Indigenous masculinity with feminine traits. In comparison to an all-knowing and reasoned European masculinity, Indigenous masculinity, sexuality, and reason was [sic] described as passionate, determined by the senses, irrational, intuitive, provocative, and whimsical."[6] As these examples underscore, the discursive terrain of gender and the body has long been a battlefield over which settlers obsessed.

The strictures placed on Indigenous bodies under invasion/colonization are particularly evident in the lives of gender-variant, nonbinary, non-cis, and Two-Spirit people. For instance, Crow tribal historian Joe Medicine Crow tells non-Native anthropologist Walter

Williams of an Indian agent who demanded Crow *badés* (*boté*), or Two-Spirit peoples, conform to Eurowestern performances of masculinity: "The agent incarcerated the badés, cut off their hair, made them wear men's clothing. He forced them to do manual labor, planting . . . trees . . . on the BIA grounds."[7] Likewise, anthropologist Sabine Lang (settler) explains that "in 1879 . . . the only surviving Hidatsa miati (male in a woman's role) was forcibly stripped of her/his female attire by the local government agent, who also dressed her/him in men's clothes and cut off her/his braids."[8] Ohlone Costanoan Esselen Nation writer/theorist Deborah Miranda's work on the gendercide of third-gender or Two-Spirit California Indian peoples offers many further examples of the physical attacks invaders aimed at people whom one Spanish soldier described as exhibiting "an excess so criminal that it seems even forbidden to speak its name."[9] Clearly, these exchanges signal dangerously disparate perspectives on gender intelligibility and the body—the Crow, Hidatsa, and California Indian people referenced here and the conquistadors, officials, settlers, and priests who try to discipline Indigenous bodies and cultural practices read gender performances and norms in profoundly different fashions. As we know, these radically differing readings have had, and continue to have, grave consequences. In each case, though, the affective terrain of the body is part of the equation and is therefore deployed in Indigenous discourses and, at the same time, in the practice of colonization.

This book pays close attention to Indigenous gender expansiveness as well as to how Indigenous people subvert attempts to contain it. More particularly, *Written by the Body* privileges iterations of gender and bodily power as lived and depicted by Indigenous people and considers how such actions and affects move between and among Native peoples to forge kinship, offer protection, and make change. The book focuses most often, then, on those who, like Sharice Davids, exist beyond the strictures of settler norms. Those figures include female-identified, Two-Spirit, and gender-variant warriors; powerful culture bearers and protectors termed here "big moms"; female wildland firefighters; Indigenous activists and leaders; and a number of self-identified non-cis folks whose creative work and actions support their nations in what I term *an erotics of responsibility*. Along the way, these conversations often consider how such folks engage with existing gender expectations, including those surrounding Indigenous and settler masculinities, since, as Hokowhitu points out, masculinity has long been a pivotal juncture at which gender intelligibility breaks down. Indigenous masculinity studies is therefore key to the project; however, on the larger level it is the body and somatic knowledge that serves as a touchstone, again and again, in the work of the writers, filmmakers, and activists centered here. Ultimately, as I'll show, the relay between the body, gender, and affect serves as a fulcrum for Indigenous literatures.

Written by the Body considers these bodily complexities and their attendant affects through the stories of powerful female-identified and gender-variant folks who take on roles that may at times cross into the realm of masculinities. As such, it's essential to note the tensions surrounding Indigenous masculinity studies that have surfaced in online exchanges and blogs, at Native American and Indigenous studies conferences, and in myriad personal discussions.[10] There are serious questions about the emerging field's move toward men and masculinity, perhaps key among them being if such a focus could reify patriarchal, antifeminist gender constructs and privilege a troubling androcentric discourse. Driftpile Cree poet/theorist Billy-Ray Belcourt voices exactly these concerns (and more) in "Can the Other of Native Studies Speak?" In this eloquent commentary on the potential limits of Indigenous studies, Belcourt contends that there "are queernesses that exist outside the traditional and the identitarian borders of indigeneity, ones that the past cannot make sense of because they emerge in the most unexpected places."[11] Belcourt questions the efficacy of Indigenous masculinity studies and argues that Indigenous studies has constituted the very subject it advocates for and that this subject rests on "the form of a Red Power–like warrior." As such, the Indigenous women, gender-variant, queer, trans, and nonbinary folks such as those considered in this book become "something of an ontological nothing, rendered as the object against which Nativeness— only ever properly male—would take shape."[12]

These sorts of obscuring renderings of gender were seen in the struggles over the 1876 Indian Act's misogynistic decree that Indigenous women who married non-Native men lost their tribal status, while non-Native women who married Indigenous men gained tribal status. This colonial mandate prohibited matrilineal inheritance and clan traditions and disenfranchised thousands of Indigenous women and children for more than the next hundred years. However, by the time the challenge came to court, colonial misogyny was, by some, being touted as Indigenous "tradition." Tanana Athabascan scholar Dian Million notes that Bill C-31, "the amendment that abolished the Indian Act's most deliberate sex discrimination, was not passed until 1985. C-31 has never fully alleviated the issues of band membership that the women sought."[13] As well, it was preceded by a legal battle that included both Indigenous and non-Indigenous opposition to the reinstatement of women's rightful status. This androcentric rhetoric was fueled by the settler norms the original act instantiated when it attempted to write a patriarchal narrative of inheritance and lineage over extant kinship models.[14] The Indian Act's claims about Indigenous kinship and status were wedded to heteropatriarchal settler demands that women be removed from traditional positions of power, rendering them, as Belcourt suggests, "something of an ontological nothing . . . the object against which Nativeness—only ever properly male—would take shape."[15]

Based on the previous example, there is precedent for the concerns that have been voiced about Indigenous masculinity studies, as seen, for example, in the face-to-face and online discussions that followed the 2016 workshop on Indigenous masculinities at that year's Native American and Indigenous Studies meeting. These conversations underscore the necessity of foregrounding nondominant iterations of gender such as female-identified, gender-variant, Two-Spirit, nonbinary, gender-fluid, and trans masculinities alongside considerations of cishet masculinity. Considering how non-cis folks more broadly—non-cis femmes and trans men, for example—negotiate, or even nullify, expectations of masculinity can undermine the reification of masculinity as any sort of natural or essential identity tied to people identified male at birth. Examining the multiple ways in which such folks engage masculinity and the body demonstrates, at the most basic level, that popular culture's hypermasculine warrior ethos is a socially engineered and inadequate understanding of the myriad ways in which Indigenous peoples live and deploy gender. Alternative, nondominant, and/or non-cis gender studies of Indigenous activisms, literatures, and films show that *masculinity is a cultural construct that shifts in context, force, and intelligibility in every iterative assemblage*. The literatures, lives, films, and activisms analyzed in this book, which range from the eighteenth-century historical accounts of warriors to current artistic productions by overtly queer and/or gender variant writers, activists, and artists, underline the fact that gender is an embodied knowledge that Indigenous peoples use as shield, as tool, or simply as play, every day.

Ultimately, an Indigenous masculinity studies that investigates how masculinities are performed outside cisgender regimes effectively queers colonial masculinity and highlights the multiple avenues by which Indigenous peoples refuse rather than reify heteropatriarchal gender norms. One such way to imagine otherwise can be found in the iterations of gender expansiveness depicted in the embodied art and activism of Indigenous peoples. To quote Belcourt and Cree, Saulteaux, and Métis theorist/writer/curator Lindsay Nixon, these imaginings "open up a space for critique that might flower queer, trans and two-spirit possibility."[16]

Masculinities outside Cishet Confines

Jack Halberstam's 1998 monograph, *Female Masculinity*, begins by asking: "What is 'masculinity'? . . . If masculinity is not the social and cultural and indeed political expression of maleness, then what is it?"[17] By looking across bodies and locations to consider this question—from nineteenth-century "tribades" and "female husbands," to early-twentieth-century "inverts," to stone butches, to trans men, to drag kings—Halberstam repeatedly demonstrates the diversity of masculinities. Throughout *Female Masculinity* he contends that while there is no single, definitive description of masculinity, "masculinity must not and cannot and should not reduce down to the male body and its effects."[18] In *Masculinities without Men?*—to date the only book-length consideration of female masculinity in literature—J. Bobby Noble likewise comments that

> contemporary studies in masculinity have intensified masculinity as a heteronormative and anxious imperative, shifting the terms from straightforward descriptions of maleness to a critical exploration of "masculinity" as a complex set of meanings. This field of inquiry suggests that masculinity (and by implica-

tion, female masculinity) is a category that alters across time, region, social class, and ethnicity.[19]

Noble's suggestion that cishet masculinity functions as an "anxious imperative" aligns with Driskill's *Asegi Stories*, which uses archival sources to demonstrate that genders and sexualities—in particular, concerns surrounding what settler-invaders historically perceived as properly performed masculinity—are intrinsic to settler rationales for colonization and conquest. These anxious masculinities have a long and troubled history on Turtle Island. But as Indigenous studies theorists like Kim Anderson (Cree/Métis), Robert Henry (Métis), Brendan Hokowhitu (Ngāti Pūkenga), Robert Alexander Innes (Plains Cree, Cowessess First Nation), Sam McKegney (settler), and Ty P. Kāwika Tengan (Kanaka Maoli) have suggested more recently, masculinity need not solely be a place of loss. Critical masculinity studies has the potential to re-see, or to use Driskill's formulation, to "re-story," masculinities, especially those that exceed or resist heteronormative imperatives.[20] In fact, it is pivotal to Halberstam's theory that *masculinities become more productive, more useful, and, in fact, more intelligible if desutured from the male body.* He imagines "the possibilities of an active matrix of exchange between male and female masculinities," contending that "if we shift the flow of power and influence, we can easily imagine a plethora of new masculinities that do not simply feed back into a static loop that makes maleness plus power into the formula for abuse."[21]

In comments about an essay that was later published in Innes and Anderson's collection, *Indigenous Men and Masculinities,* one of the reviewers stated that conversations about Indigenous masculinities should focus solely on men—clearly meaning men assigned male at birth, likely cishet—and that contributions on the masculinity of female-identified or gender-variant folks were not appropriate for the collection. Yet as Anderson explains in *A Recognition of Being,* historically there has always been play, always been movement, in acts and roles:

> Although Indigenous men and women had different spheres
> of work, they were not restricted from engaging in each other's
> work. . . . Native women had to learn essential trapping and
> hunting skills, and many contemporary women recall watching

> their grandmothers hunt, fish and trap. . . . Many nations also had greater flexibility around the gendered work roles. For example, there have always been a small number of Native women warriors in the various nations.[22]

Therefore, gender roles that in settler terms could be deemed "masculine" would not be perceived as such in Native nations—Laguna Pueblo author Leslie Marmon Silko's stories of her aunties fixing roofs and cars come to mind. Likewise, the reciprocal responsibility that shapes the roles of Haudenosaunee women, the protective acts of Beloved Women within the Cherokee clan structure, and the existence of warrior women (the focus of chapters 1 and 2) are well-known examples of female-identified people taking on occupations and/or culturally sanctioned positions that exceed any sort of binaristic understanding of gender. In addition to having roles in land allocations, clan affiliations, and conflict resolution, the women in such examples hold power, authority, and respect both within and outside the household. In these points they fit settler concepts of masculinity that situate the circulation of such cultural capital in ideologies of heteromasculinity. However, in the Indigenous cultures within which they arise, as most readers well know, none of the aforementioned actions would be considered "masculine." In fact, in many cases the very categories of masculinity and femininity themselves fracture when considered within the constellation of Indigenous gender knowledges. In thinking across such questions, then, it's important to note that *noncishet masculinities are not, as sometimes feared, about taking something away from men, but instead about envisioning how gender performances of masculinity can be ongoing, creative sites of knowledge for men, women, Two-Spirit, queer, nonbinary, trans, and gender-variant folks.*

In their introduction to *Indigenous Men and Masculinities*, Innes and Anderson recognize that there are concerns and possibilities specific to Indigenous masculinities. "Indigenous men and those who identify with Indigenous masculinities," they note, "are faced with distinct gender and racial biases that cause many to struggle. . . . At the same time, [there is a] regeneration of positive masculinities currently taking place in many communities that will assist in the restoration of balanced and harmonious relationships."[23] As the work of contemporary Indigenous studies theorists has shown, Indigenous masculinities index very different histories of gender.

Looking specifically at Indigenous masculinities and Hawaiian men in *Native Men Remade: Gender and Nation in Contemporary Hawai'i*, Ty P. Kāwika Tengan suggests that masculinity functions as a form of active Indigenous knowledge rather than as a single, discrete practice or identity. In particular, Tengan understands masculinity as a decolonial practice that has the potential to link Hawaiian men to the "religious formations, political systems, cultural practices, and relationships to land that [their] ancestors knew."[24] This is not a nostalgic return, but instead a conscious process in which "projects of nationalism, decolonization, revitalization, and reclamation produce new subjectivities of culture and gender, reworked by Hawaiian men."[25] Tengan notes that this work recognizes, and at times redresses, a number of ongoing problems, including settler-colonial incursions into traditional cultural practices and damaging stereotypes that cast Native men as violent and misogynist.

Such deconstructive analyses are radically important given that, as Brian Klopotek (Choctaw) explains, "for at least the last century, hypermasculinity has been one of the foremost attributes of the Indian world that whites have imagined. . . . These imagined Indian nations comprise an impossibly masculine race. Because of such perpetually outlandish representations of Indian gender, masculinity has become a crucial arena for contesting unrealistic images of Indians."[26] Tengan, likewise, notes that Indigenous men are also often associated with violence and that "local popular, literary, and scholarly depictions of Hawaiian men often highlight the negative stereotypes associated with the ills of colonization: high incidence of suicide, incarceration, and domestic, alcohol, and drug abuse, disturbing health and life expectancy statistics, and poor job and academic accomplishment."[27] Klopotek's and Tengan's observations about the weight of rigid expectations on, and negative perceptions of, Indigenous masculinities suggest the need to identify the fault lines in these damaging settler rhetorics. The masculinities of female-identified and gender-variant warriors and non-cis folks mark one such fault line.

THE ANALYSES OF THE BODY in *Written by the Body* therefore work in tandem with current studies of masculinity to fracture such monolithic, externally constructed, and limiting discourses about Indigenous gender traditions. A central argument of this book, then, is that *recognizing Native masculinities as not only multiple but also mobile—able to move between and among differently gendered and nonbinary bodies—requires a paradigm shift.*

Tengan brings to our attention the limits of a binary that writes hegemonic masculinities and subaltern masculinities as two opposing and discrete cultural productions:

> We need to see gendered social actors as complexly situated, located, and positioned in multiple settings and historical contexts. In doing so, we can attend to the ways in which men and women have access to different points of privilege and subordination through such positionings. . . . Hegemonies are always incomplete, allowing interplay between structure and agency—an interplay that involves and transforms indigenous ideologies of gender and power. Such an approach to hegemonic power relations allows us to explore the ways in which men and women who are complexly situated in multiple contexts can draw upon dominant gender constructs for contradictory and even subversive purposes.[28]

Thus layered examinations of gender allow for both possibilities of identifications, as well as what José Esteban Muñoz terms *disidentifications*, between and among Indigenous men, women, gender-variant, Two-Spirit, trans, and other nonbinary folks and the multiple iterations of masculinity available to them. While hegemonic masculinities may be coercive in some cases, they also may be knowingly and purposefully identified with, overtly rejected, or consciously employed as subversive tools by Indigenous people.

In his Introduction to *Masculindians: Conversations about Indigenous Manhood,* Sam McKegney addresses the potentially generative nature of Indigenous masculinities:

> In speaking with the Indigenous men and women I interviewed for this project, I've come to understand the terms "masculine" and "Indian" not only as a means of tracking colonial simulations and technologies of coercion that have served to alienate Indigenous men from tribal specific roles and responsibilities; they also act as tools for imagining and enacting empowered, non-dominative Indigenous male identities that serve the inter-

woven struggles of communal health, gender complementarity, and Indigenous continuance.[29]

Such theories of masculinity are particularly enmeshed in the nexus of community, which is one of the key places where analyses of masculinities outside Indigenous studies differ radically from those within. Hegemonic masculinities privilege, and in fact even demand, a rugged individualism (even if, ironically, this individualism is produced by the regulatory practice of mimesis). However, as scholars like Anderson and Innes, Henry, Hokowhitu, McKegney, Tengan, and more demonstrate, the construction of masculinity in Indigenous contexts often relies on group interaction and a strong sense of community responsibility. For example, as part of her work on the American Indian Fatherhood Project, which conducted 375 interviews with Chickasaw, Kiowa, Comanche, and Apache men and women on the subject of fatherhood and masculinity, Margaret Bender spoke with a Kiowa interviewee about the interactive roles of men in his present and historical community. Like many of the Kiowa people involved in the project, this speaker referenced "warrior societies, especially the Black Leggings Society, . . . as being important sources of support for adult men."[30] Though Bender is quick to point out the distinct differences in the deployments of masculinity among her collaborators, she shows, too, that tribal nationhood and communal interaction function as common tropes in Indigenous discourses about masculinity and fatherhood. In an interview with McKegney, Blackfoot artist Terrance Houle makes a similar point: "You have to get back to the idea of brotherhood that was intrinsic within almost any culture. But with Native people it was always: 'Everyone is your brother. Everyone is your sister. Everyone is your elder.' The ideas around relationships are very different. It's deeper than a blood tie."[31] Speaking of the ways settler ideologies have fractured such Indigenous relationality, Anishinaabe scholar Niigaanwewidam James Sinclair comments:

> One of the legacies of colonization has been the separation of [Native] men from their roles within families, communities, and nations. What's replaced these are hegemonic forms of corporate, neo-liberal individualist identities that ossify cultures and replace meaning with a one-size-fits-all Lockean chant of:

"Pick up your bootstraps and get on with the business of making money, buying a house, and consume, consume, consume." Indigenous masculinity is so much more than this.[32]

The facets of masculinity and the body referenced by these scholars—its productive possibility, its relationship to community, its ties to hegemonic structures—circulate in the work and activisms of the writers, theorists, filmmakers, activists, and historical figures examined in this book. From eighteenth- and nineteenth-century female-identified and gender-variant warriors to their subsequent representations in the fiction of S. Alice Callahan (Muscogee Creek), Zitkala-Ša (Yankton Sioux), Anna Lee Walters (Pawnee–Otoe Missouri), and Daniel Heath Justice (Cherokee Nation), to the culture bearers, or "big moms," of Sherman Alexie's (Spokane/Coeur D'Alene), Craig S. Womack's (Muscogee Creek/Cherokee), and Louise Erdrich's (Anishinaabe) fiction, to the female firefighters in *Apache 8* and the Indigenous leaders and activists depicted in Abenaki filmmaker Alanis Obomsawin's *Trick or Treaty?*, to Two-Spirit Ojibwe health activist and writer Carole laFavor, to the overt engagements with non-cis genders and the erotic seen in the work of queer artists and writers like Thirza Cuthand (Cree), Joshua Whitehead (Oji-Cree), and Carrie House (Diné)—each example invites a more nuanced understanding both of how infinitely faceted the performance of gender can be and how complicated the practice and process of gender intelligibility is. Much like the sun glinting off the brilliant finish of a Maria Martinez pot, every moment refracts differently. And like Martinez's innovations, each imaginative articulation is simultaneously unique and rooted in long-standing Indigenous practices, reminding us that "new" is never original, "traditional" is never static, and variations on a theme may well increase the beauty of the whole.

Why Affect? Indigenous Studies and the Body

While I almost never make blanket statements, since, as I tell my students, such claims are wrong as soon as they leave your mouth, one declaration rings true throughout this project: bodies are contextual. And here's another: bodies are relational. Let's pause for a moment and mull over some definitions: "contextual"—relating to, dependent on, what's happening around a person, place, or event; "relational"—arising from kinship, from connection, from the act of exchange. I would add to this list "embodied"—tied to, in this case, a human being, and the physical sense of that person's body, which may be what they themselves feel (cognitively or not) or what occurs when two or more bodies come into proximity. These contextual, relational, and embodied aspects of masculinities, the body, and gender intelligibility bring me to forward affect theory as a particularly applicable tool for conversations about the contours, meanings, and creative possibilities of gender in Indigenous texts.

But before turning to a discussion of the importance of affect as a productive methodology for Indigenous studies. I want to briefly engage a question put to me when I gave a paper on female masculinity at the Native American and Indigenous Studies Association in 2012. After a presentation on Erdrich, affect, and female masculinity that employed Gilles Deleuze and Félix Guattari's *A Thousand Plateaus* alongside Dian Million's work as a theoretical frame, I was asked, Why not use Indigenous feminists to make this case? Since I regularly engage Native feminists, and had in the presentation, the real question seemed to be, Why use non-Indigenous theorists like Deleuze and Guattari? My answer then and now is that theory is a tool that can be employed to liberatory ends. As Hokowhitu's extensions of Nietzsche and Foucault, Chickasaw scholar Jodi Byrd's deployment of Deleuze, Guattari, and Žižak, and Glen Cothhard's (Yellowknives Dene) return to Marx show us, non-Native theory can be a means to Indigenous ends.[33] One of the most cogent discussions of this issue appears in Banaban scholar Teresia Teaiwa's "The Ancestors We Get to Choose," where Teaiwa addresses why she includes white theorists in her Pacific studies courses:

> My experience of theory has mostly been one of valuing ideas, and in particular valuing the ability to identify connections and resonances and distinguish gaps and contradictions between models and proposals. I do not like theory when it is used as a weapon. I especially dislike theory when it is used like a silencer on a gun. I prefer to see and use theory as a frame, a magnifying glass, a key, a plow, a sail, an oar. Theory is like fiberglass as well—I have found . . . that it can get you where you want to go, faster.[34]

For a study of the rich array of non-cis genders in Indigenous texts, a powerful tool that "can get [us] where [we] want to go, faster" is affect theory. While I acknowledge there is a colonial legacy to affect theory, which Byrd engages directly in *The Transit of Empire*,[35] affect, when deployed by Indigenous theorists and read through Indigenous lenses, offers us a language with which to talk about what Million terms "colonialism as it is *felt* by those who experience it."

In her award-winning 2009 article, "Felt Theory: An Indigenous Feminist Approach to Affect and History," which is, as well, a chapter in her monograph *Therapeutic Nations: Healing in an Age of Indigenous Human Rights*, Million discusses how and why affect theory is particularly relevant to Indigenous experiences. Looking across the early writing of Aboriginal writers like Jeannette Armstrong (Okanagan), Maria Campbell (Métis), Beatrice Culleton (Métis), Lee Maracle (Sto:lo Nation), and Ruby Slipperjack (Ojibwa, Fort Hope Indian Band), Million argues that these Indigenous women "creat[e] new language for communities . . . insisting on the inclusion of [their] lived experience, rich with emotional knowledges."[36] This *felt* knowledge, which is part and parcel of Indigenous women's activism, has often been dismissed as overly emotional and therefore not the stuff of intellectual interventions. However, contrary "to the way Western knowledge works and the way most academics operate," these writers privilege that which is felt rather than any sort of disembodied and supposedly objective academic approach to structures of knowledge.[37] In this way, these embodied, highly personal narratives are themselves intellectual "frames," because, ultimately, "feelings are theory."[38] As such, Million considers what Cherokee author Betty Bell terms "the truth in the things not said."[39] Such felt truths are often held within the body and, in the work Million examines, are specifically shared among women. Indigenous women, Bell explains, "listened, and they taught me to listen, in the space between words."[40] In the end, this "space between words" represents the affective nexus of exchange in which embodied Indigenous knowledges are produced, shared, and experienced.

Affect, then, both relates to and exceeds language. For example, Million asks: "Where would the felt experience of being raped by a priest at ten years old be expressed and for whose knowledge would this experience be important? If the child has no words to name it or if her silence is enforced discursively and physically, did nothing happen?"[41] With this painful example, Million emphasizes that the privileged site of linguistic exchange cannot be the singular location of knowledge formation—the body itself must function as a site of knowledge.[42] Here, the import of nonverbal knowledges and experiences points to not only the efficacy of, but also the stark need for, affective analyses in Indigenous studies: *as a methodology, affect privileges and facilitates the lived, bodily experience of emotional knowledges.*

Bay of Quinte Mohawk writer and theorist Beth Brant also articulates this affective sense of Indigenous knowledges. Speaking about how such embodied experience survives in the face of settler invasion, she explains: "I believe memory is like a drum, one tap and one sound resonates and reverberates into our very soul. One poem, one story, one painting, and our hearts and bodies respond to the message—we are here. We remember."[43] In these accounts, the body functions as an affective repository, or what, later in this book, I call *a somatic archive of Indigenous knowledge.*

Clare Hemmings notes that, when defining affect, Silvan Tompkins, one of the foundational voices in the field of affect theory, "asked us to think of the contagious nature of a yawn, smile or blush. It is transferred to others and doubles back, increasing its original intensity. *Affect can thus be said to place the individual in a circuit of feeling and response, rather than opposition to others.*"[44] I am most interested in this sense of an interactive affective circuit between bodies. This relational, embodied way of knowing offers a window into the performance, expression, and felt experience of gender expansiveness in Indigenous histories, writing, film, and activisms. It is, after all, in the space *between* bodies and in the understandings and relationships (or rejection thereof) that gender becomes intelligible. The felt experiences of masculinities and nonbinary genders—and, in fact, gender intelligibility more broadly—are bound to this "circuit of feeling," an ever-shifting nexus of action and reaction, of receptivity, of response. However, as Tompkins's work reminds us, those affective intensities fall somewhere between bodily drives—like hunger or thirst, which are not affective—and the conscious interface of touching, feeling, and, sometimes (but not inevitably), speaking.[45]

Notably, *affect is a process,* not a thing, not a singular, bounded event that can be easily pointed to. Affect happens in the relay between bodies. Like the rippling out of a yawn, affective exchanges are not always conscious; nonetheless, they are radically interactive. The contention of *Written by the Body* is that considering how these affective cycles function in Indigenous representations of genders and the body can help the project of decolonization by revealing and undoing heteropatriarchal gender constraints. If we more effectively conceptualize nuanced iterations of Indigenous genders—both historical and contemporary—that fall outside, or perhaps more aptly, *that intentionally sidestep such limits by imagining otherwise,* we can, to return to Belcourt and Nixon, "open up a space for critique that might flower queer, trans and two-spirit possibility."

BECAUSE OF THE VAST RANGE of gender and sexualities in Indigenous cultures as well as the ever-expanding body of queer Indigenous literatures and films, the texts I consider in this book are necessarily representative rather than exhaustive. For example, the potential list of historical and contemporary female-identified and gender-variant warriors in Native North American histories is far more vast than this book could address, ranging from what Lang deems "arguably the first description of a Native American female-bodied person in a masculine role" recounted in French Jesuit missionary Jacques Gravier's sixteenth-century narrative to the many Indigenous women who serve as firefighters, political leaders, or members of today's U.S. or Canadian armed forces.[46] Methodologically, affective understandings of gender drive the lines of inquiry across the book's six chapters. The connecting link in *Written by the Body* is its steady focus on how relational networks around the body shift the ways gender becomes intelligible.

As a project, this book crosses nation-state boundaries, moving between and among Indigenous texts, histories, and activisms in both the United States and Canada. These crossings occur in part because Indigenous people have been themselves moving physically and imaginatively through these spaces since before those settler borders existed. Furthermore, in the contemporary era, Indigenous writers, activists, filmmakers, and theorists often collaborate and think across and beyond those constructed barriers, which were designed to separate, to divide, to conquer. Thus, the movement of these analyses across tribal nation boundaries—which Chadwick Allen terms a "multiperspectivism" that "must be a hallmark of trans-Indigenous literary studies"[47]—mirrors the movements of the writers, practitioners, and theorists who create the body of art and the intellectual traditions from which I draw. At the same time, even though such geographic borders are settler-imposed boundaries, they do create different histories for the Indigenous peoples engaging with these colonial nation-states. Comparisons run the risk of flattening such differences, and I am respectful of that reality and, too, want to acknowledge my position as a settler scholar grounded in American Indian studies. Keeping this in mind, I still move forward with the work at hand, not only because trans-Indigenous comparisons are so very rich but because the juxtaposition of these texts and histories allow us to see the interconnected lines of flight formed by Indigenous peoples' creative worldings, in which, so often, *they see themselves related.* Million contends that such relational practices, which contain a "nurturing inclusiveness" and are "an ideal in kinship," can serve as the basis for a polity that "interrupts absolutely."[48] With these possibilities in mind, I argue that reading across the texts and actions of female-identified and gender-variant Indigenous peoples who hold knowledge within their bodies and use it to further right relationships can highlight how such folks open pathways to teach, to protect, to heal, and to thrive.

Ultimately, *Written by the Body* situates the art, lived experiences, and complex gender ideologies of Indigenous peoples as the basis for an embodied gender theory. To do so, chapter 1, "Warrior Women in History and Early Indigenous Literatures," begins with the best-known iterations of nondominant Native masculinities—those of female-identified and gender-variant warriors. The first section of the chapter reads the archive, examining historical narratives of eighteenth- and nineteenth-century warriors who were either born into, chose, or were assigned gender responsibilities considered masculine within their cultures. The entrance of these folks into male-identified spaces illustrates the fluidity of masculine gender performances and shows how attributes of masculinity can move between and among differently gendered bodies in Indigenous contexts. The chapter subsequently considers the post-reservation era, asking how such warriors were depicted when colonial incursions ended the overt warfare on Plains territories. To answer this question, the chapter reads the first two images of warrior women in Indigenous literatures: Muscogee Creek author S. Alice Callahan's 1891 novel *Wynema: A Child of the Forest* and Dakota author and activist Zitkala-Ša's 1903 short story "A Warrior's Daughter."

Chapter 2, "Warriors, Indigenous Futures, and the Erotic: Anna Lee Walters and Daniel Heath Justice," moves to Walters's short fiction and Justice's fantasy trilogy to examine how female-identified and gender-variant warriors are depicted in the late twentieth and early twenty-first centuries. Walters's "The Warriors" addresses the intersections of gender and narrative memory in the mid-twentieth century, arguing for both the continued relevance of warrior figures in Pawnee cosmology and the necessity of challenging boundaries that limit warriorhood to a cishet domain. Justice undertakes similarly expansive work in *The Way of Thorn and Thunder,* a riveting series that celebrates nonbinary warriors, the erotic, and Indigenous futures. Together, these analyses demonstrate that both in the flesh and in subsequent Indigenous-authored textual representations, the masculinities of female-identified and gender-variant warriors center kinship narratives that privilege familial and tribal responsibilities.

Chapter 3, "Big Moms, or The Body as Archive," turns to contemporary fiction by Sherman Alexie, Craig Womack, and Louise Erdrich to analyze the affective nature of the body in the interventions made by figures I call "big moms"—larger-than-life female culture bearers who use their bodies to effect productive change for their families and nations. Centering the histories of gender expansiveness in Indigenous contexts, big moms offer narratives of relationality that privilege tribal and community well-being in kinship models outside and beyond monogamous heterocouplehood. At times these figures' power arises from a matriarchal and/or matrilineal heritage that marks Indigenous women's cultural authority, and at other times they consciously cross into a space of influence that signifies masculinity. In every case, big moms' bodies/bodily engagements effect productive change. As a result, this chapter argues that more than any library or collection of letters, *the body is a somatic archive of Indigenous knowledge.*

To further these claims about the affective power of bodies in relationship, chapter 4, "Body as Shield and Shelter: Indigenous Documentary Film," analyzes two twenty-first-century documentaries: Abenaki filmmaker Alanis Obomsawin's *Trick or Treaty?* (2014) and queer non-Native filmmaker Sande Zeig's *Apache 8: Facing Fire Is Just the Beginning* (2011), which she creates in collaboration with, among others, executive producer Heather Rae (Cherokee), of *Frozen River* and *Trudell* fame. The analyses in this chapter build on the claims for the importance of embodied knowledge established in the first three chapters. If the body archives Indigenous knowledges, then the words and actions of the female wildland firefighters and Indigenous leaders and activists highlighted in these films present an important example of exactly *how* this information is accessed, opened, and engaged in powerful affective exchanges between and among Indigenous people.

Chapters 5 and 6 pay particular attention to the junctures between and among embodiment, activism, and the Indigenous erotic. Chapter 5, "HIV/AIDS Activism and the Indigenous Erotic: Carole laFavor," extends the book's previous arguments about bodily power by presenting laFavor's life and literary history as an example of felt theory. This chapter is twofold: on one hand, it recovers laFavor's interventions into HIV prevention and health sovereignty, in which she repeatedly privileged her embodied realities as a self-identified HIV-positive Two-Spirit person; on the other, it highlights her deployment of an Indigenous erotic through readings of her two novels, *Along the Journey River* (1996) and *Evil Dead Center* (1997), the first lesbian detective fiction published by a Native author. Building on these embodied intersections of Indigenous activism and the erotic, chapter 6, "An Erotics of Responsibility: Non-Cis Identities and Community Accountability," looks to Thirza Cuthand's 2012 experimental film *Boi Oh Boi* and Joshua Whitehead's 2018 rejection of a Lambda Literary Award for his poetry collection *Full-Metal Indigiqueer* (2017) together with his 2018 novel *Jonny Appleseed*, then concludes with Carrie House's documentary film, essay, and poetry. Moving across activism, fiction, experimental film, memoir, and poetry, these chapters collectively argue that such Indigenous-focused iterations of non-cis gender reflect a form of community engagement I term *an erotics of responsibility*.

Overall, *Written by the Body* centers the lives, activisms, and artistic productions of female and gender-variant warriors, big moms, and non-cis folks to argue that their powerful interventions coalesce in an embodied gender expansiveness that *is* felt theory. Furthermore, considering the histories in which they exist, whether these folks defy, acquiesce to, or ignore colonial gender demands, their very bodies counter gendercide and resist the containment of historical trauma. Instead, as the following chapters will show, these non-cis masculinities, capacious bodily archives, and erotic sensibilities create an essential lexicon for the survival knowledges that are written in and by the body in Indigenous literatures, films, and activisms.

CHAPTER 1

WARRIOR WOMEN IN HISTORY AND EARLY INDIGENOUS LITERATURES

Greater honor was paid to her than to the Great chief, for she occupied the 1st place in all the Councils, and, when she walked about, was always preceded by four young men, who sang and danced the Calumet to her. She was dressed as an Amazon; she painted her face and wore her Hair like the men.

—Jacques Gravier, *Relation ou Journal du voyage du Pere Gravier de la Compagnie de Jesus en 1700*

In March 23, 2003, Private First Class Lori Ann Piestewa, a Hopi/ Latinx mother of a then five-year-old son, Brandon, and three-year-old daughter, Carla, was killed when the 507th Maintenance Company was trapped near Nasiriyah in southern Iraq. Piestewa, or Kocha-Hon-Mana (White Bear Girl), died at only twenty-three and was, according to the U.S. Army, the first American Indian woman serving in the U.S. armed services to die in combat on foreign soil.[1] Billy House and Mark Shafer argue that Piestewa "has become the nation's most recognizable Native American military icon since Ira Hayes helped raise the Stars and Stripes on Iwo Jima."[2] A beloved daughter, sister, and mother, since her death Piestewa has also come to embody the figure of warrior.

When speaking of the tremendous support and response he had received since his daughter's death, her father, Perry Piestewa, explained, "When she went, the indigenous people said, 'She's a warrior.' There's a warrior Kachina that signifies the warrior and they've kind of put her up on that echelon of the high end."[3] Likewise, her older brother Wayland Piestewa shared that at a powwow and memorial the day after the family was given the news of Lori's death, Lori was "renamed the 'Lady Warrior'" in recognition of her service and sacrifice.[4] Two years after her death, Hopi tribal chairman Wayne Taylor Jr. remembered Piestewa in *Indian Country Today,* saying, "Lori died a true Hopi warrior."[5] But unlike many mainstream news articles that lauded Piestewa's bravery, Chairman Taylor situated her life within the continuum of a Hopi belief system: "True Hopi warriors—such as the Hopi code talkers—serve not to kill, but to help others end bloodshed."[6] These comments and the hundreds more like them show that the discourse of warriorhood permeates articles about and memorials for Piestewa. At the same time, they suggest that despite its ubiquity, the parameters of warrior identities are themselves variable.[7]

As noted in the Introduction, the language of warriorhood has a deep resonance in Indigenous contexts, on one hand carrying the freight of settler expectations and on the other the lived experiences of Indigenous peoples. In thinking of the former, scholars have long commented that a decontextualized Indigenous warrior has come to serve as an all-encompassing symbol for settler needs and desires, thereby forming what Robert Berkhofer famously termed the "white man's Indian." From the papal bulls, to early colonial accounts of Native "savagery," to the more than one thousand Westerns produced in the twentieth century, to the ongoing deployment of "Native" mascots in U.S. and Canadian sports arenas (from primary schools to professional teams), such figures most often denote conflict and domination in colonial discourse.[8] In each of these cases the warrior is enmeshed in a necropolitical discourse that marks *them* for death and *settlers* for life. In contrast to such violent imaginings, actual Indigenous cosmologies frequently depict war and warriors very differently.

Piestewa's nation, for example, believes in the Hopi Way of peace, generosity, and spirituality. Chairman Taylor notes, "We are a nonviolent people. We do not believe in doing harm to anyone or anything."[9] Likewise, Daniel Kraker, an Associated Press reporter who lives on Hopi lands, notes that "Piestewa's death has . . . highlighted a cultural dilemma faced by many Hopi soldiers—how to balance Hopi people's traditional pacifism with an equally strong tradition of defending their Homeland."[10] While he does not fault other Indigenous people who take up the discourse of warriorhood, Cree scholar Neal McLeod rejects the appellation of warrior altogether, explaining the term does not fit a Cree worldview; in Cree, he tells us, the word "provider" is a better translation than "warrior."[11] While the ubiquitous violent images that circulate in mainstream culture speak to the destructive nature of settler portrayals, Taylor's, Kraker's, and McLeod's observations point to the nuances apparent between and among Indigenous nations' actual beliefs surrounding the gender roles and cultural occupations of warriors.

In the larger body of scholarship on Indigenous masculinities, concepts of warrior have been discussed at length precisely because Indigenous men have been bombarded with these damaging messages about how they should inhabit manhood. The relentless settler insistence on tying violence and masculinity to warriorhood has been—as Kim Anderson, Robert Henry, Robert Innes, Brendan Hokowhitu, Lloyd L. Lee, Sam McKegney, and Ty P. Kāwika Tengan (to name just a few scholars) have demonstrated—one of many ways that colonialism has affected articulations of gender among Indigenous peoples. But this is not a story of loss and victimry—there are multiple means by which such ties between unhealthy articulations of masculinity and warriorhood have been contested. Anderson and Innes have taken part in and written about programs like the Ontario Federation of Indigenous Friendship Centres' Kizhaay Anishinaabe Niin, in which, they note "training participants listen closely, hungry for knowledge about masculine roles and identities that defy those based in dominance and violence."[12] Tengan considers the regeneration of Hawaiian warrior organizations like Nā Koa and the reconstitution of masculinity on and in Hawaiian belief systems.[13] Lee has met with groups of Diné men about how masculinity can stem from and augment understandings of Diné lifeways and beliefs.[14] These examples offer just the briefest introduction to the on-the-ground work that centers Indigenous men and masculinities. While valuable, research on Indigenous masculinities has primarily focused on cishet men, leaving unexamined the warrior identities claimed for Piestewa and the women and Two-Spirit folks who came before and walk alongside her.[15]

Written by the Body steps into this gap on multiple levels. First, it decouples the warrior from the masculinity of cis-identified men assigned male at birth. This decentering of cishet Indigenous masculinity rejects the so-called white man's Indian as well as the attendant rigid strictures around masculine roles and bodies that serve to delimit the expansiveness of gender. To do so, this chapter first briefly examines the embodied labor female-identified and gender-variant warriors undertake for their families and nations before moving to an analysis of the two earliest representations of women warriors in Native American literature: Muscogee Creek author S. Alice Callahan's *Wynema: A Child of the Forest* (1891), the earliest-known novel published by an Indigenous woman; and Dakota author/activist Zitkala-Ša's 1902 short story "A Warrior's Daughter." This analytical movement from history to literature follows a chronological shift: archival and documentary accounts of Native women on the battlefield with their nations begin to wane in the late nineteenth and early twentieth centuries while literary representations of warrior women and Two-Spirits crafted by Indigenous people arise shortly after.[16] As a result, this chapter's movement from the eighteenth- and nineteenth-century archive to turn-of-the-century fiction and the next chapter's move from late-twentieth- to twenty-first-century fiction follow a distinct temporal thread in Indigenous histories and literatures in North America. Following that thread allows us to consider representations of female-identified and gender-variant warriors across selections from over a century of Indigenous literatures—from published missionary journals to newspaper interviews, from short story to novel, from sentimental romance to high fantasy. Collectively, these analyses demonstrate that both in the flesh and in subsequent Indigenous representations, the masculinities and embodied interventions of Native female-identified and gender-variant warriors, nonbinary, and/or Two-Spirit people center kinship narratives that privilege familial and tribal responsibilities. Furthermore, as *Written by the Body* demonstrates, such affective masculinities index what Dian Million terms "felt theory," Indigenous knowledges of trauma and survival held within the body. Documented in a significant array of Indigenous history, activism, film, and literature, *these survival knowledges*—as shown in this chapter and throughout the book—*construct a twenty-first-century gender theory written by Indigenous people and theorized through the body.*

Female-Identified and Gender-Variant Warriors in Indigenous Histories

With some exceptions—such as in the brief observations from Crow medicine woman Pretty Shield and Lakota warrior Rain in the Face discussed later in this section—the preponderance of extant archival materials on Two-Spirit and female-identified warriors in what is now the United States and Canada arise from the accounts of French, English, and Spanish invaders. Thus, the pens and lenses of non-Native soldiers, missionaries, and settlers provide much of the fragmentary written evidence from which we can catch glimpses into the rich lives of these warriors. As readers of this book well know, these archival records are fraught, the tenor of their descriptions often saying as much about the cultural frames of the writers as they do about the Indigenous people described in their texts. At the same time, these accounts reward careful attention because so often such individuals exceed and elude the bounds of their interlocutors. Their stories are lines of flight that allow for a multitude of possibilities beyond that intended by the writer. Thus, though hegemonic narrators may try to own the narratives of Indigenous warriors and define and defame Native peoples in their texts, the expansive ways in which such female-identified and gender-variant people inhabit their bodies, lives, and gender roles defy that containment. I turn here to a selection of historical encounters that narrate such expansive possibilities.

In her reading of the extant archival evidence of people assigned female at birth who took up masculine roles, noted anthropologist Sabine Lang names French Jesuit missionary Jacques Gravier's (1651–1708) account of a Houma chief—quoted in this chapter's epigraph—as "arguably the first description of a Native American female-bodied person in a masculine role."[17] Lang explains that Gravier's account, originally published in 1700, equates this leader's power to "a status resembling that of men in Indigenous North American cultures."[18] Gravier imagines the "femme chief" as inhabiting the space of masculinity, a line he sees as quite defined, although Lang explains that "among the Houma . . . it was not unusual for women to go to war."[19] Gravier's depiction turns on a notion of *exceptionalism,* imagining a warrior so distinct that the Calumet dance—a sacred pipe dance that was used to seal alliances and to welcome strangers with an assurance of friendship—was enacted everywhere they went. As a performance that usually included the reenactment of battle followed by the smoking of a stone pipe to signal a peace agreement, the Calumet dance engages warrior masculinities in the very fabric of its narrative. While Gravier almost undoubtedly *mis*-identified the frequency and purpose of the Calumet dance, which would not have been in constant practice to honor a single individual, Gravier's awed description situates the chief as a non-cis person of considerable status who meets the standards of warrior masculinities among the Houma people at this particular historical moment.

Writing twenty-four years after Gravier, Joseph-François Lafitau (1681–1746), another French Jesuit missionary, who spent six years (1712–17) among the Kahnawake Mohawk on the St. Lawrence River, presents a similar tale of women warriors and gender exceptionalism. In *Customs of the American Indians Compared with the Customs of the Primitive Times,* Lafitau relates this story:

> I shall tell here of a woman, who, after her husband had been taken, put to death, and eaten by his enemies, never being willing to remarry because none of the relatives of said defunct had made the effort to avenge his death, [undertook] to do so herself, and taking a bow and arrows went herself to war with men and was so successful that she took prisoners who she gave to her children to be killed. . . . Putting away all womanly actions, and taking on masculine and virile ones, she no longer wore her hair long like the other women or as she had been accustomed to doing, but adorned herself in the feathers and other things suitable to men.[20]

Lafitau's account of this unnamed woman warrior provides a rationale—a sense of familial responsibility and desire for reciprocal justice—for her deployment of what he portrays as a "virile" warrior masculinity. This description aligns with documented evidence about the masculinities of eighteenth-century Kahnawake men, who were regularly courted by both fur traders and military leaders because of "their warrior traditions and reputation for fierceness."[21] The woman warrior Lafitau describes meets this expectation and, importantly, *has access to such markers of masculine performance among her people.* Notably, she does not, however, forgo her position as mother or eschew relational responsibilities. While taking up occupations and attire perceived as masculine in this period and context, this woman warrior is still overtly situated within a constellation of relationship—with her husband, children, and network of extended family. Consequently, despite its purple rhetoric, Lafitau's narrative marks an early iteration of a pattern that recurs within the references to female-identified and gender-variant Indigenous warriors: kinship responsibilities are often referenced as that which first brings such warriors into the space of the battlefield.

While female-identified and gender-variant warriors *expand and augment* rather than subvert the gender and kinship traditions of their people, kinship and responsibility have been vacated from hegemonic accounts of warriorhood.[22] Scott Morgensen contends that colonial masculinity focuses instead on violence, surveillance, and containment and purposely works to sever Indigenous practices of relationality.[23] In direct opposition to such a fragmenting ideology, Daniel Heath Justice explains that, "In those Indigenous cultural understandings that have withstood such colonial intrusions, the status of 'human' is intimately embedded in kinship relations."[24] And, as Métis scholar June Scudeler notes, speaking of wákôhtowin, a particularly Cree sense of relatedness, kinship extends "beyond the immediate family" and blood relationship.[25] Keeping these opposing kinship epistemologies in mind, we can see how the warrior in Lafitau's account operates outside his understanding—rather than being fantastical, as his description implies, her rationale for warriorhood is, to return to Justice, "intimately embedded in kinship relations." While Lafitau clearly intends to highlight anomaly and savagery, he instead conveys Indigenous relationality when he presents kinship as engendering woman warriorhood and non-cis masculinity.

Indigenous origin stories and oral histories as well as missionary, military, and Indigenous-authored accounts all provide evidence that female-identified and gender-variant people have long stepped into spaces of leadership and warriorhood in Native nations. Thus Lori Piestewa, perhaps the most widely known contemporary Native American woman warrior, is tied to nuanced warrior traditions that arise from a deep history. Such powerful female beings include origin figures like Thought Woman (Tsichtinako) and Changing Woman (Azdaa nádleehé), seventeenth-century military and political leaders like Pamunkey werowansqua Cockacoeske and Pocasset sachem Weetamoo, eighteenth-century negotiators and diplomats like Mohawk legend Molly Brant (Tekonwatonti), and the many, many female-identified and gender-variant warriors who join forces with their kin on the battlefield well into the nineteenth century.[26] In each case such narratives exceed and revise the limited settler notions of warriorhood and masculinity: if the body of the male warrior is marked for death in settler society, the stories of the Indigenous women and gender-variant people discussed here account for generative iterations of bodily power and leadership that, to riff off José Esteban Muñoz, imagine differently.[27] With this in mind, *I suggest that rather than working as an additive to masculinity studies, research on the masculinities inhabited by female-identified, gender-variant, and/or Two-Spirit people can be centered as an avenue for productive interventions for both cis and non-cis peoples who perform such gender identities.*

Many alternately gendered Indigenous folks, whom some today would term Two-Spirit, evaded the gendercide aimed at them by settler-invaders and, in fact, as the previous examples suggest, lived their lives as respected warriors and leaders. Among those most often referenced are the Crow leader Bíawacheeitchish, or Woman Chief (ca. 1790–1830), whose story was brought to print by Edwin T. Denig, a fur trader and amateur ethnographer. Denig, who knew Woman Chief for twelve years, described their position as a leader and warrior. Captured from the Gros Ventre at ten years old, Woman Chief was adopted by a Crow family and allowed to follow their desire to pursue what would, within Crow culture, be male-identified occupations. When their adopted father died, they "assumed the charge of his lodge and family, performing the double duty of father and mother to his children."[28] Along with citing their keen sense of responsibility to their kin, which aligns with Lafitau's account of the Houma warrior he discusses, Denig repeatedly emphasizes the respect afforded Woman Chief. He notes, for example, that "when council was held and all the chiefs and warriors assembled, she took her place among the former, ranking third person in the band of 160 lodges. . . . In the meantime she continued her masculine course of life, hunting and war."[29] With at least four wives, numerous horses, and myriad successes on raids and the battlefield, Woman Chief "had fame, standing, honor, riches, and as much influence over the band as anyone except two or three leading chiefs."[30] By all accounts, Woman

Chief was a non-cis warrior who attained high status among their people and, in fact, was chosen to serve as a negotiator for the Crow along with leading war and hunting parties.

Perhaps most interesting in Denig's narrative, however, is his sense that Woman Chief's life was at the same time a story of unparalleled success and a narrative of heteronormative failure. Along with listing many of Woman Chief's accomplishments, he writes:

> No offer of marriage had been made her by anyone. Her habits did not suit their taste. Perhaps they thought she would be rather difficult to manage as a wife. Whatever the reason was, they certainly rather feared than loved her as a conjugal companion, and she continued to lead a single life. With the view of turning her hides to some account by dressing them and fitting them for trading purposes, she took to *herself a wife*. Ranking as a warrior and hunter, she could not be brought to think of female work. It was derogatory to her standing, unsuited to her taste. She therefore went through the usual formula of Indian marriage to obtain an authority over the woman thus bought. Strange country this, where males assume the dress and perform the duties of females, while women turn men and mate with their own sex![31]

Here, Denig appears torn between the tone of deep respect that runs throughout his account of Woman Chief and his inability to escape the heteronormativity of settler knowledges. While it is doubtful Denig had access to such details, he attributes Woman Chief's marriages to economic need as well as to not only a lack of interest, but also a named *fear* on the part of their male-identified peers. His prose highlights his need to make Woman Chief's action, body, and decisions intelligible within the parameters of hegemonic gender performances and heterosexual desire. By contrast, Woman Chief brings us what gender theorist Jack Halberstam terms "an anticolonial struggle, the refusal of legibility, and an art of unbecoming."[32] This particular warrior fits understandings of a Two-Spirit person, allowing us to read their perceived gender "failure" as both a critique of and a "refus[al] to acquiesce to dominant logics of power and discipline."[33] However mediated Denig's account, Woman Chief undeniably existed as a non-cis Indigenous person with the mobility to (1) inhabit the space of Crow masculinity, (2) earn warrior status within their social networks, and (3) hold a leadership role within their nation. As such, *Woman Chief's life underscores the expansive realities of Indigenous gender knowledges.*

As would be expected, extant references to warrior women multiply in the nineteenth century, a time when settler contact escalated and written chronicles of Indigenous-invader battles proliferated. Though such folks are not ubiquitous, the number of stories about female-identified and gender-variant folks who enter into battle during this era concretely demonstrates that such appearances are by no means uncommon, especially among Plains peoples. For example, The Other Magpie, a Crow woman identified female at birth, and Finds Them and Kills Them (Osh-Tisch), a Crow gender-variant person or *badé* (the Crow term for a woman assigned male at birth), are two warriors famously referenced in *Pretty-shield, Medicine Woman of the Crows* (1932)—the as-told-to collaboration between Pretty Shield (1857–1944) and Frank Bird Linderman. With these accounts in mind, noted Lakota anthropologist Bea Medicine argues, "the fact that there were a range of socially accepted roles for women in Plains Indian societies permits us to understand the role of warrior women as one aspect of this variation."[34]

Other well-known nineteenth-century Indigenous warrior women include the Southern Cheyenne warrior E'hyoph'sta (ca. 1826–1915, known, too, as Yellow Haired Woman), whose stories arise from her 1908 and 1912 interviews with U.S. anthropologist George Bird Grinnell. E'hyoph'sta is said to have gone into battle a year after her husband Walking Bear's death with the intention of dying herself. On September 17, 1868, E'hyoph'sta joined the warriors attacking Major George Forsythe's company at the Republican River in Colorado in what would later be termed by whites the Battle of Beecher Island; the war party conducted a successful multiday siege.[35] After this successful combat experience, she continued to participate in Cheyenne war parties.[36]

Grinnell notes at the end of his chapter on "Women and War," which centers E'hyoph'sta, that "women who had been to war with their husbands formed, it was said by some, a guild or society and held meetings at which no one else might be present, but, of course, the number of these women was very small."[37] While it is unclear from Grinnell's accounts whether E'hyoph'sta was part of such a group, her successful participation in subsequent battles led to her induction into the Dog Soldier Warrior Society, a predominantly male social and ceremonial organization.[38] We can see, then, that E'hyoph'sta enters not only the battlefield but also the social and political organizations that correlate with warriorhood and masculinity. Thus, while E'hyoph'sta's narrative is compelling on its own, when placed alongside the previous references we see again that although male and female roles were culturally defined and identifiably distinct among Indigenous peoples, such boundaries were also permeable—in certain cases, *female-identified and/or gender-variant people were welcomed not just into combat but also into the societies and socially sanctioned spaces of masculinity that exist beyond the battlefield.*

This recognition of Indigenous gender expansiveness holds particular impact when considered in light of the destructive and stark gender divisions demanded in hegemonic contexts. Both Mark Rifkin and Sam McKegney speak to the damage done by technologies of surveillance that surrounded gender in boarding and residential schools. Rifkin shows how enforced gender segregation was used to produce U.S. nationhood while simultaneously and purposely undermining Indigenous sovereignty.[39] In Canadian contexts, McKegney argues that "these acts of psychological, spiritual, and physical trauma constitute embroiled elements of [a] genocidal program . . . that has sought not only to denigrate and torment Indigenous women but to manufacture hatred toward Indigenous women in shamed and disempowered Indigenous men."[40] Such colonial violences demand strict divisions that actively worked to split families, erase nonbinary gender traditions, and destabilize Indigenous gender knowledges. These settler technologies, which have caused intergenerational trauma among Native peoples worldwide, are challenged by the presence of female, non-cis, and/or gender-variant warriors precisely because representations of such historical figures hold the embodied stories of another way of being in the world. It is for this very reason, as the subsequent section will demonstrate, that Indigenous writers return to such rich figures again and again. Rather than being consigned to a dusty, foreclosed past, *the stories of female and gender-variant warriors are an active presence that continues to hold resonance and power, speaking to the felt experience of North American Indigenous peoples.*

If there is one story in particular that speaks to such empowered possibility, it might be the story of Lozen. A Warm Springs Apache warrior thought to have been born in the 1840s, Lozen was said to have the capacity to sense the location of her people's enemies through prayer and spiritual intervention.[41] Lozen's story was little known outside her nation until Eve Ball interviewed her nephew James Kaywaykla and collaborated with him to write *In the Days of Victorio*.[42] Breaking a silence surrounding Lozen, her nephew told Ball his aunt "could ride, shoot and fight like a man; and I think she had more ability in planning military strategy than did [her famed brother] Victorio."[43] Kaywaykla further explains of Lozen: "I heard much of her as a warrior, but had not seen her in action. She must have been at least forty years old but was as agile as any man among us. In her youth she could outrun any of the men . . . but the men did not resent her. They were frankly proud of her and her ability. Above all they respected her integrity."[44] Further, Charlie Smith, an Apache interviewee, said, "To us she was a Holy Woman and she was regarded and treated as such. White Painted Woman herself was not more respected."[45] Significantly, Kaywaykla's and Smith's comments mark the status Lozen held in her community—a status that aligns with that afforded previously mentioned warriors like Woman Chief and E'hyoph'sta. As well, Kaywaykla and Smith introduce the intersection of warriorhood and spirituality. This node of connection between warriors and the spiritual world is entirely absent from dominant narratives about Indigenous warriorhood. Such noted absences parallel the goals of empire—in a body marked by violence, savagery, and death, there is no space for the sacred.

Lozen's import to her nation as both a military strategist and a spiritual figure circulated at a time of great upheaval for Apache people.[46] She fought and prayed at a moment when the image of the Native man as violent warrior had been consolidated by the U.S. government and mainstream press as a means of containment, a fact especially seen in media and government accounts of Apache leaders like Lozen's brother, Victorio, whom she fought alongside until his death, as well as legendary Apache leaders like Nana and Geronimo, whom Lozen subsequently joined in battle. In the face of the violent necropolitical discourses about Apache warriors that filled nineteenth-century newspapers, the story of Lozen's spiritual power, skilled tactical support of Victorio and Geronimo, and remarkable exploits to save those in danger gesture toward the ways she and the other warriors who led her people exceeded hegemonic containment. At the same time, Lozen forges a path for contemporary women warriors to follow, as chapter 4 will show in its analysis of the Apache firefighters depicted in *Apache 8.*

The significance of such female-identified and gender-variant warriors to their own tribal nations is evidenced by the living memories of such figures within their histories, a fact underscored by the oral history that surrounds Northern Cheyenne warrior Buffalo Calf Trail Woman.[47] Among other battles, Buffalo Calf Trail Woman fought in the June 17, 1876, Battle of the Rosebud (Battle of Rosebud Creek) in Montana Territory as well as the June 25–26, 1876, Battle of the Greasy Grass (Battle of the Little Bighorn), which took place just over fifty miles away the following week.[48] As with Lozen, Buffalo Calf Trail Woman's story lives not only in non-Native accounts but also within tribal history and the narrative memory of Northern Cheyenne tribal historians. In the Battle of the Rosebud, Buffalo Calf Trail Woman saved her brother, Chief Comes in Sight, through an act of heroism that brought the Cheyenne to call that conflict the "Fight Where the Girl Saved Her Brother."[49] According to Helena's *Independent Record,* in 2005, when the Cheyenne ended a hundred-year vow of silence about the Battle of the Greasy Grass, tribal historians shared further stories of Buffalo Calf Trail Woman's bravery and credited her with striking the blow that knocked George Armstrong Custer from his horse.[50] The circulation of such records within Indigenous oral and written histories attests to the fact that warrior women continue to hold relevance to contemporary Indigenous peoples and nations. Moreover, their narratives confirm Million's claim that "stories, unlike data, contain the affective legacy of [Indigenous] experiences."[51] The subversive narratives of these non-cis warriors present just such rich possibilities.

While there are so many more stories of female-identified and gender-variant warriors this chapter could include, I end this section with Moving Robe, because a *juxtaposition* of the two narratives about her participation in the 1876 Battle of the Greasy Grass expands affective understandings of Indigenous masculinities. Moving Robe (Thašína Máni, Hunkpapa Lakota, 1851–81) shared her history with Stanley Vestal (Walter S. Campbell) in 1931.[52] She references participating in at least two battles but elaborates on her experience at Greasy Grass. Moving Robe explains that after the battle commenced, a warrior alerted the camp that soldiers were coming:

> When I got to my tent, mother told me that news was brought to her that my brother had been killed by the soldiers. . . .
>
> My heart was bad. Revenge! Revenge! For my brother's death. . . . I ran to a nearby thicket and got my black horse. I painted my face with crimson and unbraided my black hair. I was mourning. I was a woman, but I was not afraid. . . .
>
> Father led my black horse up to me and I mounted. We galloped towards the soldiers. Other warriors joined in with us.[53]

Like other accounts we've seen, Moving Robe's narrative of her entry into the Battle of Greasy Grass turns on kinship obligations. According to her description, she enters the fray without hesitation and is aided by her father; her experience further reinforces Medicine's assertions about the culturally acceptable roles women have on the battlefield. She also names herself a warrior—"other warriors joined in"—making no distinctions among them.

Speaking with celebrated Dakota doctor and author Charles Eastman in 1905, Hunkpapa Lakota warrior and chief Rain in the Face (1851–1905) recounted his own memory of Moving Robe. His recollection of her participation in the Battle of the Greasy Grass is one of the stories he chose to share with Eastman while on his deathbed:[54]

> "All of us who were mounted and ready immediately started down the stream toward the ford. There were Oglallalas, Minneconjous, Cheyennes, and some Unkpapas, and those around me seemed to be nearly all very young men.
>
> "'Behold, there is among us a young woman!' I shouted. 'Let no young man hide behind her garment!' I knew that would make those young men brave.
>
> "The woman was Tashenamani, or Moving Robe, whose brother had just been killed in the fight with Three Stars. Holding her brother's war staff over her head, and leaning forward upon her charger, she looked as pretty as a bird. Always when there is a woman in the charge, it causes the warriors to vie with one another in displaying their valor," he added.[55]

Notably, Rain in the Face's recollection situates the presence of women warriors at such battles as somewhat, but by no means entirely, uncommon. His statement "Always when there is a woman in the charge" suggests that such events occur frequently enough to create a recognizable pattern of behavior. His description is in many ways conventional in terms of gender norms: Rain in the Face references Moving Robe's physical appearance—she is both dainty and attractive, "pretty as a bird"—and also recalls using the young woman's presence to incite masculine bravado: "Let no young man hide behind her garment!" The latter implies a gender divide absent in Moving Robe's own description and attends to certain well-documented Lakota cultural expectations about manhood and bravery. Yet, when examined further, Rain in the Face's depiction also foregrounds the interactive, affective nature of more expansive Indigenous gender performances.

In his analysis of female masculinity in Caribbean contexts, Ronald Cummings discusses the way such gender articulations circulate:

> Gender performances, productions and meanings are embedded in the realm of the social. Recognition serves to frame masculinity in terms of a series of iterations: recurring performances, images, perceptions and discourses which not only reinforce hegemonic masculinities but also serve to make female masculinities visible and readable as social and discursive sites of relation.[56]

In placing Cummings's claim alongside Rain in the Face's description, we can recognize how Moving Robe's physical presence alters the psychology of battle and simultaneously reinforces the highly contingent nature of masculinities as a whole. Importantly, Rain in the Face explicitly contends that expressions of Indigenous masculinities shift because of the affective force woman warriors have on their male-identified counterparts. If we follow Rain in the Face's logic, Moving Robe's presence literally causes the acts and expectations of Indigenous masculinity to be first verbally hailed ("Behold, there is among us a young woman!"), then externally and internally acknowledged among warriors ("making those young men brave"), and, finally, adhered to, which "causes the warriors to vie with one another in displaying their valor."[57] While Cummings suggests and I agree that hegemonic masculinity makes female masculinity legible, I'd add that *the bodily encounters of warrior women transform performances of Indigenous masculinities.* As recalled in Rain in the Face's narrative memory, Moving Robe's presence on the battlefield makes the malleable nature of masculinity and the attendant expectations of masculine behaviors among Lakota men more visible.

Along with highlighting these narratives of Indigenous gender expansiveness, *Written by the Body* situates such Indigenous knowledges as the very foundation of masculinity studies. *Indigenous women and gender-variant warriors aren't an alterity in masculinity studies—an aside or supplement—they serve as a fulcrum for more nuanced understandings.* Considering a like intervention in light of their work on the Anishinaabe warrior Ozaawindib (also known as Yellow Head), Two-Spirit Métis and Sault St. Marie Nishinaabe scholar Kai Pyle contends:

> Despite two centuries of fragmented and distorted representation, Ozaawindib's story remains important to Ojibwe people. A full account of her life would place her in even deeper context as an agokwe, a woman who went to war against the Dakota people of Mni Sota Makoce, the daughter of a prominent leader, a U.S.-designated chief in her own right, a woman who liked to drink socially on occasion and who sometimes got in fights, a good hunter and a swift runner, and above all as an Ojibwe person. To define her story only through the disgust of John Tanner or the exaltations of Henry Rowe Schoolcraft does a violence to her and to all the people today that would benefit from hearing her story, especially Two-Spirit Ojibwe people.[58]

If we consider Pyle's comments about Ozaawindib alongside the other examples shared here, we can confirm a number of points. Female-identified, non-cis, and gender-variant people regularly stepped into warrior roles within their nations, a fact that discredits endless settler demands for the cishet male-identified warrior figures they love to place on battlefields, football jerseys, and cinema screens. Further, as Pyle suggests, recovering and returning to these actual histories benefits Indigenous people. To return to where this chapter began, although dominant newspaper accounts often use words like "first" to speak of Lori Piestewa, she exists within an Indigenous tradition of like women and gender-variant warriors and leaders who still have stories to tell, knowledge to share. When read together, these narratives emphasize links between kinship, warriorhood, and gender expansiveness and underscore the ways such relationships circulate in the cultural memory of Indigenous people.

Such shared memory is essential to the transformative stories analyzed in the rest of this chapter, which turn from Indigenous histories to women and gender-variant warriors in Indigenous imaginations. These memories are maintained in Indigenous oral and written histories, as we've seen. At the same time, they also exist in creative expression, most notably that of literature and film. In *Why Indigenous Literatures Matter,* Justice argues that "Indigenous literatures are the storied archives—embodied, inscribed, digitized, vocalized—that articulate our sense of belonging and wonder, the ways of meaning-making in the world and in our time."[59] To chart this creative narrative archive, the second half of this chapter turns to Callahan's *Wynema* and Zitkala-Ša's short story "A Warrior's Daughter." An analysis of these two earliest representations of women warriors demonstrates how such figures index—in Callahan's case the affective limits of, and in Zitkala-Ša's the extensive possibilities of—gender expansiveness in early-twentieth-century Native American literature. Chapter 2 then moves to the contemporary period, juxtaposing the realist fiction of Pawnee/Otoe-Missouri writer Anna Lee Walters's 1983 short story "The Warriors" with Justice's fantasy series *The Way of Thorn and Thunder: The Kynship Chronicles,* arguing that these imaginative expansions build on and extend Indigenous narrative memories about female-identified and gender-variant warriors by mapping the contours of affective embodiment and the Indigenous erotic.

The Rupture of S. Alice Callahan's Women Warriors in *Wynema: A Child of the Forest*

In turning to the reservation era and the first iteration of warrior women in Indigenous literature, the rest of this chapter finds not literatures that speak of Indigenous "continuity and presence," but rather those of rupture and absence.[60] The earliest novel published by an Indigenous woman in North America, Muscogee Creek author

S. Alice Callahan's *Wynema: A Child of the Forest,* includes depictions of Lakota women who join the battle at the Wounded Knee Massacre, which took place on December 29, 1890, shortly before the novel's 1891 publication.[61] Yet despite the fact that Callahan was actually a contemporary of some of the female-identified and gender-variant warriors previously referenced in this chapter—she was born in 1868 and died in 1894—her depiction of her characters' entrance into armed conflict comprise a radically different affective resonance than do the historical accounts of warriors like Woman Chief, E'hyoph'sta, Lozen, Buffalo Calf Trail Woman, Moving Robe, or Ozaawindib. Muscogee Creek/Cherokee scholar Craig Womack has famously called *Wynema* a text filled with "intentional misrepresentation," asking, "What are we to make of this author, then, who is purposefully writing to satisfy white stereotypes?"[62] We can consider this question in light of Callahan's introduction of women warriors in the hastily appended final chapters of the novel, which turn to the days just before and after Wounded Knee.[63] In light of the previous histories, I want to suggest Callahan's portrayal of these women and this historical moment represents what Justice calls a "rupture" in relationality. Such challenges to Indigenous kinship speak of physical and psychic "violence, violation, fragmentation" and "pain."[64] Yet, he maintains, and I agree, that "ruptures, too, can be read. The absences tell stories of their own."[65] While Callahan's imaginative rendering of warrior women troubles rather than transforms, her textual ruptures raise significant questions, including how and why might *Wynema* represent an affective response to women who step into the role of warrior?

In the sampling of historical narratives that began this chapter, female-identified and gender-variant warriors are marked as exceptional in courage as well as in the strategies and execution of combat. While their presence in combat was not ubiquitous, their participation, especially in the context of the Lakota to whom Callahan refers, made cultural sense. "Whether Plains Indian women participated in military activity directly or supported it in an indirect way," Medicine explains, "it is clear that they saw their own well-being and that of their kin and community in terms of a social system which revolves around warfare."[66] Thus, Lakota warrior women would support rather than undermine this social system and would operate, as well, within the kinship structures that map alliance and familial and national connections within a Plains ideology. Speaking of such axes of relationship in *Oglala Women*, Marla Powers describes the movement of kinship ties, saying that Plains people understand themselves and their place in the world through interlocking levels of affiliation: "An individual belonged to the *tiyošpaye* 'band,' the *oyate* 'tribe,' and finally the Teton."[67] These maps of belonging brought Plains women to the battlefield, and once there, as Rain in the Face notes, their bodies held significant affective possibilities. We can surmise, then, that in late-nineteenth-century Indigenous contexts a warrior woman's presence in combat *furthers* rather than hinders the possibility of a successful outcome in a military engagement.

The presence of Indigenous women in combat represents a bodily intensity filled with possibility. However, Callahan's Plains women, while driven by concerns of kinship that might at first seem similar to those of historical warrior women, function on a radically different affective plane. Physically, Callahan defines her female Lakota characters through what W. E. B. Du Bois famously called the impenetrable veil of race. Lacking any individualizing detail, Callahan's women are literally absent. Haunted and haunting, they are described only as "dark figures," who "[creep] stealthily from [their] tent[s]" (88).[68] When the novel's forty women and children depart for the soon-to-be-battlefield at Wounded Knee Creek, they are likewise "dark figures, running, sliding, and falling along the dark road in the bitter night" (88). The racialized rhetoric in this scene is heavy with a sense of inevitability—a classic trope in dominant Ghost Dance and Wounded Knee narratives—Callahan's tone leaving readers no doubt that the women are heading toward their death.

In addition to being circumscribed by darkness and loss, the Lakota women's entrance into the conflict at Wounded Knee Creek situates them *as a direct cause for the loss*. The narrator explains:

> The Indians were slaughtered like cattle, shot down like dogs. . . . To add to this consternation, on turning about toward his camps, [the Lakota leader, Wildfire] beheld the women who had followed them to battle, instead of going to the reservation as they had promised and started to do. . . . As they rushed into the line of battle where they more unfitted the men for fighting.
>
> "Good and gracious Father, Miscona! *You have lost the battle for me*," groaned the chieftain. (89; emphasis added)

As seen here, Callahan crafts a jarringly different picture of women's presence in battle than that offered by the historical record. Rather than spurring the men to perform greater acts of valor and/or claiming their own culturally sanctioned place in the conflict, as in Rain in the Face's comments about Moving Robe, the presence of Callahan's warrior women on the battlefield index liability and loss.

Further, Callahan confines her Lakota women to a limited narrative of kinship that privileges marriage and heterocouplehood as the text turns on the romances of its two protagonists, Genevieve and Wynema. Rifkin discusses the ways U.S. government Indian policies and boarding schools attempted to instantiate monogamous couplehood in place of Indigenous modes of collectivity.[69] Narrow definitions of heterocouplehood came to stand in for the more expansive understandings of kinship exemplified in most Indigenous cosmologies. These selfsame logics of heteronormativity constrain Callahan's images of the Lakota—the power of Lakota women, the historical acceptance of Plains women on the battlefield, and the flexibility of Lakota gender roles are all noticeably absent from *Wynema*. Instead, as Susan Bernardin notes, the text "represent[s] Lakota women as sympathetic maternal figures" characterized primarily through their "mother-love."[70] While Callahan gives us an image of Plains women with the agency to join their husbands in battle, gender complementarity vis-à-vis the possibility of women who fully inhabit the role of warrior fighting alongside male counterparts is not considered. By contrast, *Wynema* offers a reductive version of kinship and women warriors, erasing the existence of such very real figures and substituting in their stead dark symbols of sentiment that are racialized, gendered, and coupled according to hegemonic nineteenth-century mores.

To read *Wynema* through Justice's ideas, in their very unknowability the Lakota women signal a rupture in relationship between and among Indigenous people that is fostered by settler sentiments. On one hand, Callahan was drawn to address the massacre. Yet on another, her narrator's simultaneous empathy for and distancing from Plains people reveals a rift, a rupture, in that selfsame logics of recognition. Even while Callahan claims relationship to, in the words of her dedication in the first edition of the novel, "the Indian tribes of North America who have felt the wrongs and oppression of their pale-faced brothers," Callahan's Lakota are both hopelessly primitive and doomed to extinction. As numerous critics have pointed out, the preface to the novel most specifically exemplifies this identificatory schism: in it, Indians are a "they" and "them" of which Callahan herself is sometimes a part and sometimes not. And, since the question of to whom one is related holds great sway in Indian country, Callahan's waffling about kinship is a weighty matter. Bernardin turns to Callahan's dedication to address this fragmentation, gesturing toward its use of "familial terms that invite readerly sympathy for Indians."[71] However, "in the first several chapters an authorial voice overtly marked as 'Anglo,' seemingly belies the publisher's certification [of Callahan's Indigeneity] by repeatedly using 'we' to demarcate narrator and audience from 'them'—the Indians being described."[72] Callahan's Creek Indians are subsumed under the novel's decidedly Anglo version of late-nineteenth-century feminism, which, while recognizing some aspects of women's rights, privileges the cult of domesticity in its elevation of marriage and monogamous couplehood for the novel's two central characters. Callahan's Lakota, by contrast, are almost entirely stripped of cultural beliefs, historical relevance, and personhood. If, as noted affect theorist Silvan Tomkins contends, "the shame response is literally an ambivalent turning of the eyes away from the object toward . . . the self," then perhaps that "deeply ambivalent" act informs the rhetorical absence of Callahan's warrior women.[73]

Claiming Gender Exceptionalism: Zitkala-Ša's Woman Warrior

The contrast between the first two iterations of Native American warrior women in literature could not be starker. Arising from the pen of famed Yankton Sioux author Zitkala-Ša (Red Bird), the short story "A Warrior's Daughter" functions not as rupture but as a clear and present narrative memory that "emerges from" a tribally specific "worldview and spirituality."[74] "A Warrior's Daughter" originally appeared in a 1902 issue of *Everybody's Magazine* and was later republished in Zitkala-Ša's 1921 collection of short stories and autobiographical essays, *American Indian Stories*. A well-known warrior herself, who campaigned for Native American rights and suffrage, Zitkala-Ša, or Gertrude Simmons Bonnin, was born in 1876, eight years after

S. Alice Callahan. She published her debut essay in *Harpers* in 1900, nine years after H. J. Smith and Company released *Wynema* and a year before *Old Indian Legends,* the first of Zitkala-Ša's two collections, came to print.[75]

While we know more about Bonnin's life than Callahan's, in part because of the former's fame during her lifetime, there is no question that the two seem to have had radically different early childhoods, at least until Zitkala-Ša left the Yankton Sioux Reservation for boarding school in Wabash, Indiana, around 1884. Callahan grew up ensconced in the upper echelons of the Muscogee (Creek) Nation. Her family was said to be "rich in gold or stock and in control of Muscogee politics. Black slaves tilled their land and herded their cattle while they rode in carriages."[76] Zitkala-Ša, by contrast, casts her preboarding-school childhood as more like that of Callahan's protagonist Wynema than Callahan's own. For example, when describing her seven-year-old self, Zitkala-Ša comments: "Loosely clad in a slip of brown buckskin, and light-footed with a pair of soft moccasins on my feet, I was as free as the wind that blew my hair."[77] The Yankton author and activist depicts her early childhood as an idyllic period of innocence before the fall of her years in boarding school. Additionally, while the two young women both show marked commitments to feminist ideals, Zitkala-Ša embraces a more overt sense of independence, challenging a heteronormative status quo in ways that Callahan, in her extant letters and novel, does not.[78] These differences in affiliation and upbringing may account for the radical difference between the characterizations of the Plains warrior women found in each of their texts.

As we turn from Callahan's novel to Zitkala-Ša's "A Warrior's Daughter," we see that the title and opening scenes of Zitkala-Ša's piece create an expectation that the narrative will focus on a warrior father's love for, and a young suitor's courtship of, the daughter of a famed warrior; however, Zitkala-Ša has something else in mind entirely. Instead, she shows that in Dakota contexts the bravery, courage, and daring inherent in a warrior masculinity can run from father to daughter. Tusee, the "warrior's daughter," is not merely a female relative of a warrior but is herself the embodiment of every aspect of her paternal heritage—she rides, strategizes, performs acts of daring, and, as we'll see, ultimately succeeds where her suitor fails in making war on Dakota enemies. By the end of the story, in stark contrast to Callahan's doomed and ineffectual Lakota women, Zitkala-Ša's protagonist embodies a productive, protective, and affective form of female masculinity that hinges on familial relationship and tribal responsibility.

"A Warrior's Daughter" begins by detailing the strengths of "the chieftain's bravest warrior," thereby emphasizing the central traits of the signifier "warrior" in Zitkala-Ša's estimation. According to the omniscient narrator, the warrior in question had previously undertaken "heroic deeds" to gain his status and was, as well, "one of the most generous gift givers to the toothless old people."[79] In addition, the narrator emphasizes his great love for his then eight-year-old daughter, Tusee. Thus, within the first pages of her text, Zitkala-Ša's readers are schooled that "true" warriors are brave figures who act with heroism, evince a deep generosity, and hold pronounced respect for kinship ties.

Early in the story, the contours of a warrior's bravery are further defined through a subsequent exchange between the protagonist, a now-grown Tusee, and her unnamed suitor. A test of the suitor's bravery and correspondingly, according to Tusee's father, the young man's worthiness for Tusee's partnership in marriage, requires "an enemy's scalp-lock, plucked fresh with [his] own hand" (143). In "Dakota Warfare," Ruth Landes speaks to the necessity of such acts, contending that for the Dakota people, "bravery, under the circumstances defined as honorable, was . . . a criterion of mature responsible maleness."[80] In many ways, the largely white audience of *Everybody's Magazine,* the original publication venue for "A Warrior's Daughter," would be both familiar and at ease with this narrative of masculinity: the young suitor's "test" mirrors the dominant values of bravery and heroism tied to iterations of hegemonic masculinities, as does the patriarchal narrative in which a father sets the terms of his daughter's betrothal.[81] However Zitkala-Ša's allusion to the practice of scalping, with its popular connotations of primitive savagery and its connection, for non-Native audiences, to the frightening stereotype of the savage warrior would at the same time have made the familiar strange.[82] This latter iteration of a potentially violent masculinity most likely titillated mainstream readers who embraced a settler nostalgia for a romanticized West, as the ongoing popularity of traveling performance troupes like Buffalo Bill's Wild West Show under-lined.[83] The scene turns, then, on a specter of Indigenous masculin-ity weighted—at least for hegemonic readers—with expectations of violence. While traditionally in Sioux (Lakota, Dakota, Nakota) cul-tures a warrior was thought to exhibit bravery, fortitude, generosity, and wisdom, in the eyes of most dominant U.S. audiences at the turn of the twentieth century, an Indigenous warrior was the vicious and static actor of western-themed dime novels.

Even in her twenties, Zitkala-Ša was consistently aware of audi-ence expectations, as demonstrated in her letters and public appear-ances. For example, in speeches she employed theatric rhetorical flourishes and often shed her everyday dresses to don pantribal garb. Patrice Hollrah explains that at times Zitkala-Ša "seems to play on the romantic notion of the noble savage in the pristine Eden of the 'New World.'"[84] Such decisions highlight Zitkala-Ša's rhetorical savvy and ability to manipulate audience expectations for her own ends. Such is the case, as well, in "A Warrior's Daughter," where she uses the power of expectation and anomaly to seize and keep her readers' attention. In this instance that power hinges on certain scripts about the per-formance of masculinity. She first teaches the audience about the virtues of a warrior masculinity in Dakota culture, then teases with her allusion to practices her settler readers would likely perceive as marking "savage" masculinity, and finally turns, with sleight of hand, to what for dominant readers would be an entirely unexpected gender performance—that of female masculinity.

As with the historical women warriors with whom this chapter began, Tusee's performance of a warrior masculinity is animated by a commitment to kinship on multiple levels. On one hand, Tusee has fallen in love with the young man who seeks to wed her. When her fa-ther sets the challenge before her lover, contending that he must com-plete a warrior's act of risk and bravery to win Tusee, she explains: "My father's heart is really kind. He would know if you are brave and true" (143). The narrator further states that Tusee "wished no ill-will between her two loved ones," thereby equating her filial attachment to her father with her romantic tie to her lover (143). As a result, when her lover fails at his appointed task and, instead, is taken cap-tive, Tusee does not merely grieve; she acts in light of these aforemen-tioned emotional and familial obligations.[85] These obligations to her lover and family combine with her subsequent actions to frame Tusee as a woman who, for the benefit of her family and nation, participates in warrior practices traditionally situated as the domain of men.

Tusee, in fact, epitomizes the figure of the warrior woman from the moment she leaves her family's lodge to follow her suitor into battle. She is by no means the only woman to attend the war party, yet the difference between the narrator's depictions of Tusee and of the other women is striking. The "brave elderly women" follow on "ponies laden with food and deerskins" to perform the important obligations of preparing food and tending camp, as would have occurred in many Plains war parties. In Zitkala-Ša's characterization of Dakota gender responsibilities, all the women except Tusee pack, cook, and strike camp while the men hunt and attack (the unnamed) Dakota enemies. By contrast to the older women, Tusee, unburdened by stores, joins the group attired "in elaborately beaded buckskin dress" (144). Additionally, the narrator characterizes the protagonist with images of strength and bravery more common to descriptions of warrior masculinity: "Proudly mounted, she curbs with the single rawhide loop a wild-eyed pony. It is Tusee on her father's warhorse" (144). The ceremonially dressed young woman is able to tame this spirited mount with ease, which highlights Tusee's command of horsemanship—an important attribute of Plains warrior identity in the late eighteenth and nineteenth centuries—and parallels her equine abilities to those of her warrior father. At this point in the story, then, Tusee already operates in a space of gender exceptionalism. As a result, even before Tusee springs into action to save her beau from the enemy, Zitkala-Ša depicts her as an example of a Plains warrior woman.

Tusee's bravery and success explicitly reflect her inheritance from her father and her embodiment of the key virtues of warrior masculinity. Armed with a knife and a burning need to prevail over her enemy, Tusee stalks toward the enemy's victory dance "with a panther's tread" (146). Her actions here and throughout the scene are infused with courage and boldness as she single-handedly plans and executes her lover's rescue.[86] Speaking of such acts in an early essay on Plains war practices, Marian W. Smith maintains that "war honors" among Plains peoples include "fearlessness, the capacity to make successful surprise attacks, the power to overcome an antagonist or show superiority to him, and the ability to carry out successful war projects. All of these were connected with the warrior's relationship with the supernatural."[87] Likewise, Paula Gunn Allen notes:

> In English, the term "war" means soldiers blasting away at military targets for the purpose of attacking or defending territory, ideals, or resources. In the tribal way, war means a ritual path, a . . . spiritual discipline that can test honor, selflessness, and devotion, and put the warrior in closer, more powerful harmony with the supernaturals and the earth.[88]

Tusee manifests the facets of an Indigenous warrior identity as described by Smith and Allen—she acts with daring and successfully completes an audacious plan that brings her face-to-face with an enemy combatant whom she kills. Moreover, the fulfillment of Tusee's subsequent prayer—"All-powerful Spirit, grant me my warrior-father's heart, strong to slay a foe and mighty to save a friend" (146)—aligns her with the spiritual properties of a warrior masculinity emphasized in stories about Lozen. The warrior's daughter thus embodies every aspect of her father's identity, not only exhibiting exceptional horsemanship but also demonstrating bravery, stealth, expert strategic skills, and a deep tie to Dakota spirituality.

While Tusee herself epitomizes the same masculinity that characterizes warrior women in Indigenous traditions, hers is only one of the many images of Indigenous masculinity that circulate throughout the rescue scene. The warriors from the opposing camp are identified as "lusty" and "naked," invoking the classic specter of a hypersexualized, primitive, and threatening masculinity, while her lover's failure in warfare likewise marks him as improperly gendered: "haggard with shame and sorrow," his now-abject figure is mocked by the enemy as they celebrate their victory (148). This ritual display in which the victor's performance of hypermasculinity rests on the body of the defeated recurs when an enemy "warrior, scarce older than the captive, flourish[es] a tomahawk in the Dakota's face" (148). The sole witness to this exchange, Tusee deems it "a living death" (148). We see, then, the slippery nature of warrior masculinity as it moves between and among the bodies in the narrative, shifting from the suitor to the enemy combatant to whom he loses in battle, and finally stabilizing in Tusee, who bests both young men in the art of war. The consummate image of her father, Tusee, by the final accounting, emerges as not only the best but also as *the most properly masculine* of the young warriors who appear in the text.

By the conclusion of "A Warrior's Daughter," Tusee frees her lover and kills the young warrior who captured and humiliated him, demonstrating her prowess and counting the final coup of the story. Importantly, when she delivers the death blow to her enemy, Tusee "gives a wild spring forward like a panther for its prey," her hissed rebuke—"'I am a Dakota woman!'" (150)—the last words the young man hears before her knife ends his life. As the warrior falls at her feet, the narrator explains: "The Great Spirit heard Tusee's prayer on the hilltop. He gave her a warrior's strong heart to lessen the foe by one" (151). Exhibiting careful planning, stealth, and spiritual favor, Tusee drops the guise of temptress, which she employed to lure the now-dead young man from the victory dance, and subsequently enters the arena disguised as an old woman. Through these lightning-fast shifts, Zitkala-Ša suggests that both male and female gender performances are malleable constructions that women can deploy for the benefit of themselves and their people, a claim reinforced by the story's conclusion.

In the final moments of the piece, Tusee rises from her hunched disguise to take on a warrior's physical strength and free her lover:

> "Come!" she whispers, and turns to go; but the young man,
> numb and helpless, staggers nigh to falling.
> The sight of his weakness makes her strong. A mighty
> power thrills her body. Stooping beneath his outstretched arms
> grasping at the air for support, Tusee lifts him upon her broad
> shoulders. With half-running, triumphant steps she carries him
> away into the open night. (152–53)

The array of gender roles embodied in the rapid-fire conclusion of Zitkala-Ša's short story is dizzying. Tusee inhabits both the part of a young girl attracted to her enemy's display of virility, and an old woman, bent by the dual burdens of age and labor, all the while acting as a strong, decisive Dakota warrior. Moreover, the vehement claim to Dakota womanhood made while plunging a knife into the belly of her enemy emphasizes the fact that all these aspects of her identity—her ingenuity, her bravery, her desirability, her responsibility, her femininity, and, yes, her masculinity—coexist within the strong body of a woman warrior.

The Affective Circuit of Female Masculinity in "A Warrior's Daughter"

Stepping back from an overview of how "A Warrior's Daughter" crafts and subsequently develops the facets of a warrior subjectivity, we can consider, too, what makes this representation particularly affective, as well as what can be gained by reading Zitkala-Ša's depiction of gender expansiveness through such a lens. To do so, I return to the final scenes of the story.

The ever-shifting identities seen throughout Tusee's rescue of her partner point to the fact that her warrior masculinity relies on active exchange. In fact, her gender-fluid performances exemplify noted affect theorist Brian Massumi's contention about the way affect (which he terms "intensity") "infolds contexts . . . volitions and cognitions" in cyclical and often preconscious sites of contact.[89] Tusee's body exists in that space of transition—always becoming what it is not, changing according to context, need, and the play of bodies upon one another. This play is necessarily relational, since Tusee inhabits gender in light of situational and community needs. As well, her transformations point to the body's *inherent* indeterminacy—the body is always in flux, never quite reaching its destination.[90] There is therefore no fixed point, no single action, that creates a warrior. Instead, Zitkala-Ša suggests that warrior identity *is* the body in action. These fluid shifts from one point to another speak to the constellation of gender possibilities in, and to the expansiveness of, the Indigenous gender knowledges Zitkala-Ša depicts in the early twentieth century.

I want to suggest here that using affect theory to understand the many gender performances through which Tusee moves—from warrior's daughter, to consummate rider, to temptress, to old woman, to strong warrior-savior—shows us something particular about Indigenous representations of warrior masculinity. Or at the very least, about Zitkala-Ša's particular representation of that role. As we've seen, "A Warrior's Daughter" teaches us there is no singular point at or to which Indigenous masculinity or a warrior woman's identity can be calibrated. Despite having spent the first section of this chapter offering historical examples of such figures, an affective reading of Zitkala-Ša's story suggests we still cannot concretely or correctly say, "a warrior woman is x." Is a warrior woman a cis woman who goes into battle to avenge her husband? Is a warrior woman an unmarried figure with spiritual powers who scouts the location of an enemy to save her brother, to protect her people? Is a warrior a gender-variant person accepted into masculine-identified spaces but identified as a woman in many settler encounters? In each case, extant historical narratives say yes; however at the same time, as contemporary readers, we recognize that *the contexts* of these warrior masculinities *differ* and *the embodied movements that create them range widely in action, duration, and intensity.* Through her characterization of Tusee, Zitkala-Ša helps her early-twentieth-century readers recognize the then-radical argument that there is no one act to, or in which, the fluidity of gender can be tethered. It is Tusee's constant bodily movement through a myriad of possible roles that makes her a warrior—she is, in fact, still changing at the very moment of the story's conclusion.

The most notable example of the affective change Zitkala-Ša imagines comes in the story's final paragraph, when the narrator explains how, after Tusee finds her lover unable to support himself, "the sight of his weakness makes her strong" (153). Her warrior identity, this unruly iteration of masculinity, intensifies through the unspoken play of body upon body. Just as Rain in the Face described Moving Robe's transformative effect on the battlefield, here too the felt interaction between and among bodies engenders what seems to be a preconscious shift. Thus when Tusee inhabits a Dakota warrior masculinity, with its call for bravery, daring, strategy, and selflessness, her body answers that need with a "mighty power" that "thrills her" (153). Clearly cast as a physiological response, this affective reaction offers something more than the intellectual acts of planning Tusee previously performed. One of the earliest affect theorists, Baruch (or Benedictine de) Spinoza, proposes that "the body cannot determine the mind to thought, neither can the mind determine the body to motion nor rest, nor anything else," and that "what the body can do no one has [yet] determined."[91] Much as Spinoza suggests, in this final scene Zitkala-Ša represents the body as affectively responding to an unprecedented call for strength, thereby enabling Tusee to complete what should be a herculean task—lifting the nearly inert body of a grown man and running with him to safety. In this act, masculinity, which heretofore has been seen in Tusee's abilities, decisions, and actions, intensifies through an embodied response to affective forces that literally expand the body's physical capacity. Making gender intelligible in this instance, then, means *understanding how Indigenous writers forward the active, affective nature of the Indigenous body in relationship.*

As this chapter demonstrates, "A Warrior's Daughter" pulls from a particular thread of cultural memory to highlight the gender expansive roles available to Dakota women. Zitkala-Ša looks to a precontact economy of gender and recognizes it as one in which Indigenous women had more freedom than she herself encounters at the turn of the twentieth century.[92] Yet an affective reading of the story teaches us this and so much more. Analyzing the fluctuating expressions of Tusee's warrior masculinity causes us to appreciate *how gender can be useful,* how it can become a tool in the Plains context of the narrative. Unlike Callahan's limited depictions of women in battle, Zitkala-Ša suggests that such flexible gender performances benefit Indigenous community and contends, as well, that the boundaries of Plains gender roles are fluid enough to affectively respond to a community's specific needs. She also proposes that valued aspects of behavior, which in Dakota contexts are often attached to masculinity, can be passed from father to daughter. As a result, reading Zitkala-Ša's depiction of a nineteenth-century warrior woman through an affective lens transforms our contemporary understanding of what happens when a Native woman enters a space coded as masculine. When Tusee employs female masculinity as one among many options available to her, using it purposefully and, in fact, joyfully, her body responds by offering her an affectively generated power. And given the historical warrior traditions engaged in the first section of this chapter, this affective power is not radically transgressive, as it would most likely have been perceived by dominant audiences at the point of its publication, but is, instead, well established.

The complex and layered iterations of historical and literary warrior identities broaden discussions of Indigenous gender representations in the early twentieth century, reminding us not only that warrior women like Lori Ann Piestewa have always held powerful and active roles in protecting their families and communities but also that they exist within a long-standing and expansive array of Indigenous gender knowledges. Zitkala-Ša purposely evokes such knowledges, affirming the fact that, as Justice contends, "Indigenous literatures are storied archives—embodied, inscribed, digitized, vocalized—that articulate our sense of belonging and wonder, the ways of meaning-making in the world and in our time."[93]

CHAPTER 2

WARRIORS, INDIGENOUS FUTURES, AND THE EROTIC

Anna Lee Walters and Daniel Heath Justice

> Expressing our sensualities, sexualities and genders without
> stigma is the work of warriors. And perhaps this is our power:
> though we have been forgotten, suppressed and lost, we still
> persist—with love.
>
> —Lindsay Nixon, "Making Space in Indigenous Art for Bull Dykes
> and Gender Weirdos"

As we move from the turn of the twentieth century into the mid- to late twentieth century, warrior women, so prevalent in eighteenth- and nineteenth-century representations, are not initially evident in extant literary publications, though they remain alive in Indigenous oral history and memory. So while Mohawk writer E. Pauline Johnson's 1913 collection *The Moccasin Maker* presents strong and unconventional female characters, overt reference to female warrior traditions do not appear. The same can be said for Mourning Dove's (Christine Quintasket, Salish) collaboratively produced texts: *Cogewea the Half Blood: A Depiction of the Great Montana Cattle Range* (1927) and *Coyote Stories* (1933).[1] Likewise in Ella Cara Deloria's (Dakota) *Waterlily*, which was written in the 1940s though not published until 1988, we see strong, complex female characters but no specific allusion to warrior women or Two-Spirit people. Additionally, like Zitkala-Ša, women such as Deloria, Laura Cornelius Kellogg (Oneida), and Ruth Muskrat Bronson (Cherokee) were active in politics and could themselves be argued to follow a warrior women tradition given dominant gender mores and expectations of the early to midcentury period.[2]

Female-identified and gender-variant warriors return to Indigenous fiction in the post-Renaissance era, as this chapter will demonstrate. While there are innumerable texts that could be considered here, the two selections analyzed bring important and different representational aspects of woman and gender-variant warriors in Indigenous literature into the equation. Anne Lee Walters's "The Warriors" directly engages what happens at the intersections of gender and cultural memory in the mid-twentieth century. "The Warriors" points toward both the continued relevance of warrior figures in Native oral histories more broadly, and Pawnee traditions specifically, as well as to the necessity of working to explode cishet, male-focused boundaries of warriorhood. Although the pairing may initially seem unlikely, I argue that Daniel Heath Justice undertakes similar expansive work in his twenty-first-century fantasy series *The Kynship Chronicles*.[3] While Walters interrogates the place of cis-identified Indigenous women in warrior paradigms, Justice addresses nonbinary warriors, the erotic, and Indigenous futures. In doing so he answers an important question Cree scholar Dana Wesley posed at the 2015 Native American and Indigenous Studies conference about where "queer, trans, and two-spirit life would dwell inside" "imagining[s]" of Indigenous futures.[4] In both cases, *these story lines directly confront and reframe narratives about warriors by placing women and gender-variant figures as the axis upon which an affective understanding of gender turns.*

Warrior Nation: Female Masculinity as Cultural Continuity in Anna Lee Walters's "The Warriors"

Like Zitkala-Ša, Pawnee/Otoe-Missouri writer Anne Lee Walters offers a short story in which the facets of a warrior identity move between male- and female-identified characters. In "The Warriors," which appeared in Walters's short story collection *The Sun Is Not Merciful* (1985) and was later reprinted in Paula Gunn Allen's landmark *Spider Woman's Granddaughters* within a section likewise titled "The Warriors," Walters imagines a warrior ethos that flows between and among two Pawnee sisters—the narrator, Pumpkin Flower, and her younger sibling, Sister—and their uncle Ralph, a Korean War veteran and traditional singer. The action begins in the late 1960s, moves into the girls' early teen years, and then concludes when the girls, now in their twenties, attend their uncle's funeral; the entire piece is narrated from an unidentified point in their later lives. Throughout her short story, Walters builds a complex discourse about a Pawnee warrior identity that rocks between redemption and loss, posing the underlying question: *What is a warrior in the latter half of the twentieth century?*

The narrator's uncle carries with him and shares narrative memory as he teaches about Pawnee history, legend, and song, which are, he explains, living reminders of "precious things only the Pawnees know."[5] Each time he sees his nieces, he shares stories within which "warriors dangled in delicate balance" (112). In fact, the narrator explains that "Uncle Ralph talked obsessively of warriors," narrating the legend of the Pawnee warrior Pahukatawa and details of momentous battles in which "painted proud warriors . . . shrieked poignant battle cries at the top of their lungs and died with honor" (112–13).[6] Clearly, the girls' uncle, a veteran who struggles with alcohol addiction, longs for all the productivity and power a warrior masculinity signifies. If in 1902 Zitkala-Ša imagines a warrior ethos as encompassing bravery, daring, and selflessness, Walters's character, who lives nearly three-quarters of a century later, sees the tenets of a warrior masculinity as an expression of a nationhood he fears lost to the world.

According to Walters's short story and to most, if not all, Indigenous understandings of warriorhood, generosity is as much a part of a warrior ethos as bravery. Consequently, warriors accept the responsibility to feed and clothe their people, often hunting for those who cannot hunt for themselves much like Tusee's father did in "A Warrior's Daughter." Uncle Ralph demonstrates how this valued tenet of warrior responsibility continues into the mid-twentieth century when he regularly arrives at his sister's house bearing gifts of food because, the narrator explains, "Pawnee custom was that the man, the warrior, should bring food, preferably meat" (118). The girls' uncle also works for the good of the nation by carrying on Pawnee cultural traditions. Uncle Ralph teaches the girls Pawnee language and is called on by others because of his skilled drumming and singing: "They said he was only one of a few who knew the old ways and the songs" (118). Yet, even while he claims and enacts a warrior identity, their uncle simultaneously laments the passing away of all that makes up a Pawnee warrior's world, saying, "Young people nowadays, it seems they don't care 'bout nothing that's old. They just want to go to the Moon" (117–18). Though not explicitly stated, the chasm represented by contemporary disinterest in Pawnee culture seems to be, at least in part, the impetus behind Uncle Ralph's steady decline into alcoholism, which eventually leads to his homelessness.[7] The implication, then, is that warrior traditions, which represent the best of Pawnee cosmology, are at risk of vanishing, disremembered and unaccounted for.[8]

Despite the specter of such seemingly irredeemable loss, Walters's story, like Zitkala-Ša's, narrates an inheritance in which warrior masculinity passes through kinship lines from male-identified to female-identified characters. In "The Warriors" the girls/young women take up a warrior identity as a form of cultural continuity. Consequently, formerly male cultural practices are handed down from uncle to niece in the same way Tusee inherited the central attributes of her father's warrior masculinity. We see this as Uncle Ralph teaches the girls Pawnee language and history, which he distinctly describes as part of a Pawnee warrior tradition. However, even as these exchanges occur, Uncle Ralph himself does not imagine the girls as warriors; warriors for him are the stuff of his legends and histories, and in those histories as he relates them, warriors are always and only cis men. Thus, after Uncle Ralph sings a warrior song and Sister dances a war dance, all three laugh. The narrator explains: "Sister began to dance the men's dance. She had never danced before and tried to imitate what she had seen. Her chubby body whirled and jumped the way the men moved theirs" (118). When her uncle sings her "an *Eruska* song, a song for the warriors," she steps into that location, her body affectively answering his call to action (118). Though Sister's steps are clumsy, her dance serves as an embodied claim to her Pawnee inheritance.

In *Indians in Unexpected Places*, Dakota scholar Philip J. Deloria asks "how we might revisit the actions of Indian people that have been all too easily branded as anomalous."[9] One common reaction to such anomalies is what he terms an ideological chuckle. "The safest response to . . . strangeness"—such as Sister's attempt to perform a male-identified dance for warriors—"is often laughter, which takes direct aim at the impossibility of the image. A chuckle can reaffirm the rightness of one's broadest cultural expectations."[10] The laughter after Sister's dance, while not unexpected, confirms Uncle Ralph's and even the girls' own gender expectations—their shared amusement tacitly maintains that women are not warriors. Furthermore, Uncle Ralph's reactions throughout the piece underscore his continued belief in that fact. When the narrator asks him overtly, in what she correctly suspects will be the last time she sees him, "Uncle Ralph, can women be warriors, too?," he laughs much as they laughed together at Sister's war dance (123). Answering her question with an amused query of his own—"'Don't tell me you want to be one of the warriors too?'"—he "hug[s] her merrily" (123). Though he loves his nieces fiercely, Uncle Ralph's ideological chuckle defines a warrior masculinity as one wedded solely to cisgender men. Even as the sisters follow him, raptly absorbing the Pawnee language, cultural history, and traditions he imparts, Uncle Ralph laments the disinterest of "young people nowadays" and the loss of Pawnee identity; he mourns the fact that he is the last of the Pawnee warriors.

These exchanges emphasize the need for sustained cultural memory about women warriors and also illustrate the fragmenting effects of limited conceptions of warrior identities. When contemporary settler norms rigidly circumscribe the boundaries of warrior identity by binding it specifically to the bodies of those identified male, it ossifies, becoming the express opposite of the fluid possibilities we saw it represent in "A Warrior's Daughter." Jack Halberstam's contention that "masculinity must not and cannot and should not reduce down to the male body and its effects" carries significant weight in this scenario, since such reductive readings of gender threaten the efficacy of cultural transmission.[11] In fact, *in a paradigm that denies the place of women warriors, gender ceases to function as a tool and instead becomes a trap.* Perhaps bringing this trap into view by acknowledging the longstanding existence of warrior women in Indigenous cultures and thus the efficacy of female, gender-variant, and non-cis masculinities addresses the objections of those who imagine Indigenous masculinities as limited to cis bodies identified male at birth. Such considerations resonate with Justice's argument about the productive function of anomaly: "Neither good nor evil, potentially helpful or harmful to established social categories and hierarchies, the anomalous body . . . represents profound powers and transformative possibility."[12] In Justice's reading, discomfort becomes beneficial, even necessary. And such is the case in Walters's "The Warriors," where, if women lack the capacity to become warriors, gender trumps nation to call for the end of a line. With these potential ruptures in mind, we can see how discomfort and unsettling expectations such as those aroused by the anomalous figure of the woman warrior and the concept of female masculinity actually augment rather than challenge understandings of Indigenous masculinities.

As in the final scene of "A Warrior's Daughter," in "The Warriors" the female inheritance of a warrior masculinity manifests in affective bodily responses. For example, Sister's first overt claim to a warrior identity occurs in direct reaction to the girls' encounter with the hobos who haunt the text. Symbols of dispossession, a loss of kinship relations, and a loss of community, the hobos evoke a visceral response from Sister. The narrator shares two such encounters with indigent men who come to the hobo camp not far from their house. Each conversation defines a different aspect of Sister's sense of her Pawnee heritage and incites her claim for two types of affective relationship—one with her nation specifically and one with Indigenous people more broadly.

While their parents attempt to instill fear in the girls, urging them to avoid the hobos, Uncle Ralph situates the men in relation to the Pawnee. He explains that hobos "see things in a different way. Them hobos are kind of like us. We're not like other people in some ways and yet we are. It has to do with what you see and feel when you look at this old world" (113). Uncle Ralph suggests that for the hobos, as for the Pawnee, the felt experience of the world is different. When speaking of the Pawnee, Uncle Ralph discusses this difference as "beauty": "For beauty is why we live. . . . We die for it, too" (112). However, the girls' conversation with "a black man with white whiskers and fuzzy hair" challenges their uncle's narrative of relationality (114). As the girls and the hobo regard each other, the narrator "remember[s] what Uncle Ralph had said and wondered what the black man saw when he looked at us standing there" (114). Thus the hobo's response—"Indians is Indians, I guess"—to Sister's question—"Know what kind of Indians we are?"—shocks both girls. Sister vehemently denies this erasure, employing her uncle's words in an outburst that shows both how she perceives herself and also how she has internalized her uncle's narrative of Indigeneity: "Not us! We not like others. We see things different. We're Pawnees. We're warriors!" (114).

Much like when she stepped into the performance of the war dance, when Sister recites their uncle's oft-repeated words, his warrior subjectivity becomes her own. In addition, the imbricated fields of self-recognition and tribal nationhood coalesce within her newly claimed identity. In "Nearly Utopian, Nearly Normal," Lauren Berlant contends that "citizenship, in its formal and informal senses of social belonging, is also an affective state, where attachments take shape."[13] We see this attachment in Sister's immediate affective response—flush, wrinkled forehead, instinctive anger. She viscerally, reflexively, rejects a limiting pluralism that would elide her Pawnee citizenship. Instead, she overwrites the specific history of her people onto the hobo's generic statement of multicultural sameness by claiming a warrior identity.

At the same time, however, when the body in front of them is markedly that of a Native person, the girls privilege a connection to a larger sense of Indianness, though that bilateral claim for relationality means differently than it did in the flattening assertion that "Indians is Indians." When faced with an Indigenous hobo who repeatedly claims with annoyance that he "ain't got no people!," the narrator explains, "Sister . . . turned and yelled. 'Oh yeah? You Indian ain't you? Ain't you? . . . We your people!'" (116). The affective nature of Sister's responses returns us to Brian Massumi's contention that "the body doesn't just absorb pulses or discrete simulations; it infolds *contexts*, it infolds volitions and cognitions that are nothing if not situated."[14] Sister's bodily responses might look similar—reddened cheeks, quickened breath, verbal outburst—however, they recognize the difference between and among bodies and, concomitantly, they recognize, react to, and build relationship. Importantly, these affective encounters bring Sister to recognize both viscerally and cognitively the felt parameters of a warrior identity; here, the delineation of such subjectivity relies not on the mercurial performance of gender but instead on her deeply rooted connection to Pawnee nationhood and belief systems. As a warrior, Sister claims reciprocal relationship and responsibility, the very facets of the Pawnee world that Uncle Ralph imagines will vanish into the sunset with his passing.

Throughout the story, the girls recognize and gradually embrace their heritage as the next in a long line of Pawnee warriors. As a result, when guests at Uncle Ralph's funeral say "Ralph came from a fine family, an old line of warriors" (123), that statement is no end of the trail. The girls claim that inheritance, *their* inheritance, as Pawnee warriors, following in their uncle's footsteps and maintaining a Pawnee worldview. In the final scene of the story, the then-twenty-something narrator says to her sister, "I wanted to be one of his warriors"; Sister places one hand to her own chest and reaches out her other to touch her sister, answering: "You are. . . . We'll carry on" (124). Sister's actions underscore the *physicality* of their embodied knowledge of Pawnee warrior traditions, her touch combining with her words to further emphasize the felt nature of Indigenous practices and the way bodies, nationhood, and warrior identities coalesce.

Throughout Walters's piece, a rhetoric of cultural loss vies with a rhetoric of transformation, leading us back to this section's initial contention that, with this rocking between possibilities, Walters asks: *What is a warrior in the latter half of the twentieth century?* Her answers acknowledge the potential pain of being a Pawnee man who inhabits a warrior masculinity in the late 1960s and early 1970s. Ralph's courage, his cultural awareness, his knowledge of tribal history and traditional belief systems should afford him a position of respect, much as that earned by the warriors in the eighteenth- and nineteenth-century histories in chapter 1. However, in his mid-twentieth-century moment, Uncle Ralph finds himself out of step with a world that views his warrior identity as anachronism, entertainment, or logo. But even while acknowledging the potential pain of a twentieth-century male-identified warrior, Walters simultaneously refutes a hegemonic reading of Pawnee culture and warrior traditions as historical relics, substituting in its stead a narrative of Indigenous futurity in which warrior traditions not only exist but also continue to expand and change. The sense of Indigenous cultural traditions as always already a thing of the past invokes Raymond Williams's contention about the limited range of the mainstream historical imagination:

> In most description and analysis, culture and society are
> expressed in habitual past tense. The strongest barrier to the
> recognition of human cultural activity is this immediate and

regular conversion of experience into finished products. What is defensible as a procedure in conscious history, where on certain assumptions many actions can be definitively taken as having ended, is habitually projected, not only into the always moving substance of the past, but into contemporary life, in which relationships, institutions and formations in which we are still actively involved are converted, by this procedural mode, into formed wholes rather than forming and formative processes. Analysis is then centered on relations between these produced institutions, formations, and experiences, so that now, as in that produced past, only the fixed explicit forms exist, and living presence is always, by definition, receding.[15]

Williams helps us recognize the flawed ideological processes by which dynamic cultural practices become the discrete stuff of history, by which the present marches in a straight line toward its vanishing point. Such limiting and limited processes are exactly that which Walters's story refutes. Through Uncle Ralph's laments, Walters highlights the psychological impact of a historical enclosure in which warriors exist solely in memory—Ralph is ultimately undone by this decimating belief, losing sight of both himself and his familial connections in its destructive shadow. Through the girls' embodied experience of a warrior identity, Walters rejects the possibility that a "living presence is always, by definition, receding." Pawnee warriors, and warrior women more generally, are not artifacts of the past; they are living, breathing, changing beings in the present. As the narrator and Sister affectively experience their culture—hearing it, speaking it, seeing it, dancing it, naming it, claiming it—their bodies, their senses, their memories, and their emotions constitute an affiliative archive of Indigenous practice, of Indigenous knowledge, of Indigenous presence. Women warriors are not only aspects of an Indigenous past, as Zitkala-Ša argued, but also, according to Walters, the launching point for Indigenous futures.

Warriors, the Erotic, and Indigenous Futures: "Long-Term Visioners" in Daniel Heath Justice's *Kynship Chronicles*

Turning from Walters's short story to Daniel Heath Justice's fantasy series *The Way of Thorn and Thunder: The Kynship Chronicles,* with its focus on the fictional world of the Folk, the Indigenous inhabitants of Justice's Everland, moves us further into the space of imagined possibilities and warrior futures. Justice builds from several literary traditions to give us his kick-ass, polyamorous Kyn warrior, Tarsa'deshae. Arising from Indigenous histories and literary legacies of female-identified and gender-variant warriors as well as from the long-standing literary tradition of high fantasy fiction, Justice's hero expands our previous sense of what warriors signify in Indigenous literatures. While S. Alice Callahan offered the first instance of women warriors in late-nineteenth-century Native fiction, Zitkala-Ša taught early-twentieth-century readers that key aspects of a Plains warrior masculinity—bravery, daring, tactical abilities, and deep connection to an Indigenous spirituality—can exist in the body of a cisgender Indigenous woman. Writing in the latter half of the twentieth century, Anna Lee Walters envisioned those same traits as part of a felt theory—knowledge carried in the body from the present into the future. Both Zitkala-Ša and Walters suggest that such embodied knowledge can be passed through kinship lines regardless of sex or gender. Likewise, both writers depict affective circuits: in their texts, warrior identities and warrior masculinities index familial responsibilities and national identifications through the felt experiences of the body. We turn here to Justice because of what his fantasy trilogy adds to this conversation about female-identified and gender-variant warriors: *The Way of Thorn and Thunder* allows for *a recovery of the place of the erotic in a warrior ethos.*

Justice's warriors privilege a sense of kinship that encompasses multiple genders and desires. At the most basic level, this broad understanding of kinship is evidenced by the fact that the Indigenous inhabitants of Everland have a three-gender system—she-Kyn, he-Kyn, and zhe-Kyn—and warriors can occupy any of these genders. This contrasts with the human figures in the text, who, as allegorical European settler-invaders, adhere to strict heteronormative and cis-normative binaries in gender, religion, and power. The cosmology of *The Way of Thorn and Thunder* thus includes analogies to both the sort of gender-expansive traditions inhabited by figures like Woman Chief and Ozaawindib and to the settlers who attacked such gender expansiveness. Importantly, the Indigenous characters in Justice's fiction reflect the wide range of bodies, actions, and desires that exists among historical and present-day Indigenous warriors. But his work moves beyond a simple narrative of inclusion: Tarsa, the central warrior of Justice's text, allows us to consider what the extant historical record does not—*how the erotic undergirds an affectively articulated warrior masculinity.*

A significant number of Indigenous studies critics have recognized the importance of the erotic in Indigenous contexts. Paula Gunn Allen and Beth Brant (Bay of Quinte Mohawk) both reclaim the intersections of bodies and desires, providing early articulations of the erotic. In *Writing as Witness,* Brant argues that such work is a healing tool for Indigenous peoples, "a way to mend . . . broken circles," and "give sustenance."[16] Importantly, she also explains that while the erotic includes "sex and/or sexuality," a "broader cultural definition . . . [is] at work here. Strong bonds to Earth and Her inhabitants serve as a pivotal edge to [Indigenous peoples'] most sensual writing."[17] Since the turn of the twenty-first century, Craig Womack (Muscogee Creek/Cherokee), Qwo-Li Driskill (Cherokee), Deborah Miranda (Chumash/Ohlone Costanoan Esselen Nation), Kateri Akiwenzie-Damm (Anishinaabe), Robert Warrior (Osage), Mark Rifkin (settler), and myself, among other scholars, have argued for an acknowledgment of the centrality of the erotic to Indigenous literature, lives, and nations.[18] Justice, too, has been among those critics who have reclaimed an erotic sensibility in his creative and critical writing. In *The Way of Thorn and Thunder* he depicts the erotic as an intrinsic part of his protagonist's attainment of a healthy warrior identity and an essential aspect of Indigenous collectivity.[19]

As *The Way of Thorn and Thunder* begins, readers encounter a Feaster, a semi-giant with rock-hard skin and an insatiable appetite, who has been driven from his mountain home by human encroachment. Leaving a path of destruction in his wake as he ravages Kyn towns, the ancient creature offers us our first view of Namshéké, the Redthorn she-warrior who will earn the name Tarsa'deshae (She-Breaks-the-Spear) after the conclusion of this successful battle. Joined by six other Redthorn she-warriors, Tarsa and her Kyn companions overcome the Feaster by virtue of their bodily possibility. Each of the seven was "in their moon-time" in which they possessed a "cyclical power [that] made *all* the she-Kyn doubly powerful."[20] Justice's opening scene thereby invokes the fecundity of the female body as a source of strength rather than shame as he draws from beliefs common among Indigenous nations.[21]

This space of possibility, in which the body extends protection and power, expands when Fa'alik, a zhe—or third-gender—Kyn, ritually disposes of the Feaster's remains. The narrator explains that zhe-Kyn "straddled the male and female worlds in all things . . . moving between the blood of war and the blood of the moon without fear" (10). Drawing from this bodily wellspring, "Fa'alik drew the group together and, singing a song of healing and reconciliation, drove the flames into the monster's chest" (10). In this scene, this Two-Spirit figure functions as a bridge, holding a cleansing and restorative potential within their gender-variant body much as the Redthorn warriors drew strength from their menstrual blood. As in Zitkala-Ša's and Walters's fiction, this literary depiction operates affectively, centering a narrative of relationship nurtured by somatic intervention. Justice draws on an archive of Indigenous knowledge to imagine this bodily potential and construct his speculative world.

I want to pause for a moment to note the importance of such work. Until perhaps the 1970s and 1980s, high fantasy and speculative fiction imagined futures and alternate histories that were too often both white and heteronormative. In his analysis of science fiction and race, noted Afrofuturisms scholar Isiah Lavender III quotes Richard Dyer's comment that in the annals of speculative fiction, "whites are not of a certain race, they're just the human race."[22] Offering ethnoscapes as a theoretical frame through which to identify and challenge such whitewashed alternative realities and visions of the future, Lavender explains: "The ideas and histories that the text uses, defines, discards, renovates, and invents define and situate the ethnoscape. The ethnoscape foregrounds the human landscapes of race and ethnicity. . . . It both fabricates and reconceptualizes racial difference, enabling us to unpack sf's racial or ethnic environments and to think about human divergence in social behaviors."[23] In The Way of Thorn and Thunder we encounter an ethnoscape that draws on long-standing Cherokee memory and history—the novel is, in fact, an allegory for Cherokee removal. In Justice's ethnoscape, as we will see, women, gender-variant people, and kinship are vital to Indigenous nationhood, and warrior traditions are about responsibility rather than savagery for all genders of the Folk. In light of these facets of his alternate universe, in the process of imagining otherwise, Justice reveals and subverts the *original* science fiction narratives of the land that is currently North America: the myth of terra nullius, the doctrine of discovery, and the ongoing settler mantra of manifest destiny.

Such work is necessary and valuable. Riffing off the Afrofuturisms movement and coining the term "Indigenous futurisms" in her Introduction to *Walking the Clouds* (2012), the first anthology of Indigenous science fiction, Anishinaabe scholar Grace Dillon calls for "Native writers to write about Native conditions in Native centered worlds liberated by the imagination."[24] Two-Spirit Oji-Cree scholar and creative writer Joshua Whitehead takes this further, commenting on the ways speculative fiction can address "the temporalities of Two-Spirit, queer, trans, and non-binary Indigenous ways of being."[25] Looking at the history of queer Indigenous art, particularly, Cree, Saulteaux, and Métis theorist/writer/curator Lindsay Nixon notes that in the very recent past, "gender-variant and sexually diverse Indigenous artists weren't, or perhaps weren't permitted, to create art that drew from their bodies, genders and sexualities for content that was being shown in major galleries, and therefore canonized."[26] It is essential, then, not just that Indigenous writers and artists employ fantasy and speculative fiction to reimagine the past, envision alternate modes of being, and look toward the future, but also, specifically, that Indigenous queer, gender-variant, and sexually diverse folks are both creating it and represented in it. To return to Wesley's question about where "queer, trans, and two-spirit life would dwell inside" "imagining[s]" of Indigenous futures—one answer would be within the complex worlds of Justice's fiction.

The fact that Justice crafts Tarsa's warrior identity as emerging from an embodied Indigenous erotic presents an example of such layered imagining. Her initiation into the Redthorn warrior society and her bodily manifestation of the Kyn's most sacred symbol, the wyrwood tree, directly arise from an erotic sensibility. As I have discussed elsewhere, the rites of passage for this Redthorn warrior in Justice's Everland include the painting of the body, bodily marking with thorns, and sex with the Two-Spirit figure who ritually burned the Feaster's remains.[27] Sexual desire functions here as a gateway to a Redthorn warrior ethos. Further, like every other part of the Redthorn initiation, such erotic exchange is shared and celebrated as a central part of a warrior's strength—it is, in fact, that which *enables* transition. Keeping in mind Lavender's call "to unpack sf's racial or ethnic environments," we can see how, in *The Way of Thorn and Thunder,* Indigenous erotic desire overtly counters colonial narratives about the body. Jessica Danforth, the founder and executive director of the Native Youth Sexual Health Network, points out that in "North America and in Australia and New Zealand . . . the very thought of sexuality was purposely taught as shameful. . . . Western settler society brought over sexual shaming."[28] Dian Million names such shame a settler weapon—a "debilitating force" and "an old social control."[29]

Justice directly refutes such iterations of shame. Thus, Tarsa recalls her sexual experience with Fa'alik as a source of strength when she undergoes the bodily pain and attendant fear as her powers as a Wielder—a person able to access the *wyr,* or the spiritual power of the land—first begin to emerge. This allusion to Indigenous cosmologies that include both land and desire as essential to spiritual enlightenment aligns Justice's world with Brant's definition of erotic wholeness in which "sex and/or sexuality" combine with "strong bonds to the Earth and Her inhabitants." Tarsa's memories of her initiation into the Redthorn warriors underscore these connections:

> Fa'alik smiled broadly, helped her stand, and presented her to the group as one of their own. It was the first time that she'd ever *belonged.* . . . Every moment of that night—from the body marking, the dancing, and the feasting to the tender love-making with Fa'alik that followed . . . had been a reminder of all that was perfect and beautiful and balanced in the world. They'd all known who they were, and she was one of them— they belonged to those tree-covered mountains. The night had been warm, the Redthorns had rejoiced, and [Tarsa had] been fully, vibrantly, alive. (22)

In this scene, the Redthorn warriors' balance—an integrated matrix of body, desire, and land—adds community inclusion and solidarity to the previously discussed traits of bravery, daring, generosity, and spirituality that serve as vital aspects of a warrior ethos. Justice's woman warrior thus exhibits the daring and strength of Zitkala-Ša's Tusee and the commitment to cultural continuity of Walters's Pawnee sisters while also functioning as a fully realized *erotic* being, an aspect of a warrior ethos heretofore unrealized in the depictions of warriors we've considered. And, notably, nonheteronormative sex is one of the avenues through which Tarsa accesses this new role and its attendant responsibilities.

Even with only these few examples in mind, we can see that the ethnoscape of Justice's Everland presents an explicit critique of settler narratives that repress(ed) the expression of the erotic in Indigenous communities. In the historical processes of European settlement of the Americas, or what Ann Laura Stoler terms "the colonial order of things," European invaders depicted "the libidinal energies of the savage, the primitive, the colonized [as] reference points of difference" in a "sexual discourse of empire."[30] In the process, as scholar-activists like Womack, Miranda, Justice, and Driskill have shown, Indigenous people were "stolen from their bodies."[31] To instantiate this radical shift in Indigenous practices (or at least the appearance of such a shift), settlers employed sexual violence both overtly, in the form of rape and murder, and more insidiously by attempting to pervert Indigenous beliefs about the value of the body and the productiveness of the erotic as a means of subjugation. Further, healthy iterations of Indigenous masculinity as inhabited by male, female, and alternately gendered peoples were exoticized and/or vilified; in settler imaginaries, war and warriors, which in Indigenous contexts were tied to familial and tribal responsibilities, were incorporated within narratives of conquest in which sex was marked as a form of debasement and conquest. In *The Way of Thorn and Thunder,* Justice uses the realm of high fantasy to reclaim Indigenous erotic productivity by integrating such practices into Kyn cosmology and linking them with the Kyn's survival of the human encroachment that drives the Folk from their land.

Justice weaves the erotic into the fabric of Kyn life and, in the end, depicts it as central to the recovery of their people, land, and culture. Within the narrative, the erotic is at times directly related to sex and sexuality and at times tied instead to the broader pattern of Kyn life and beliefs. Thus, Tarsa is depicted as bisexual and polyamorous, and her sexual desire and emotional attachments play a pivotal role in her life as she enters into Kyn leadership during and after the Kyn's forced removal from their homeland. Notably, her entrance into leadership arises from Tarsa's abilities as a Redthorn warrior and Wielder—

abilities that, as we've seen, are tied to an embodied erotic. It makes narrative sense, then, that some of the most erotic moments in the text relate to Tarsa's connection to the land and the *wyr*, the power that courses through it.

A prime example of the tie between land and the Indigenous erotic can be identified when Tarsa fully and intentionally accepts her power as a Wielder during her encounter with the Eternity Tree, one of the most sacred of all entities in Kyn spirituality. In this scene, just as in her initiation into the Redthorn warrior society, the erotic acts as a channel that ushers Tarsa from one state to the next. The Eternity Tree, as the first wyrwood tree, is the "physical manifestation of Zhaia, the first mother of the Kyn, the source of the *wyr* in the Everland, and the living covenant between the folk and the land" (597). To offer context, shortly after Tarsa joins the Redthorn warrior society and slays the Feaster, she has a rare physical transformation that marks her as having a deep connection to the *wyr*. But given the changing ways of many Kyn, including her closest family, this manifestation of spiritual power marks her not as beloved healer or spiritual counselor, as it would have in past eras, but instead as outcast. To follow the ways of the *wyr* and learn to manage her physical and spiritual gifts, Tarsa must leave her family, who has abandoned Zhaia and the traditional ways of the Eld Green for human beliefs about Luran and the way of the Celestials. Tarsa departs from her birth home in Red Cedar Town with her aunt Unahi, a Wielder, or Greenwalker, who likewise has been forced out of the community because of her own spiritual powers and cultural beliefs in the old ways.

Tarsa initially experiences her embodied connection to the land, which allows her to physically manifest thorns, for example, or even to violently rend trees, rocks, and earth, as threatening—a violent curse rather than a gift. These negative emotions about her bodily potential vis-à-vis the *wyr* are brought about by the Kyn's shift from an Indigenous cosmology to settler practices and beliefs, drawing a clear parallel to the ways the sexual discourse of empire affected those upon whom it was forced. Therefore, when she begins to manifest her power, Tarsa is confined and abandoned in a pit of iron, a metal that poisons Kyn and would eventually kill her. In this ethnoscape, to use Justice's words, adherence to "settler nationalism"—here analogized as the isolating beliefs of the Celestials—focuses "on individualism in opposition to community," thereby creating "lonely and isolated subjects of an ultimately unaccountable state authority."[32] In that state of isolation, with no tutelage or comfort, Tarsa equates her connection to the *wyr* and the bodily power that arises from it with shame—she sees herself as monstrous. The novel depicts her path out of this darkness as she gradually gains Indigenous knowledge and finds community with her aunt Unahi and the society of Wielders to whom she belongs. Tarsa's experience with the Eternity Tree is the physical and spiritual manifestation of that process; it marks a moment in which she finds herself related, reminding us that, in Indigenous contexts, "kinship makes peoples of us through responsibilities to one another."[33]

Through Tarsa's physical, emotional, and spiritual encounter with the Eternity Tree, Justice argues that sexual colonization and its attendant shames can be overcome. As I'll show, that conversion from shame to love comes through the power of the erotic—further, an erotic that explicitly flows through and from the land, which invokes the sensuality of the natural world, the spiritual realm, and the meld between those incarnate spaces and the corporeal body of a Kyn warrior. For example, as Tarsa draws nearer to the Eternity Tree, she experiences "a rising anticipation" and a "bloodsong throbbing against her skin" (150).

> As she neared the end of the tunnel, Tarsa heard a soft, low rustling in the distance, a gentle pulse on the air that sent sudden tremors through her sensory stalks from wave after wave of pure, unbound *wyr*. She stopped and clutched the damp wall, gasping from the intensity as the sensual charge throbbed through her body, trailing down through every hair and length of flesh. Her entire body trembled with awareness, and she let the feeling wash over her for a long time, until her body grew accustomed to the rhythmic sensation. (152)

The diction here evokes sex and desire as the erotic power of the land fills Tarsa. When she enters the pool surrounding the Eternity Tree, "she stepped forward into the water and felt it caress her body. Her clothing dissolved; there was no barrier between her flesh and the rippling touch of the water. . . . The air was afire with energy, like a new-birthed storm, but she felt no more fear or shame" (155–56). The scene depicts both spiritual orgasm and physical rebirth, as Tarsa literally transforms through the animate power of the *wyr*. Thus, when Tarsa emerges from the pool, naked, she does so physically changed; the "azure sigils" on her face and body—"a sign of her true face and matured Awakening"—mark her access to the ancient Indigenous knowledges that make her a true Wielder (158). As well, much as she was welcomed into the Redthorn warriors, so too is she met and celebrated by the community of the Wielders' Circle. Isolated no more, Tarsa is ushered into a web of relationship and responsibility by the erotic power of the *wyr*.

While we have seen warrior women in battle, with family, and in prayer, Justice's depiction of this juncture between a warrior spirituality and an Indigenous erotic evokes the ties that have long been depicted between warrior identities and virility. In dominant narratives, these ties were historically distorted: rather than being seen as inherent to a productive warrior spirituality, the erotic aspects of a warrior masculinity were cast as fundamentally dangerous. With these histories in mind, we see the significance of Justice's ethnoscape: The Way of Thorn and Thunder *integrates a fully realized Indigenous erotic—its connection to sexuality, land, and the intersections between the two—into a warrior identity, presenting a layered recovery of Indigenous bodies and belief systems through a speculative narrative.*

I turn to a final example of the complex warrior identities in Justice's novel to discuss how these images, like others examined in this and the previous chapter, operate affectively. Thus, though set in an alternate reality, Justice's warriors—male, female, and third-gender—show how the Indigenous body not only contains the felt experience of colonialism but also functions as a means through which Indigenous actors supersede settler violence. As with Zitkala-Ša's depiction of Tusee, here, too, movement and active presence characterize the Indigenous body in affective relationship.

In Justice's fantasy world, the Folk, the larger collective of Indigenous groups to whom the Kyn belong, are attacked and forcibly removed from their homelands after an illegal treaty, The Oath of Western Sanctuary, is signed. Much like the Cherokee removal that serves as the allegorical referent for the text's events, the Kyn's desperate trek out of Everland includes widespread devastation and loss. Part of that devastation centers around the destruction of that sacred, other-than-human being that brought about Tarsa's transformation: the Eternity Tree is hacked down in an attempt to deliberately sever the Greenwalker Kyn from their physical, emotional, and spiritual connection to the land. The narrator explains, "After the Tree fell, the dying began" (409). The Kyn subsequently walk what they term the "Darkening Road" away from their capital, the peace city of Sheynadwiin, westward toward the land of their relocation. However, the grim trek brightens when a spiritual wonder comes to light: the Eternity Tree still lives. Remarkably, that life exists within the body of Tarsa'deshae.

The plot twist that allows Tarsa to physically manifest the spirit of the Eternity Tree demonstrates how fantasy can take affect up a notch. Thus, Baruch Spinoza's comment that no one has yet determined the limits of what a body can do is nowhere more evident than in the realm of Justice's imagined Indigenous futurities.[34] When the Eternity Tree is cut down by Celestial Kyn, Tarsa, who is present at the event, takes on its power to spiritually and physically heal. Her touch causes a "cool emerald flame" to flow between her body and the body of the being with whom she has contact; in that exchange "the spirit-deep exhaustion [of the trail] vanish[es]" until there is "no more pain, no more fear" (425). Importantly, too, a being that receives Tarsa's healing touch also then become themselves an embodied, active receptacle for the Eternity Tree and all it represents in Justice's novel. This somatic exchange, which occurs as soon as Tarsa lays hands on another, offers an imaginative way to undertake the sort of affective work Million identifies in which "felt experiences" serve "as community knowledges."[35] Here, *the warrior's body is more than active, it is generative:* by employing the speculative possibilities of science fiction, Justice offers us a world within which the affective exchange between bodies represents community reconstruction and decolonial empowerment.

In an interview with Sam McKegney for *Masculindians,* Justice discusses his depiction of Tarsa, expanding on how he understands the warrior identities her character displays:

> A warrior to me is somebody who fights the good fight with everything they can with love at the centre of their concern.... Tarsa's driving force at her best is love. And that's the kind of

warrior she had to be. So she goes from being a blood warrior, where she has to shed blood, to becoming an advocate
for peace. But even as an advocate for peace, she's a warrior.
The difference is, she's looking for other alternatives and is
paying attention to the particular kind of balance that peace
requires. . . . The Greenthorn Guardian that she becomes the
head of, these are long-term warriors, these are long-term
visioners. They're about building, they're about growing things.
And that's the kind of warrior she becomes and embodies by
the end.[36]

This idea of warriors as "long-term visioners" offers us a powerful
way to understand not just *The Way of Thorn and Thunder* but also
the broader affective potential of warriors' bodies and stories and
the power of the erotic. For so long, dominant narratives of loss
circumscribed warrior identities and, concomitantly, Indigenous
masculinities—warriors were savage and therefore ended up justifi-
ably dead, or were noble and conveniently heading off into the sunset to bravely and sadly die. As Cree scholar Dallas Hunt explains,
"settler futures" were "therefore premised on the denial of Indigenous
futures."[37] Within this settler binary, Indigenous knowledge systems
that allow for and embrace women and gender-variant warriors are
nowhere to be found. As a result, warriors and Indigenous futures
were imagined as antithetical from one another. Such belief systems
mirror Uncle Ralph's fear that, in contemporary society, a warrior's
destiny is to vanish. *Wynema*'s Lakota women on the battlefield at
Wounded Knee offer one such tale of inexorable loss. Yet ultimately,
these first chapters of *Written by the Body* show that historical and
literary accounts of women and gender-variant warriors can instead
serve as living narratives of embodied possibility and cultural continuity that look toward Indigenous futures. As such they imagine
otherwise for warriors of all genders and identifications by *recasting
eroticism and warriorhood in Indigenous terms, from Indigenous bodily
knowledges.* Because as Lindsay Nixon argues so powerfully in the
epigraph to this chapter, "Expressing . . . sensualities, sexualities and
genders without stigma is the work of warriors. And perhaps this is
our power: though we have been forgotten, suppressed and lost, we
still persist—with love."[38]

CHAPTER 3

BIG MOMS, OR THE BODY AS ARCHIVE

Indigenous women articulate a polity imagined in Indigenous terms, a polity where everyone—genders, sexualities, differently expressed life forms, the animals and plants, the mountains—are already included as the subjects of the polity. They are already empowered, not having to argue for any "right" to recognition; they form that which is the polity, that which is respected and in relation. That kind of polity would do more than "reform" any relations; it would bring us beyond "representation."

—Dian Million, *Therapeutic Nations*

This chapter turns to culture bearers, ass kickers, and rule breakers who use the affective influence of their ample bodies in ways that hegemonic culture often associates with cisgender men. I call these women "big moms." Big moms are Indigenous women who consciously use their bodies to forward dynamic, affective relationships in the service of their nations. They are women who, to gesture toward Dian Million, are "already empowered," constructing expansive polities for their families and nations.[1] The big moms I discuss here are frequently aunties, mentors, and advisers—rather than biological mothers—who stake fierce claims to kinship and shoulder more than their share of familial and community responsibilities. As such, big moms offer narratives of relationality that privilege tribal and community well-being and move beyond and outside the strictures of monogamous heterocouplehood. At times these women's strength arises from a matriarchal and/or matrilineal cultural heritage in which such corporeal beings and activities would be anything but masculine, since they mark Indigenous women's cultural authority; at times they consciously cross into spaces of influence that signify masculinity. As a result, not every big mom evinces the sort of bodily masculinity previous chapters considered, but as with female-identified and gender-variant warriors, big moms, too, use the affective power of their bodies to effect productive change.

We begin with the mother of all big moms, Big Mom from Spokane/Coeur d'Alene author Sherman Alexie's 1995 novel *Reservation Blues*. I turn our attention here not despite, but *precisely because of* Alexie's own problematic history, which came to light in the 2018 charges of sexual harassment I discuss at the end of this section. Big Mom is a literary culture hero who indexes a particular kind of embodied power and a way to move past the very toxic masculinity Alexie himself has displayed. I argue that Big Mom shows how one can imagine complex gender representations and critique damaging iterations of masculinity and still, in the end, be caught in the ever-expanding tangle of cishet settler gender structures that authorize the objectification and abuse of women.

In embarking on this analysis, I acknowledge up front that one approach would be to ignore the literary legacy that arises from the pen of a writer flawed in this particular way. My work in no way refutes that approach—as a person who has experienced both sexual abuse and harassment, I recognize the validity of disengagement as a protective strategy. But silence and erasure are not the only way to confront troubling histories, and here I choose to bring the problem directly into critical conversation. In doing so, I use a character from Alexie's own oeuvre to shine a light on the snare of settler masculinity. After first sketching out the possibilities of big moms' embodiment and power, the chapter considers how damaged masculinities and the reverberations of abuse function as a trap. In the end, I argue that big moms—not only the fictional characters from Alexie's *Reservation Blues,* Craig Womack's *Drowning in Fire,* and Louise Erdrich's Birchbark House series, but also the very real Indigenous women in the documentaries discussed in the following chapter—provide a framework for disentanglement.

What Bodies Remember: Big Moms and Somatic Archives

A pivotal character in Alexie's first novel, *Reservation Blues*, Big Mom is a fixture on the Spokane Indian Reservation, which serves as the text's central locale. The first epigraph, attributed to Charles Mingus—"God's old lady, she sure is a big chick"—sets the stage for our encounter with Big Mom and the spiritual power she epitomizes.[2] Famed Mississippi Delta blues guitar player Robert Johnson arrives on the reservation after dreaming of Big Mom's potential to heal. Johnson believes Big Mom "might save him. A big woman, she arrives in shadows, riding a horse. She rode into his dreams . . . with songs he loved but could not sing because the gentleman might hear."[3] Throughout the text, Big Mom is described as "big"—she is "over six feet tall," "thick and heavy," "huge"—the height and breadth of her body aligning with the depth of her spiritual power (202, 204). Her physical form challenges settler norms that demand thinness and even frailty in women's bodies, an important caveat, since settler narratives often evacuate power and desirability from women who are physically large. Further, along with being the force that might liberate Johnson from his legendary bargain with the devil at the crossroads, Big Mom serves as a repository for Spokane historical knowledge, which she experiences and also carries in her body.

In many ways, given the wide-ranging depictions of Big Mom's influence and spiritual abilities, it's clear why Spokane scholar Gloria Bird critiques her as a stereotypical "figure . . . exalted to mythical disproportions."[4] Bird highlights Big Mom to argue that here and elsewhere in his work, Alexie trades in hyperbole—Bird's essay is, in fact, titled "The Exaggeration of Despair in *Reservation Blues*." Bird makes excellent points in this case. Such exaggeration *is* a hallmark of Alexie's work: he deploys mainstream expectations of Indigenous identities as a source of his humor, often trades on pan-Indian tropes, and, especially in his early work, presents characters and plots in which "postmodern irony rules."[5]

At the same time, as we saw in previous chapters, such larger-than-life figures recur from nineteenth-century Indigenous literature to the present. Crossing the temporal boundaries of several centuries, Big Mom's exceptionalism aligns with that of Zitkala-Ša's Tusee, Daniel Heath Justice's Tarsa, and the Indigenous warriors upon whom they are based. Moreover, Big Mom experiences the physical and psychological trauma of the Spokane people's genocidal encounters with settlers much as Craig Womack's Lucy Self does in Creek contexts, as we'll see later in this chapter. And, like Lucy, while Big Mom physically contains the lived histories of that trauma, she simultaneously presents a way to move beyond it. Her expansive body holds multitudes. As another figure who fits the parameters of characters Daniel Heath Justice has called "long-term visioners,"[6] Big Mom offers what we might term *affective understanding:* her abundant figure contains not just the felt experience of colonialism but also the felt experience of Indigenous persistence and resurgence. Ultimately, fictional characters like Tusee, Tarsa, and Big Mom acknowledge a real-world fact: more than any library or collection of letters, *the body is a somatic archive of Indigenous knowledge.*

Recently, scientific studies have reinforced the idea encapsulated by N. Scott Momaday's trope of memory in the blood: the body holds and passes on knowledge in the form of inherited memory. Brian G. Dias and Kerry J. Ressler, researchers at Emory University, found that mice inherit bodily reactions that rely on information learned by previous generations. They conclude that their findings "[highlight] how generations can inherit information about the salience of specific stimuli in ancestral environments so that their behavior and neuroanatomy are altered to allow for appropriate stimulus-specific responses."[7] This study exploded from the scientific community into the popular press precisely because of the impact it holds for the way we understand the intersections of history and the body. Dias points to just such possibilities when he expands on the ramification of these findings: "From a translational perspective, our results allow us to appreciate how the experiences of a parent, before even conceiving offspring, markedly influence both structure and function in the nervous system of subsequent generations."[8] Given that Dias and Ressler's research focused on the intergenerational transfer of fear conditioning, perhaps the most painful hypothesis to arise from this equation is the possibility that *historical trauma persists within the body at a cellular level.*

Thus when Big Mom hears the gunshots when U.S. Army colonel George Wright orders more than eight hundred Spokane horses to be killed, that horror—embodied by physical recoil, tears, mental and physical shock, and mourning—subsequently becomes a "transgenerational epigenetic inheritance."[9] Alexie's narrator, Thomas Build the Fire, seems to understand this fact, as evidenced in his description of the events: "The first gunshot . . . reverberated in [Big Mom's] DNA" (9). The historical trauma of this gunshot, which epitomizes the collective weight of settler violence, recurs over one hundred years later, when Junior, a member of the Coyote Springs blues band, takes his own life in response to the cycles of dysfunction that have followed colonial incursions into Spokane lives.[10] In their article "How Bodies Remember," which focuses on the felt experience of political violence in Chinese society after the Cultural Revolution, Harvard researchers Arthur Kleinman and Joan Kleinman consider similar possibilities regarding the body's manifestation of historical trauma, asking: "How do political processes of terror (and resistance) cross over from public space to traumatize (or reanimate) inner space and then cross back as collective experience? How does the societal disorientation caused by a crisis of cultural delegitimation become a bodily experience?"[11] This chapter suggests that these sociosomatic processes occur not just in the individual body but also in the affective transit between and among bodies.

Yet as this book has demonstrated in its readings of warrior masculinities, affect does not exist solely in the space of trauma. If historical violence persists as an embodied reality, and intergenerational trauma exists at the cellular level—if settler violence is, in fact, a physically inherited reality—can't we also surmise that *the survival mechanisms that have enabled Native people to live before, through, and beyond such trauma must also be memories in the blood?* A central concern of this chapter, then, is how the figures of big moms—women who are acknowledged as valued culture bearers, formidable aunties, and shrewd political leaders—forward this kind of embodied survivance.

Reservation Blues suggests that Big Mom—who, according to the narrator, has lived for generations—takes that choking loss of settler trauma and transforms it into a medium that has the potential to heal: music. To effect this transformation, Big Mom reclaims the very bodies of the horses themselves: "She saved the bones of the most beautiful horse she found and built a flute from its ribs" (10). Writing of the historical event to which the novel alludes, Stefanie Pettit, a correspondent for the *Spokesman-Review,* contends that the 1858 slaughter has been deemed "one of the most brutal, inexplicable and traumatic acts of the mid-1800s war between the U.S. government and Native Americans of the Inland Northwest."[12] The site, which today is known as Horse Slaughter Camp, long presented physical reminders of the horrific killings. According to Pettit, "more than 50 years later, the bleached bones of the horses could still be seen along the river."[13] Notably, this was not the only case of such atrocities. In September 1874, U.S. Cavalry commander Ranald S. MacKenzie performed a similar act, seizing fourteen hundred Comanche horses and killing a thousand.[14] The bones that make up Big Mom's flute have a chilling historical correlation. But much as Justice uses fantasy to reclaim the ties between an Indigenous erotic and a warrior sensibility, so here we see a larger-than-life culture bearer gesture toward *the corporeal possibilities that survive in the wake of trauma.*

Speaking of how sociosomatic responses encode such trauma, Kleinman and Kleinman offer a powerful explanation of what happens when the body archives history:

> Symptoms of social suffering, and the transformations they undergo, *are* the cultural forms of lived experience. They are lived memories. They bridge social institutions and the body-self as the transpersonal moral-somatic medium of local worlds . . . [to] reveal what those local worlds are about; how they change; and what significance they hold for the study of human conditions. That is to say, bodies transformed by political processes not only *represent* those processes, they *experience* them as the lived memory of transformed worlds. The experience is of memory processes sedimented in gait, posture, movement, and all the other corporeal components which together realize cultural code and social dynamics in everyday practices.[15]

There are a number of significant concepts here that overlap with understandings of affect as employed in *Written by the Body*. Kleinman and Kleinman's research reinforces Brian Massumi's claim that the body enfolds contexts at both conscious and preconscious levels.[16] Additionally, if we revisit Million's contention that "feelings are theory" in conjunction with the argument that the bodily expression of historical trauma can be identified even in the everyday practices of walking, standing, or sitting, we can better understand the specific ways in which affect helps us see *how* the body functions as a theoretical *and* physical site—or a somatic archive of Indigenous knowledge.[17]

Moreover, Indigenous contexts enable us to extend Kleinman and Kleinman's schema. Since knowledge must be shared in the majority of Native cosmologies, it exists in the space of communal exchange. Important dreams or feats of bravery, for example, were and still are recounted among groups as shown in the histories referenced in chapter 1. Even when certain instances of Indigenous knowledge are not appropriate for larger distribution, such as in the case of some sacred encounters or spiritual practices, there is often still an exchange between a tribal member and a spiritual/ceremonial leader and/or medicine person.[18] Thus while Kleinman and Kleinman focus on what happens to the "local" body (the body of the individual) in the wake of trauma, of primary interest to this analysis is what happens to Indigenous knowledges when bodies are placed in juxtaposition and/or conversation, when affect is considered not individually but communally. *Reservation Blues* posits that such interactive bodily exchanges can occur through the process of hearing and making music, a social and spiritual medium and also one that demands bodily engagement.

A trickster figure, a spiritual figure, the embodiment of cultural continuity, Big Mom, who is rumored to have walked across the surface of the Spokane Reservation's Benjamin Lake, suggests that music carries the potential to free the body from its bondage to physical and psychological trauma. Medical practitioners and researchers Carolyn J. Murrock and Patricia A. Higgins explain that music, "which is both science and art," is also "a form of non-verbal communication that can elicit a broad spectrum of emotions."[19] Music has had proven success as therapy for stroke survivors, Parkinson's patients, and people living with Alzheimer's and similar diseases.[20] And among Indigenous peoples, as noted Ojibwe scholar Brenda J. Child explains, "traditions of song and dance help restore the balance that is drained by bodily sickness and deliver spiritual sustenance."[21] Like affect, music is about movement, about interaction, and about the body in connection. Musicologist Marie Strand Skånland points out that music's "impact . . . derive[s] from the *relationship* between music and the person. In other words, music is not merely a stimulus that 'acts' on listeners; it offers opportunities to the people who engage with it and provides its benefits based on the ways in which people interact with or *appropriate* it."[22]

Thus, by forwarding Big Mom's music as a healing form of affective exchange, we can consider the redemptive possibilities of posttraumatic *survival* narratives rather than inherited trauma alone. For example, when Big Mom plays the flute each morning, she does so to "remind everybody that music created and recreated the world daily" (10). In this scenario, an active, process-oriented understanding of music offers present-day hope and looks toward Indigenous futures. As literary scholar Janine Richardson points out, in *Reservation Blues,* "music acts on memory and could be a healing force for those willing to submit to its powers."[23] Speaking of the importance of hearing and feeling the sound of a jingle dress, for example, Child explains that "in the Ojibwe world, spiritual power moves through air and sounds hold significance."[24] Even for folks without fully functioning cochlea, music is felt, and that sound is subsequently interpellated through bodily vibrations and/or a resonant hum that lingers in the body's core.

Importantly, Skånland also suggests that music subsequently requires participatory interaction as folks choose to (or choose not to) "engage," "interact," or "appropriate" that which the body hears/feels.[25] So while music necessitates physical relationship and can evoke response, it also requires a certain level of conscious exchange—the felt circuit that enacts healing can also be denied. *Reservation Blues* suggests that such denial occurs when internalized trauma limits the body. In these cases, inherited and contemporary traumas form a seemingly unbridgeable block to productive futures, as seen in reactions to Robert Johnson's blues. When Johnson sings the blues, vibrations of pain, of joy, of sorrow manifest "a new road" for the Spokane who encounter his powerful music.[26] However, the narrator maintains that some listeners remain stuck in old somatic maps, neuropathic highways carved by "car wrecks, suicides, murders" (174). This transgenerational settler inheritance populates the body like cancer when, the narrator explains, "they buried all of their pain and anger deep inside, and it festered, then blossomed, and the bloom grew quickly" (175). In a troublingly rapid multiplication cycle, one cell divides into two and two divide into four, until a carcinogenic experience of lived and inherited pain threatens to consume everything in its wake. It is precisely this sort of traumatic doubling that leads to Junior's suicide. As antidote to such narratives of exponential despair, Big Mom represents a character whose body archives *both* historical trauma *and* embodied healing. A long-term visioner who imagines Indigenous futures shaking free from the clinging tendrils of trauma, Big Mom creates art with the bones of genocidal practices and also, with the very breath of her body, invites those around her into sociosomatic relationship.

Notably, Big Mom's performance of such a powerful female identity, which encompasses an acknowledged influence among those on the reservation and beyond, evokes brash and troubling iterations of cishet masculinity from several of the young men in the novel. Thus, while she may perform gender differently from the female and gender-variant warriors of the previous chapters, Big Mom's cultural power still incites masculinity, bringing it into visibility, much as we saw evidenced in the affective exchanges that surround the warriors in chapter 1. It is here, then, that *Reservation Blues* most overtly addresses the trap of settler masculinity, or what Morgensen terms "colonial masculinities," which are a "creation of conquest."[27] As Innes and Anderson note, such toxic masculinities encourage Indigenous men "to achieve their privilege through the oppression of those who are perceived from a hegemonic masculine perspective as" somehow less than.[28] Big Mom's power and ample form transgress *dominant* expectations of ideal womanhood and, at the same time, reveal an insistent cishet version of Indigenous masculinity that, though critiqued in *Reservation Blues,* as we'll see, also ironically marks Alexie's own troubling history in the present day.

One example of the overt cishet masculine performances that erupt in response to Big Mom's somatic abundance can be found in Victor Joseph's actions and attitude. While Thomas recognizes Big Mom as "a bigger part of God" than most people, Victor mocks Big Mom's attempts to help Coyote Springs, the band Thomas, Victor, Junior, Checkers, and her sister, Chess, form in the wake of Johnson's arrival on the Spokane Reservation. Though Big Mom's larger-than-life chords "[knock] everybody to the ground," Victor refuses to acknowledge her affective power (206).[29] Like the characters who deny the transformative possibilities of the blues in the novel, Victor clings to sociosomatic maps etched by trauma rather than acknowledge Big Mom's (or any other woman's) cultural knowledge. Notably, his performative masculinity, which materializes as a weary cynicism, arises directly from settler narratives that write Indigenous manhood in limited hegemonic terms. In fact, Victor's machismo relies on acts of disregard and emotional and physical violence that align with dominant beliefs about Indigenous men's stoicism and savagery rather than on Native ideologies that link productive iterations of masculinity to reciprocal responsibility and the intricate web of kinship obligations. To further reinforce his I-don't-give-a-shit facade, Victor mocks Big Mom's status as culture bearer and denigrates her explanation of music's importance: "Shit. . . . This is all starting to sound like a New Age convention. Where are the fucking crystals?" (207). By contrast, Big Mom mentors Coyote Springs precisely because of her investment in the sort of reciprocity and cultural/relational responsibility Victor eschews. Moreover, her attempt to support, teach, and advise Coyote Springs stems from her confidence in Indigenous survivance—she holds this out to Victor, offering him the possibility of transformation, the possibility of redemption. Choosing bluster over belief, Victor continues to needle Big Mom until she walks out of the house, temporarily leaving Coyote Springs to their own devices. With his actions, Victor challenges Big Mom's cultural authority and vision of Indigenous futures, implying that the embodied knowledge she offers the band carries no more weight than empty sound and fury trumpeted by charlatans.

Victor and Big Mom's encounter recalls Skånland's argument about music as participatory relationship. While Big Mom's body can function as an Indigenous archive of both trauma and survivance, she offers productive knowledge through *an economy of relational exchange*—music and healing must be mindfully recognized and consciously accepted. The transit of knowledge between bodies, to again quote Skånland, "offers certain opportunities to the people who engage with it and provides its benefits based on the ways in which people interact with or appropriate it."[30] Victor's ongoing performance of a tough-guy cynicism and ennui severs that collaborative possibility; accordingly, through an affective reading of Big Mom we see how a masculinity that rests on hegemonic rather than Indigenous understandings of gender short-circuits long-term visioning.

The late Anishinaabe elder, orator, and teacher Basil H. Johnston speaks of these sorts of short circuits in a conversation with Sam

McKegney. In a discussion about the cultural shifts residential schools caused in articulations of Indigeneity, Johnston contends that

> we have to get back to old values. For example, . . . the loss of a sense of duty. The whole emphasis is on rights—"My rights are being violated," "My rights are being infringed upon." There's not a word about duties. To us, a right is a *debnimzewin*. But each right is also a duty. . . . And so we have to go back to some of these values: responsibility, duty, right.[31]

This sense of reciprocal responsibility that Johnston identifies as integral to Indigenous understandings is, within Johnston's nation, historically passed down through the Indigenous women on whom characters like Big Mom are patterned. "The principal teachers [in Anishinaabe culture] were the grandmothers," he explains. "They were the holders and keepers of wisdom. Not so much the men, but it was the women."[32] Alexie sets Big Mom up as just such an Indigenous culture bearer. In doing so, he crafts a vivid and all-too-close-to-home picture of how masculinities that denigrate rather than respect women—and female authority more specifically—can cause some cishet men to reject the possibility of right relationship that big mom figures ultimately represent.

These affective intersections between masculinity and powerful womanhood and the conflict between toxic masculinity and female embodiment recur throughout the novel. For example, the scene between Big Mom and Victor in which Victor mocks Big Mom's power and questions the validity of her spiritual vision—"Where are the fucking crystals?" (207)—is quickly followed by a like encounter between Big Mom and Michael White Hawk, the nephew of the tribal council president, which is framed by the narrator's comment: "Victor wasn't the first Indian man to question Big Mom's authority. In fact, many of the Indian men who were drawn to Big Mom doubted her abilities. Indian men have started to believe their own publicity and run around acting like the Indians in movies" (208). In an aside that directly comments on and critiques the primitive savagery of the Hollywood warrior trope—what McKegney terms a "socially engineered hypermasculinity"—Big Mom offers Michael recovery in the place of violence.[33] She tells "the toughest Spokane Indian man of the late twentieth century" that "music is supposed to heal" (208).

However, Michael, despite his brilliance at the saxophone, sees only conflict in the masculinity he performs: "'But Big Ma,' White Hawk said, 'I'm a warrior. I'm 'sposed to fight'" (208). Big Mom's counter— "Michael, . . . you run around playing like you're a warrior. You're the first to tell an Indian he's not being Indian enough. How do you know what that means? You need to take care of your people" (208)—recalls the nuanced iterations of masculinity examined in previous chapters, in which kinship considerations, generosity, and tribal and familial responsibilities comprise the warrior masculinities taken up by women and gender-variant warriors and depicted by twentieth- and twenty-first-century Indigenous writers. Such complex exchanges are shut down by Michael's shortsighted, misogynistic retort: "You don't know what you talkin' 'bout. . . . You jus' a woman" (208).

While Big Mom literally embodies cultural continuance, showing how the body can archive trauma, memory, *and* survivance, the scenes addressed above demonstrate how impoverished or oppositional understandings of masculinity actively refuse the rich possibilities of such affective exchange. Kim Anderson discusses these oppositional disjunctions as a "loss of balance . . . experienced in our families, communities, and nations linked to gender relations."[34] She emphasizes that the often-troubling consequence of such imbalance "becomes a struggle against the systems, policies, and institutions that were enforced upon us by the colonizer. It is not a simplistic struggle against men or individuals."[35] Speaking of the impact of residential schools on gender, McKegney discusses how a larger "genocidal program . . . has sought not only to denigrate and torment Indigenous women but to manufacture hatred toward Indigenous women in shamed and disempowered Indigenous men."[36] The patterns in Victor Joseph's and Michael White Hawk's reactions to Big Mom exemplify the systemic loss of balance to which Anderson and McKegney refer and also touch on exactly the sorts of claims lodged against Alexie. In these textual examples, and in the charges of sexual misconduct aimed at Alexie, masculinity ceases to carry with it the productivity and the twinned sense of kinship and responsibility that Johnston describes, which returns us to a key claim of this book: limited or binaristic concepts of masculinity, which so often arise from settler ideologies, endanger Indigenous futures. By contrast, the cultural work of big moms and long-term visioners reminds us that gender has served and can continue to serve Indigenous communities as a generative tool that benefits the entire polity.

To employ Ty P. Kāwika Tengan's theory, such recoveries actively "re-member" Indigenous gender. Tengan defines "'re-membering' masculinities" as "a type of gendered memory work that facilitates the formation of group subjectivities through the coordination of personal memories, historical narratives, and bodily experiences and representations."[37] Though Tengan focuses on "Kanaka ʻŌiwi (Native Hawaiian) warriorhood and masculinity in the context of Hawaiian nationalism and decolonization," the concept of re-membering gender serves as a broader tool of Indigenous theory.[38] Importantly, Tengan explains that the creation of such integrated understandings of gender are community ventures. To reframe in light of my arguments, we can see how re-membering gender necessitates a shared sociosomatic relationship, thereby offering one answer to the question of what happens to Indigenous knowledges when bodies are placed in conversation: *gender can be re-membered in the affective exchanges promoted by female-identified and/or gender-variant warriors and big moms, and, as well, by men who reject colonial masculinities to work in tandem with them.*

Ultimately, this section indexes the possibilities of affective connection between bodies and also engages how such possibilities are short-circuited. My analysis shows, as well, how the body can archive multiple forms of Indigenous knowledge. While some of these forms are painful, such as the epigenetic traces of historical trauma, Big Mom's embodied recoveries also suggest that the body likewise can hold and share Indigenous experiences of survivance. Importantly, the transit of such productive knowledge relies on the forging of sociosomatic bonds. If the body *is* an archive of Indigenous knowledge, then that archive must be accessed, opened, and engaged through active—though not necessarily verbal—interchange between and among Indigenous people. In other words, the possibilities embodied by big moms, whose ample bodies index and affectively share Indigenous knowledges, necessitate a dynamic interaction that can be enabled or deflected by differing articulations of masculinity.

I CONCLUDE THIS SECTION by turning to Sherman Alexie's alleged predatory behaviors and the ways they enact the very iterations of toxic masculinity that *Reservation Blues* critiques. The revelations that Alexie is said to have made inappropriate sexual remarks, pursued young women, and used his literary stardom to lure women into relationships—or at least into bed—call for a conversation about how the intersections of gender and power can become a weapon rather than an ethical responsibility. Attending to what toxic masculinity looks like as well as to how masculine power, when wielded with ill intent, can damage individuals, relationships, and careers, demonstrates the importance of big moms in life and literature. The painful irony is that, based on the stories shared by the three women who agreed to speak on the record, Alexie engaged in the same toxic behaviors his work critiques.

Early in 2018, in the midst of the #MeToo movement, accusations began circulating about Alexie's misconduct. Brendan Kiley and Nina Shapiro, reporters for the *Seattle Times,* suggest that the initial public thread appeared in the online comments that arose in response to a January 4, 2018, *School Library Journal* piece, "Children's Publishing Reckons with Sexual Harassment in Its Ranks."[39] Within a few weeks of these comments, Litsa Dremousis, a Seattle writer, began a Twitter thread about women who accused Alexie of abuse.[40] These events crystallized around a March 5, 2018, NPR story that described a pattern of abuse in which Alexie "traded on his literary celebrity to lure them into uncomfortable sexual situations."[41] Three writers— Jeanine Walker (settler), Elissa Washuta (Cowlitz), and Erika Wurth (Apache/Chickasaw/Cherokee)—went on the record with accounts of Alexie's sexual misconduct and abuse of his literary clout. Their stories had power, and in light of the ensuing public outcry his book tour was halted, numerous awards and scholarships were renamed, and his ever-rocketing career came to an almost immediate standstill. Alexie declined the 2018 Carnegie Medal and, before retiring from the public eye, issued an apology. In it, he notes: "There are women telling the truth about my behavior and I have no recollection of physically or verbally threatening anybody or their careers. That would be completely out of character. I have made poor decisions and I am working hard to become a better man who makes healthier decisions."[42] It can be argued that this "apology" leaves much to be desired in terms of a real engagement with *debnimzewin,* what Basil Johnson termed the duties and responsibilities of masculinity. As

Michi Saagiig Nishnaabeg scholar Leanne Betasamosake Simpson notes, when harm has occurred, relationship must be rebalanced: "Restorative processes rely upon the abuser taking full responsibility for his/her actions in a collective setting."[43]

While there have been no official charges filed, the stories these women share combine with Alexie's own admission of guilt (as hedging as it may be) to point to the fact that while Alexie was able to imagine better in his fiction, he mirrored the damaging structures of hegemonic masculinities in his own behaviors and, to date, seems to have taken no real restorative action. Alexie is, of course, by no means alone here. Cherokee writer and social media influencer Adrienne Keene noted in her blogpost, "The Native Harvey Weinsteins":

> I think about my friends' strong, beautiful faces and bodies, and I think about the shit they've been put through by some of your faves in Indian Country. The men we uphold as examples, as our "famous Indians," our important leaders to be admired. The ones who have "made it." The actors, the musicians, the athletes, the activists, the writers, the DJs, the politicians, the government workers, the business owners, the motivational speakers, the professors. I've heard so many stories. From heartbreaking, terrifying stories, to mundane, run-of-the-mill sexual harassment stories—the ones that should be horrifying but happen so often we've become numb.[44]

Keene's post tackles the larger effects of trauma—the fear, the pain, and the ever-present sense of danger such experiences instantiate among Indigenous women. She addresses power gone awry, and masculinity employed to coerce and to contain. The stories Walker, Wurth, and Washuta share position them as women who reject—or at least find a means to work past—the numbness to which Keene refers. They chose to speak publicly because the years of silence, the years of whispers about Alexie, served no one.[45] And, while these discussions are traumatic in their own right, they are, we know, necessary. In their choice to call for change and, concomitantly, to refute toxic masculinities, these writers echo the long-term visioners who came before them and demand a more productive future for Indigenous women.

Ultimately, with my analysis of *Reservation Blues*, I want to suggest we take what's productive from Alexie and use it for good, use it to spark conversation about the very issues that led to his public downfall. Furthermore, while his celebrity and his own openly acknowledged trauma had damaging consequences for him and others, his work influenced generations of writers. To teach a survey of Native literature and not acknowledge Alexie is like ignoring the elephant in the room. Whether we choose to teach Alexie in such a survey and highlight the controversy and ensuing consequences or choose to explain why we no longer teach Alexie, we *must* continue to have these difficult conversations.[46] There is no question that there should be serious outcomes for what he did. Yet at the same time, to erase the historical record, to tell every Indigenous kid who read Alexie and saw themselves represented in his vivid and funny images that their feelings were false, that his work has no value, has its own problematic consequences.

Alexie's characters, the hope he offered, the futures he imagined, especially as the young man he was when he wrote *Reservation Blues*, are visions that still hold value. Big Mom offers redemption in the face of misogyny. Her embodied possibility acknowledges the ways masculine performances can fuck us up, as well as suggesting that indexing and naming such toxicity can potentially offer a way out, a way through, for flawed human beings. In *Reservation Blues*, neither Victor nor Michael heeds Big Mom's advice that they break loose from the ensnaring systems of settler masculinity. And though Alexie had the ability to identify the problem of toxic masculinity in Indigenous contexts, and the imagination to forward a strong woman to embody an antidote, the testimonies of Jeanine Walker, Erika Wurth, and Elissa Washuta and the memories of those who could not go on record suggest that Alexie, like his characters, became a participant in the very colonizing structures he critiqued.

Jazz, Gender, and Dreaming History: The Body as Affective Process in Craig S. Womack's *Drowning in Fire*

As we've seen, big moms archive Indigenous knowledge, teach survivance, and challenge toxic masculinity. Yet, while the presence of Big Mom could affectively *incite* masculine performance, she did not herself *perform* masculinity. Broadening the parameters of big mom figures, this section and the next turn to characters who model socio-somatic relationship while also encompassing and expanding representations of non-cis masculinities. Like Big Mom, the big moms who fall into this category participate in affective exchange—their bodies archive Indigenous knowledge of historical trauma and survivance and also serve as embodied repositories of Native intellectual traditions.

One example of a big mom who evinces aspects of masculinity as she simultaneously archives and extends sociosomatic knowledge of tribal history can be found in Craig Womack's groundbreaking novel *Drowning in Fire* (2001). Womack's text is notable for a number of reasons, among them the fact that it is the first novel since Carole laFavor's *Along the Journey River* (1996) and *Evil Dead Center* (1997) written by a queer Indigenous writer to include a queer Indigenous protagonist.[47] Additionally, given that laFavor's books had fallen off the literary radar by the early 2000s, Womack's text was, for most readers, the first of its kind and is rightly considered a marker for the more overt rise of queer Indigenous studies that occurred early in the twenty-first century. *Written by the Body* will look at length at laFavor's literature and activism in chapter 5; here I return to the concept of big moms with an analysis of Womack's Lucy Self. Though not the center of the novel, an honor that goes to the queer Mvskoke (Creek) character Josh Henneha, Lucy, Josh's aunt, presents another iteration of a big mom figure.[48] Lucy adds a biological auntie to the mix of big mom figures and also, and importantly, evinces a seemingly heterosexual (though by no means heteronormative) non-cis masculinity. An analysis of Lucy's character reinforces the significance of the affective transit between and among bodies, showing how even in the aftermath of sexual violence such exchanges can function as a path to physical, psychic, and cultural healing in Indigenous contexts.

There are a number of parallels between Big Mom and Lucy that bring me to read the latter as a big mom—a woman who kicks ass, takes names, and produces productive change through the iterations of Indigenous memory she carries in her body. Like Big Mom, Lucy serves as a culture bearer—in this case for Mvskoke, rather than Spokane culture. In the first chapter of Womack's novel, set in 1964, we are introduced to Lucy through the eyes of her nephew Josh, who rests on her lap as she heals his earache with story and tobacco smoke. Encircled by his aunt's arms, Josh studies her hands, which are "calloused and rough like a man's."[49] Josh imagines his aunt's body as all encompassing. Her larger-than-life figure has the capacity not only to cradle him but also to envelop his uncle, whom Josh envisions "crawl[ing] up into her lap and clasp[ing] stained fingers around [Lucy's] waist while she held on to him in the darkness" (8–9). In this opening scene of the text, Lucy comforts and heals Josh, recounts Mvskoke origin stories, and details familial history. She, like Big Mom, is a figure whose body holds a multitude of healing possibilities for those who enter into affective relationship with her.

Additionally, we again encounter scenes in which music serves as an affective space with potential to heal, or at least mitigate, embodied experiences of trauma. In this case, music further signals Lucy's performance of aspects of non-cis masculinity. As he rests amid the curling tendrils of tobacco smoke, Josh calls for Lucy to pull out her trumpet rather than tell him an origin story. When she refuses because of the late hour, he protests: "But everybody says you play all night in bars" (4). Though he knows better than to say the words aloud, Josh subsequently thinks: "I never have seen the kind of place she's talking about, but I sure heard people go on about it and how a woman has no business there. According to some of them I shouldn't even be staying over at Aunt Lucy's house" (4). Josh's words suggest that Lucy's playing, however well known in the community, marks her as transgressing hegemonic gender restrictions. These restrictions are explained by the bandleader of the Oklahoma City Blue Devils, Walter, who references the cultural and economic limits of women's opportunities to play jazz publicly in the early part of the twentieth century. When Lucy approaches him about taking up the trumpet to replace Walter's passed-out-drunk horn player, Walter answers: "Lucille, you might could pass as colored, since you're darker than some of these high-yeller horn boys, but you'll never pass for a man. . . . Now, if you was a singer, Lucy, that would be another story entirely. They'll 'low that. But you can't play a horn on the stand 'less you got one in your britches, too" (93). Lucy response—"You ain't seen me in overalls" (93)—addresses her awareness that she often exceeds dominant gender expectations for women's appearance. Both in her musical performance and in her attire, Lucy resists heteropatriarchal norms that attempt to dictate female behavior and circumscribe opportunities for women; at the same time, her experiences show that in the twentieth century, the culturally sanctioned possibilities for crossing into the locations, occupations, and attire of alternate genders are significantly fewer than those available to the Indigenous women of the previous centuries.

Womack repeatedly depicts Lucy as masculine in appearance—for example, along with commenting on Lucy's work-roughened hands in his 1964 vignette, in 1978 Josh describes his eccentric and now-aging aunt as "wearing men's overalls with a pencil protector in the pocket. She had on a men's pair of black-framed nonprescription glasses" (89). Her kin, as Josh's matter-of-fact descriptions of his aunt show, find nothing particularly extraordinary about her assuming masculine attire and/or demeanor. In more public spaces, however, Lucy encounters pressure to conform to early-twentieth-century gender restrictions. As a result, while Lucy attains her dream of playing in a band, her presence in Oklahoma City music venues requires that she participate in a rather blatant form of passing.[50] Because a female trumpet player is beyond the pale in 1920s Oklahoma jazz clubs, the only way Lucy can perform is for a male instrumentalist, the second trumpet, to fake it: she hides behind a partition and produces the gorgeous notes he mimes. The poorly skilled horn player thus garners the accolades for Lucy's significant talent—an example of the realities that powerful, smart women have lived with in dominant culture for hundreds of years. Looking back on this experience years later, Lucy explains to Josh: "Now, that's where I got all my wind from; I had to blow twiced as hard as any trumpet player of my time, hidden off behind the bandstand like that" (94). Here, Womack takes bodily exclusion and turns it into corporeal possibility. I want to suggest that Lucy's "wind," like that of Big Mom's flute, represents Indigenous persistence in the face of cultural opposition. Importantly, in both cases those survivance narratives are psychic *and* physical realities that are literally expressed through the breath and body of women.

Lucy's reveries about her days in the Oklahoma City Blue Devils beg the question of *what happens when productive bodily exchanges are short-circuited, when certain limited iterations of masculinity take on cultural capital, and other, more complex iterations are refused.* Though the management's decision to exclude women might, as she claims, offer lessons in tenacity, on the bandstand Lucy's bodily expressions are circumscribed by a singular demand for cis masculinity. Speaking of the history of gender and jazz in the latter part of the twentieth century, Nichole T. Rustin explains that "myths about black musicians' genius" cast them as visionary "black men embodying ideals of manhood . . . and masculinity."[51] Horn players, then, were expected to embody both blackness and cishet maleness. And even in the postwar period, twenty-some years after Lucy would have played, "young girls [were] taught their proper social roles, which certainly did not include working as a jazz musician. Singers dominated the respectable place of women in popular music; female instrumentalists were much harder to find."[52] Despite Lucy's musical prowess, the dominant—though not familial—cultural perceptions of her physical body therefore limit the public expression of her art. In his depiction of this exclusion, Womack emphasizes the low level of expectations for hegemonically approved iterations of heteromasculinity. In fact, the bar for cisgender masculinity is so low that it can be acceptably performed even by a passed-out trumpet player or one "who couldn't swing even if he was in a fistfight" (94). Given that the first trumpet player is unconscious and the second incompetent, obviously neither of these men presents the sort of idealized versions of Black masculinity Rustin describes as endemic to jazz musicians. Here, masculinity boils down to perceptions about and privileges accorded to those identified male at birth. This calls to mind Morgensen's contention that the "entire project of cultural genocide rested on implementing a colonial sex/gender binary."[53] While Morgensen describes boarding and residential school systems, the same colonial logics are alive and well in 1920s Oklahoma, where settler binaries are still employed to contain and constrain women.

Interestingly, the cross-cultural connections/disjunctions at work in the jazz orchestra are reminiscent of those explored in *Reservation Blues* when Robert Johnson enters the space of the reservation and approaches an Indigenous culture bearer, Big Mom, for healing. The healing Big Mom affords, while grounded in the embodied memory of Indigenous history, can extend beyond the realm of Indigeneity—like her body, Big Mom's affective reach is capacious. Performing a comparable search for healing, Lucy, who flees her own iteration of the devil, enters a space historically marked not only for men but also specifically for African American men. Walter alludes to this fact with his comment that Lucy "might pass as colored" but not as a man, a remark pointing not only to the expectation that jazz players are male and African American but also to the history of Creek intermarriage and the racialized politics of skin color in and around the Muscogee (Creek) Nation.[54] In each case, whether speaking of perceptions of gender or national/cultural affiliation, the boundaries of identity are imagined as discrete and quantifiable. And, once imagined as such, those boundaries are subsequently policed as if they were measurable iterations of the real. By contrast, Lucy's crossing, like Johnson's, invokes the possibilities of affective intercultural relationship.

A consideration of the intersections between expectations of masculinity and the space of the jazz club evokes the overlaps between hegemonic perceptions of African American and Native American masculinities. In the eyes of dominant culture, a specter of violence infuses both—there is a long, well-documented history of settler narratives that cast African American and Native American men as libidinal threats to white womanhood. (This reminds us why Justice's recovery of the erotic is so essential.) Yet even while misrepresented and maligned, certain iterations of Black and Native masculinities exist, as well, in a similarly constructed space of coerced acceptance. An example of this pattern can be seen in the fact that Native American actors performed for the entertainment of white viewers on the Hollywood screen while African American musicians did likewise for white audiences in certain blues and jazz clubs. Though actual Black and Native masculinities were and are both internally varied and radically divergent from those consumed in the popular movies and clubs that cater(ed) to white audiences, such complexity was— and still is—not often recognized in hegemonic venues. To return to Womack, Lucy's experience of jazz clubs picks at the seams of similarly neat distinctions surrounding race, gender, and performance. Along with collapsing the accepted binaries of gender and culture by participating as an orchestra *player* rather than as a singer, Lucy finds solace in jazz riffs that have the potential to speak the truth of a long-standing pain she never voiced. Much like Anna Lee Walters's characters claim kinship with African American hobos, Womack depicts

Lucy's deeply embodied performances of an African American musical genre as emerging from a shared experience of historical trauma.

If Robert Johnson's devil finds him at the crossroads, Lucy's devil emerges from systemic settler attacks on Indigenous lands and cultures. Womack undoubtedly crafts Lucy as representative of the many Indigenous women who live through and with the trauma of psychological and sexual abuse enabled by the violence of empire. As a young girl, Lucy is persistently assaulted by her white father; she also witnesses the aftermath of her father's sexual abuse of her cousin Jennie, one of her closest childhood friends. The girls' mistreatment, which haunts Lucy for the rest of her life, exists within a nexus of settler trauma. Lucy's white father basically kidnaps a young Creek boy from his grandmother's care to gain access to his land allotment. He also attempts to isolate Lucy and her mother from Creek community by keeping them from attending the Green Corn Ceremony, calling Native gatherings "the devil's work," discouraging Creek language use, and refusing to allow Lucy's mother to have relatives in their house. Nearly every aspect of Mvskoke culture is attacked by these prohibitions, which challenge the validity of Indigenous land claims, spirituality, language use, cultural practices, and kinship relations. When taken together, Lucy's father's proclivity for land theft and his abuse of young Indigenous girls resonates with the history of Indigenous–white relations in North America by resting on the simultaneous conquest of Native lands and bodies.

In terms of situating these occurrences within the parameters of this project, the trauma Lucy experiences at her father's hands is both an individual event and a larger symptom of settler invasion and genocide. These painful intersections reside in her body and present themselves in reflexive action as much as in the conscious mind. Lucy's felt experience, like Big Mom's, underscores Kleinman and Kleinman's argument that

> bodies transformed by political processes not only *represent* those processes, they *experience* them as the lived memory of transformed worlds. The experience is of memory processes sedimented in gait, posture, movement, and all the other corporeal components which together realize cultural code and social

dynamics in everyday practices. The memorialized experience
[of embodied history] merges subjectivity and social world.[55]

Lucy's body thus serves as both the vehicle for and the expression of
trauma—her memories of abuse erupt during flashbacks in which
rage threatens to consume her. These violent corporeal experiences
endanger those around her just as the initial events endangered—
and continue to endanger—her. Such explosive iterations of embodied trauma underline the affective nature of posttraumatic stress—
situated in bodily memory, these somatic experiences are at times not
controlled by conscious decision. For example, in the midst of one
episode of rage, Lucy realizes she has a butcher knife aimed at one of
her own children (126). Triggered by flashbacks of her father, Lucy
acts reflexively. She describes the feeling of such an event, saying that
sometimes "the darkness would cover me and pound inside my head"
(124). Like Alexie, then, Womack addresses how painful somatic
maps can threaten to spread cancerously to the next generation. In
the latter case, Lucy's body archives, enacts, and extends intergenerational settler trauma, presenting an all-too-painful iteration of, to return to Million, "colonialism as it is felt by those who experience it."[56]
However, much as Big Mom takes up the flute in *Reservation Blues*,
Lucy turns to the trumpet as a way to mediate, if not entirely eradicate, the reverberations of abuse. She confronts the felt experience of
colonialism through music.[57]

Aboriginal health activist Jessica Danforth notes that "traditional
forms of medicine and health centre around people's sexuality, which
is really their bodies and their bodily rights, and their bodily sovereignty. And autonomy, . . . because when we lose control of our bodies, we lose control of our nations."[58] Memories of just this sort of loss
of control bring Lucy to immerse herself in music. She comments:
"Here's the part that breaks my heart. Jennie and I never said a word
about [the abuse]. I wanted to protect her from all the ugliness, but
I couldn't ever ask her. How could I? We didn't even have words for
it. . . . All the stories that pour out of me now began that day I seen
Daddy and Jennie in the Ford" (123). Using music as a means to both
articulate and recover from this heartbreak, an adult Lucy explains:
"On weekends I went to Oklahoma City, and I hid behind my partition and blew like a sonofabitch. . . . That rage made me hit notes no

man could ever dream of" (123). Her comments here resonate with Ralph Ellison's description of the function of blues. He argues:

> The blues is an impulse to keep the painful details and episodes of a brutal experience alive in one's aching consciousness, to finger its jagged grain, and to transcend it, not by the consolation of philosophy, but by squeezing from it a near-tragic, near-comic lyricism. As a form, the blues is an autobiographical chronicle of personal catastrophe.[59]

In these scenes, the brutal experience of Lucy's sexual assault reverberates from self to family, from body to nation. It ripples out from the point of origin, which is both her father's abuse and, simultaneously, settler incursions into the Creek polity. However, as we've seen previously in this chapter, *trauma is not the only possible somatic event the body can archive*. Like the air Big Mom blows through her flute, which calls Indigenous people to look toward the future, Womack depicts Lucy's "wind"—her trumpet-playing—as *a bodily expression of survivance*.

Key to her identification as a big mom, Lucy's survivance strategies entail not just acts of self-preservation but also a lifetime of mentoring, nurturing, needling, and passing on Mvskoke history to those she loves. The stories housed in her body and the relationships they engender require affective transit between and among bodies. In fact, as with her music, with Lucy's oral history, "stories form bridges for other people to cross, to feel their way into another experience. That is the promise of witness."[60] As we saw in the previous section, music's effects on the body offer practitioners a way to speak the unspeakable and also a way to forge connections with audiences who practice active, embodied listening. Just as the previous section argued about Alexie, here, too, we see a situation in which silence is not the answer. Lucy kept her and Jennie's sexual abuse close to her chest for so many years, as do so many survivors. She explains:

> I, Lucille, smoking words on my tongue, dreaming of whippoorwill calls, casting swirled memories on the waters, has stories too dark to tell. A life of talking, and I ain't told some of them to anybody. . . . I can step in and out with my stories just like that; the band rests, and I take my chance to solo,

play my words against the piano, bass, guitar, drums of the
rhythm section while everybody else falls quiet. And if they're
listening right, if they take in the words, not just hearing them
with their ears but soaking them up through their body openings, when it's their turn to stand up and sound out, they'll play
all the better themselves for it. (111–12)

In this scene, jazz provides a grammar for the ongoing experience of
sociosomatic trauma. Following this logic, if Lucy's body archives
familial and historical trauma, we see that her breath—the most important corporeal tool of a trumpet player—encourages generative
understanding—survivance knowledges—to be "soak[ed] . . . up
through . . . body openings" in a conscious act of affective exchange.

In their Introduction to *Body & Society*'s special issue on affect,
coeditors Lisa Blackman and Couze Venn discuss a process-oriented
model of affect. The question, they argue, is not what affect *is* but
what affect *does* for understanding. Affect helps us interpret bodies
and embodied experience differently—rather than static entities
to be acted upon, *bodies can be perceived more accurately as enfleshed
processes.* Blackman and Venn suggest that "in the shift to bodies as
processes (rather than fixed or unchanging objects or entities) . . . affect is invoked to gesture toward something that perhaps escapes or
remains in excess of the practices of the 'speaking subject.'"[61] This
understanding of affect helps provide a language for the articulation of both the trauma and survivance knowledges that big moms
carry in their bodies. These entwined structures often exist outside
of language, which is why envisioning them as embodied processes
moves us toward a closer (though by no means exact) sense of their
form and function. Following this line of thought (or line of flight,
for you Deleuzians), *when we envision the body as a somatic archive, we
are not talking about a static entity—about the archive as a discrete, sin-
gularly located object/place where history is contained and entombed—
but instead about the body holding active, shifting, enfleshed processes of
memory and history with the power to mediate, or even disrupt, recurring
cycles of sociosomatic trauma.*

While the embodied language of jazz, as well as sociosomatic reactions to music more generally, present one discursive process for
the transit of enfleshed knowledges, another exists in the movement

of embodied history. Womack suggests that Mvskoke histories can be shared via the conduit of dreamscapes as well as through written texts, oral narratives, ceremony, shell shaking, and song. In "Intense Dreaming," Million maintains that dreaming

> is the effort to make sense of relations in the worlds we live, dreaming and empathizing intensely our relations with past and present and the future without the boundaries of linear time. Dreaming is a communicative sacred activity. Dreaming often allows us to creatively sidestep all the neat little boxes that obscure larger relations and syntheses of imagination. I also believe that dreaming, theory, narrative, and critical thinking are not exclusive of each other. They form different ways of knowing.[62]

The communicative, creative, and sometimes sacred experience of dreaming, which most often circulates in the fluid space between preconscious and conscious activity, allows historical knowledges to be shared between and among community members. If we continue to read the ample figures of big moms as somatic archives of Indigenous knowledge, we can further recognize them as figures that are especially likely to take part in such active dreaming, since it encourages embodied historical exchange.

Like breathing or sneezing, dreams are (in most cases) not something we mindfully control; yet, as the movement of our bodies in sleep (from the small-scale jump or twitch, to increased breathing and heightened pulse, to full-blown sleepwalking) and the measurement of our brain waves during REM (rapid eye movement) sleep show, dreams fully engage our cognitive capacities. Both scientists and laypeople, for example, report finding the answers to thorny theoretical problems in that state of bodily repose rather than in their daily, fully conscious work routine. Notably, in considering the parallels between aspects of dreaming and Indigenous belief systems, during the stage of our sleep cycles in which we dream—REM or stage four sleep— the rules of space and time realign; chronological, linear, and/or teleological thinking hold no sway in dreamscapes. Thus dreamscapes, which have flexible space-time continuums, better align with Indigenous cosmologies that allow for nonchronological connections between and among locations, time periods, people, and the other-than-human world. At the same time, in dreams, the brain accesses the hippocampus, the cradle of memories, and the amygdala, which holds/triggers emotional responses. And though a dreamer's eyes usually remain closed, the visual cortex fires repeatedly, just as it does when one is looking, open-eyed, at an image or the world around one.

Thinking about the direct connections between the practice of dreaming and the somatic exchange of Indigenous knowledge brings up another important aspect of dreaming: our memories are tied to our dreams. In "Cognitive and Emotional Processes during Dreaming," an article based on their neuroimaging of the brain, Martin Desseilles, Thien Thanh Dang-Vu, Virginie Sterpenich, and Sophie Schwartz note that "memory consolidation processes occur during REM states."[63] In fact, they point out that "a large body of data support the involvement of sleep in memory."[64] Likewise neuroendocrinologists Björn Rasch and Jan Born show that during sleep our memories are retrieved and reinforced.[65] Therefore dreaming and memory are intimately connected.

Mirroring the contours of dreamscapes, the chapters in *Drowning in Fire* move fluidly in time and space, shifting narrator, tense, era, and location both among and within chapters. Along with the present-day story line that follows Josh through his 1970s adolescence and later into his adult relationship with Jimmy in the 1990s, Womack unfolds key moments in early-twentieth-century Creek history through a series of dream experiences. In her capacity as a big mom, a figure that archives cultural knowledge and extends embodied healing to her family and community, Lucy functions as a direct conduit for many of these chronological shifts and cultural exchanges. Her depiction aligns with Leanne Simpson's observation that "dreams and visions propel resurgence because they provide . . . both the knowledge from the spiritual world and processes for realizing these vision. Dreams and visions provide glimpses of decolonial spaces and transformed realities that we have collectively yet to imagine."[66] These imaginative possibilities are Lucy's legacy. In fact, even after she has begun to show signs of age-related cognitive impairment, she continues to hold and share Mvskoke historical memory. Moreover, her interactions with Josh show how such embodied historical traces can transit between and among physical bodies and temporal locales. Josh gains the cultural knowledge that sets him at ease with his sexuality and also reconnects to his Creek heritage through the conduit of Lucy's spoken stories and shared dreamscapes. In fact, across the nearly one hundred years of history the text presents, connections to the healing power of a Mvskoke cosmology are bound to acts of dreaming: much as Million suggests, *dreaming functions as an affective process that can mobilize Indigenous knowledges.*

Speaking of *Drowning in Fire,* Michele Henry maintains that "through Josh's active listening over the years his Aunt Lucy invites him to enter her stories, experience them, and share them with others. [Eventually] Josh is able to fly into Lucy's world through his imagination, and she ushers him into this shared world."[67] Henry continues: "It is clear in this narrative that the oral tradition is not fixed by one person but continually reentered and re-experienced through each participant. . . . Within the Creek worldview it is permissible for Josh to enter into Lucy's story and remember it for himself as a participant in the Creek community."[68] The cultural transaction to which Henry alludes affirms the creative potential of affective exchange. Moreover, the cyclic movement of memory, dreaming, and history returns us to Blackman and Venn: "In the shift to [recognizing] bodies as processes . . . affect is invoked to gesture toward something that perhaps escapes or remains in excess of the practices of the 'speaking subject.'"[69] While the speaking subject carries significant import in cultures with strong oral traditions, here Creek history is located in shared dreamscapes that are *bodily experiences* rather than the stuff of language, underscoring Lucy's argument that significant events cannot always be articulated through the medium of the spoken word. In this equation, then, the corporeal expression of Mvskoke tradition circulates in and through the embodied landscape of dreams. *History itself can therefore be perceived as a felt emotional knowledge or, in other words, an affective experience.*

Long-Term Visioners and Masculine Practices: Louise Erdrich's Affective Traces

In their previously referenced article, "How Bodies Remember," Kleinman and Kleinman ask: "What are the interactive processes through which societies remember? How does societal memory tangibly work? How is it socially experienced?"[70] To consider how the somatic interventions of big moms might help us answer these questions, I turn to Louise Erdrich's Old Tallow, a recurring character in the first three volumes of her series of children's books, which began with *The Birchbark House*, a novel that follows an Anishinaabe family and community through a season of their lives on Moningwanaykaning (The Island of the Golden-Breasted Woodpecker, or Madeline Island) in 1847.

While there are many powerful female characters in Erdrich's *The Birchbark House*, the charismatic Old Tallow serves as the best example of a big mom, an ample figure whose body serves as an archive of Indigenous knowledges that are shared to promote healing and community wellness. Additionally, Old Tallow gestures toward the reach of big moms, who, whether single, polyamorous, married, or widowed—or any combination of those—can be cisgender or can embody aspects of what we might now term a Two-Spirit identity. Old Tallow, like Lucy, offers another iteration of non-cis masculinity; however, while Lucy's masculinity was primarily shown within familial settings, Old Tallow's oft-acknowledged masculinity circulates overtly within the larger public arena of the Anishinaabe community to which she belongs. The Birchbark House series, then, expands this chapter's analysis of affective embodiment by reminding us of what has always been true—the range and breadth of masculine performances in Indigenous contexts.

As a big mom, Old Tallow, like the previously referenced female-identified and gender-variant warriors, is marked by a power that exceeds the bounds of the generally accepted conduct for females in Anishinaabe cultures. The narrator describes Old Tallow as "a rangy woman over six feet in height" who is "powerful, lean, and lived surrounded by ferocious animals more wolf than dog and fiercely devoted to her. Old Tallow could bring down a bear with her pack of dogs, her gun, or even [her] razor-sharp spear."[71] Additionally, Omakayas, the novel's seven-year-old protagonist, explains, "Old Tallow was afraid of nothing" (20). In the majority of her descriptors, Old Tallow violates common behavioral expectations for Anishinaabe women: she lives alone, goes out at night, hunts large game, and entirely ignores the niceties of female attire by wearing ragged dresses, worn moccasins, and "a white man's hat with a heavy brim" that she is rarely seen without (22). Like Lucy, then, Old Tallow consciously sidesteps the most common gender norms of dress and occupation for her particular place and time—in this case, those of Anishinaabe women during the mid-nineteenth century.[72]

Old Tallow, who is known for her gruff and at times even hostile demeanor, exhibits the same expansive body as Big Mom—both women are over six feet tall and depicted as physically and psychologically powerful. She also enters into similar affective relationship with others and, as we will see, uses her physical body as a conduit for tribal healing. In "'Manly-Hearted Women': Gender Variants in Louise Erdrich's Birchbark House Books," Don Latham marks Old Tallow's choice of dress as an aspect of her behavior that characterizes her as "gender variant." Latham points to the history of Two-Spirit people in such contexts and reads Old Tallow and Two-Strike, a contemporary of Omakayas, as gender-variant figures. He contends: "The depiction of gender variants in the Birchbark House books differs from that of white tomboys in the classic tomboy novels of the nineteenth and early twentieth centuries in that the gender variants are not put under any pressure to change the gender roles they have adopted."[73] As a big mom whose non-cis masculinity, or gender-variant performance, affords her affective movement, Old Tallow nurtures and mentors those she loves. This generative bodily capacity arises *precisely because* she steps outside more commonly prescribed gender roles.

The Birchbark House opens with a key flashback that centers Old Tallow and emphasizes her fearless and selfless nature even though she herself is not present in the scene. In a prologue titled "The Girl from Spirit Island," voyageurs who have come to Lake Superior to gather and trade furs discover an island upon which an entire Anishinaabe community has been decimated by smallpox. Looking uneasily at the bodies from the shore, the men see only one living being—a crawling baby. However, rather than risking exposure to the disease by rescuing her, as a group they return to their canoes, abandoning the child to her fate. The narrator explains what happens as they paddle away from the baby:

> One man had tears in his eyes. His name was Hat; he thought
> of his wife and decided he would tell her about the baby. If
> there was anyone in the world who'd go and rescue that little
> girl, it was his wife. He shivered a little as he thought of her.
> He couldn't help it. Tallow, she was called, and sometimes she

scared him with her temper. Other times, he was amazed at
her courage. He grimaced in shame—unlike him, his wife was
afraid of nothing. (2)

The text begins with Hat's description of his wife's courage and concludes with the reveal that Tallow not only rescues that baby, later
named Omakayas, but also that she puts her husband out of her house
because she deems him "a fearful fool" after he leaves the child to die
(236). Tallow's affective interventions—she puts first her body (by
entering the path of the settler contagion) and then her emotions
(by telling Omakayas, the recipient of a tremendous amount of Old
Tallow's gruff love, of her rescue and adoption) on the line—thus
frame the narrative of *The Birchbark House.*

The first of these somatic interventions circles expectations of cisgender Anishinaabe masculinity. Tallow's scorn of Hat's inaction signals his compromised masculinity and contains an implicit demand
for a relational responsibility and ethic of care that he abdicates. Her
rescue of the abandoned infant ultimately stresses that to *successfully*
perform Indigenous masculinity, one must protect, nurture, and
sacrifice for other Anishinaabe people. The definitions for masculinity and bravery that Old Tallow extend as she tells an eight-year-old
Omakayas the story of her rescue from Spirit Island therefore align
with the warrior masculinities discussed in chapter 1. And though
she makes little of her actions, readers can see that in contrast to her
husband, Old Tallow herself exhibits all of the valued aspects of those
productive masculine performances—courage, selflessness, leadership, and a strong sense of group responsibility. Moreover, she puts
herself in physical danger to enact these ethical considerations. In this
way, her body functions as a vehicle for healing and cultural reconciliation. Much as warrior women put their bodies in the line of enemy
fire for their families and nations, so too does Tallow risk bodily harm
and death to rescue a baby from the throes of a smallpox epidemic.
Furthermore, when Tallow subsequently places the orphaned child
with an Anishinaabe family, she reaffirms and, in fact, reinforces the
Anishinaabe kinship philosophies that Hat denied when he valued
his own life over that of the baby.

While, according to her husband's description, Tallow had long
since exhibited the sort of productive non-cis masculinity associated with Plains warrior women, we might situate the moment of

Omakayas's rescue as the primal scene of Tallow's big mom-ness (as well as, perhaps, the moment when she fully takes up the performance of masculinity and in the process trades the name "Tallow" for "Old Tallow"). While her brusque nature, large stature, and solitary living arrangement initially seem to situate Old Tallow outside corporeal relationship with others, the movement of Tallow's body into the path of danger places her into a long-term affective relationship with Omakayas and her adoptive family. Old Tallow builds and extends kinship relations through this affective exchange: she works with and for the family's well-being, and they reciprocate by taking care of her when, for example, she suffers frostbite after an injury during a sudden freeze. Their intimately connected, complementary relationship is fueled by Old Tallow's gender variance.

This affectively expressed relationship is evident even in Old Tallow's death in the third book of the series, *The Porcupine Year*, which occurs when she sacrifices her body and life to honor the kinship bond she shares with Omakayas's family. When, after being compelled to leave their beloved home on Moningwanaykaning under pressure from settlers and the U.S. government, the family find themselves starving in the deep of winter, Old Tallow, despite the weakness of her body, attempts to hunt and kill a massive bear to save them all. She dies locked in the bear's embrace, giving her life in a final, successful attempt to sustain those she loves.[74] In this way, she inhabits a relational role similar to those of the previously analyzed big moms who also sustain their loved ones and communities through embodied healing practices. Recalling Johnston's words—"a right is a *debnimzewin*. But each right is also a duty"—Tallow chooses a larger sense of reciprocal relationship, taking seriously the duties and responsibilities of her gender-variant position and the affective bonds it has allowed her to create and maintain even when doing so means her death.[75]

Looking across these representations, Tallow's courageous and selfless responses construct a non-cis masculinity that enables the novel's young readers to better understand the flexibility of Anishinaabe gender roles as well as to more clearly perceive the cultural expectations for *cisgender* Anishinaabe masculinity. For example, readers of *The Birchbark House* can appreciate the severity of Hat's violation of the expectations and responsibilities of Indigenous

masculinity *precisely because* of Tallow's embodied response—
*Tallow's non-cis masculinity makes legible the contours of what, among
the Anishinaabeg of her time, would be appropriately performed cisgender masculine relations.* Furthermore, upon her return Tallow subsequently chooses right relationship over marriage ties, emphasizing that Anishinaabe kinship obligations exceed the boundaries of
heterocouplehood, an idea at odds with hegemonic understandings
of the latter. And, as we've seen, by articulating a more responsible
form of masculinity, Tallow forwards societal restoration: she returns
an orphaned Anishinaabe baby into the arms of the Anishinaabe people and makes the ultimate bodily sacrifice by valuing the survival of
the extended kinship unit over the needs of the individual. With these
representations, Erdrich suggests female and/or non-cis masculinity
has the power to reconstitute productive relationships that not only
support but also ultimately maintain and expand the Anishinaabe
nation.[76]

CONSIDERING Old Tallow's and Lucy Self's correlations to Big Mom
develops the commonalities between and among such powerful female culture bearers, aunties, and mentors. Sometimes invoking
forms of non-cis masculinity and sometimes simply taking up
the cultural power that is their earned and/or inherited right as
Indigenous women, the strong female characters, or big moms,
crafted by Sherman Alexie, Craig Womack, and Louise Erdrich are
perhaps most prominently marked by a deployment of bodily knowledge: their bodies archive Indigenous knowledges and they use those
knowledges to help those in their community thrive rather than simply survive. Throughout all these examples, the body acts as a complex apparatus of knowledge production and cultural renewal: in
other words, as long-term visioners who play music, tell stories, and
dream futures, big moms reveal the healing and history already encoded in and by the body.

CHAPTER 4

BODY AS SHIELD AND SHELTER
Indigenous Documentary Film

> We used to make our own wood in them days. We even cut the
> tree down, hand logged, sawed it by handsaw. We took all of
> the blocks down with these things rolling them. . . . We were real
> skookum women. Today I couldn't do it.
>
> —Carrie Joe, quoted in Susan Roy and Ruth Taylor, "'We Were
> Real Skookum Women'"

As Carrie Joe notes in her comments about a photograph of a group
of smiling Shishálh First Nation women rolling massive pieces of
cedar, women did the work that needed to be done.[1] Much of this
work involved labor-intensive efforts that non-Natives would code as
masculine; however, as Joe explains, such work *was* always the work
of women. In fact, a significant body of literature shows that women
whom settlers read as gender crossing were, in reality, completing
necessary tasks for their people that they themselves likely did not
see as remarkable. Because settler binaries of gendered occupation
have been strictly enforced, powerful Indigenous people like those
discussed in the previous chapters could often be improperly masculinized through colonial logics. By contrast, the big moms and
female-identified and gender-variant warriors examined to this point
in *Written by the Body* have all worked within Indigenous paradigms
and accessed and archived Indigenous narrative memory through
their felt experiences. As Dian Million argues, these felt experiences
coalesce in an embodied Indigenous theory.

While chapters 2 and 3 centered literary readings of such felt knowledges, this chapter turns to documentary film to consider how the affective experiences of female-identified and gender-variant warriors and big moms resonate in these nonfiction representations. It's important to first note that fiction and documentary film are not antithetical—literature is not divorced from contemporary Indigenous experience, and documentary film is not an unfiltered window into some pure reality, as has been repeatedly recognized in film studies. In fact, speaking of the history of Indigenous documentary film, Pamela Wilson comments that "we might speculate that the entire question of 'empirical truth versus fiction' regarding a film's subject matter is a construction imposed from a dominant Western cultural mindset; 'truth' claims themselves are culturally specific."[2] While some audiences might value a historical version of "the real" over the literary, there is, of course, a fluid intersection between the two.

There are crucial reasons to move between and among differing genres of literature and film. Key among them, to paraphrase the title of Daniel Heath Justice's important book, is the fact that *Indigenous literatures matter*. This claim rings true on a number of levels. I think, for example, about the many young queer/nonbinary Native American and Aboriginal folks who have commented to my coeditors and me that the poetry and fiction in *Sovereign Erotics* served as a lifeline as they came of age. In addition, as the next chapter (on HIV activist Carole laFavor) will highlight, literature is and has always been a common form of expression for social justice advocates—one need only skim tribal papers from the 1960s and 1970s to see how central poetry is to the calls for sovereignty and coalition in the Red Power era. Poetry, fiction, and documentary film are complementary, each offers a means to chronicle the world and, as well, a means to change it. Looking at the first wave of fiction and autobiographical literature from Aboriginal women writers that began in the 1973 with Métis writer/activist Maria Campbell's *Halfbreed*, Million points out that such literature offers "a history that can be *felt* as well as intellectualized."[3] Embodied fictional and autobiographical narratives of this sort take down the barriers that colonial logics place between "the personal and political."[4] Documentary film has the capacity to do similar work.[5] Like the histories and fiction analyzed in the previous chapters, then, the two documentary films that serve as the focus of this chapter highlight the embodied connections at the heart of *Written by the Body*. In this light, this chapter does not turn to documentaries to offer something *more* valid than, say, Erdrich's depiction of Old Tallow or Justice's Tarsa; rather, it constitutes a parallel reading that extends the usefulness of affective paradigms and further considers the powerful intersections of gender, kinship, and the body in Indigenous narratives.

As gestured toward by the epigraph, Indigenous women's physical labor is not an anomaly but a common occurrence—women do what needs to be done to support their kin networks and nations, and such work is complementary to the work done by folks of other genders, not contradictory. Indigenous nations include a multitude of female-identified and gender-variant folks who provide this sort of affective exchange to their communities by consciously using their bodies as shield, shelter, political commentary, and/or protest in the service of their families and nations.[6] Female-identified and gender-variant warriors, be they aunties, culture bearers, and/or big moms, routinely get the job done—whether that job be to protect, to fight, to feed, to teach, to grieve, to heal, or to love. Their stories extend our understanding of how meaning emerges from the intersections of embodied labor and Indigenous bodies in relationship. To stake this claim, chapter 4 analyzes two twenty-first-century documentaries that depict contemporary Indigenous women who literally place their bodies on the line for their communities: Abenaki filmmaker Alanis Obomsawin's *Trick or Treaty?* (2014) and non-Native filmmaker Sande Zeig's *Apache 8: Facing Fire Is Just the Beginning* (2011), which she creates in collaboration with the female firefighters she interviews.[7]

The Body as Activism in Alanis Obomsawin's *Trick or Treaty?*

It would be difficult to talk about how contemporary Indigenous women employ their bodies in the service of their nations in the present day and not turn to the texts and events of the Idle No More movement. As most readers will know, in November 2012, Jessica Gordon (Cree/Anishinaabe, Pasqua First Nation), Sylvia McAdam (Cree), Sheelah McLean (non-Indigenous), and Nina Wilson

(Nakota/Plains Cree, Kahkewistahaw First Nation) held a teach-in at Station 20 West in Saskatoon, Saskatchewan, to protest omnibus Bill C-45, a Harper administration initiative that ignored Aboriginal sovereignty and Canadian government treaty obligations. Using the Facebook page IdleNoMoreCommunity and the Twitter hashtag #idlenomore, these teacher–activists planted the seeds for a grassroots political movement of rallies, protests, and flash-mob round dances launched as a national day of action on December 10, 2012. On that same day, Attawapiskat Chief Theresa Spence began a hunger strike, which she undertook to demand that Prime Minister Harper and David Johnston, the governor general of Canada, meet with her and other First Nations leaders on treaty concerns.

In her 2015 film *Trick or Treaty?*, renowned filmmaker Alanis Obomsawin follows the rise of the Idle No More movement and the legacy of Treaty 9, or the James Bay Treaty, through the lens of two linked events: Chief Spence's hunger strike and the journey of the Nishiyuu walkers—six young James Bay Cree men and their guide and relative, Issac Kawapit—who trekked 1,600 kilometers (990 miles) from the Whapmagoostui First Nation community to the steps of the Canadian Parliament in Ottawa to support Chief Spence and Idle No More. By hinging this story of activism and solidarity on these particular political actions, the documentary centers the affective power of bodies, thereby highlighting how bodily responses to oppression are key aspects of contemporary Aboriginal resurgence and Indigenous futures.[8] Obomsawin's film aligns with the previous analyses in *Written by the Body*: in *Trick or Treaty?*, Indigenous people deploy their bodies as affective models of protection through which Indigenous pasts, presents, and futures coalesce to foster sovereignty and community well-being.

Chief Spence is introduced by a palimpsest of voices in Obomsawin's documentary. The first is that of National Chief Shawn A-in-chut Atleo, a hereditary chief from the Ahousaht First Nation, speaking at the Assembly of First Nations. A member of the press asks Atleo if it's "appropriate" that a reporter was escorted off Attawapiskat land. Atleo turns the question back at the reporter: "Is it appropriate that First Nations ranked around sixty-seventh on the UN Human Development Index when Canada ranks in the top seven?" He continues: "Amnesty International released a report that said that there's a grave human rights crisis among First Nations in Canada. Is that appropriate?" Atleo further references, with tears, his experience of going to the morgue with a family to identify the body of their daughter. In relation to this story, he points to the large number of murdered or missing Indigenous women whose deaths and disappearances remain unaddressed, asking, "The question is, is that appropriate?" Atleo's final words—"We are at a tipping point"—resonate with an urgency echoed in the subsequent sequence. The panning shots of an Idle No More rally move across dancers, drummers, and the crowd of land protectors/treaty rights advocates holding signs and banners. The frame pauses and tightens on a woman holding up a large flag: the top a sun across a background of undulating blue stripes; the bottom a Union Jack flag with a British crown upside down at its center. She states forcefully, while dancing to the beat of the drum, "Today the sun rises for our people forever. Our children." The scene cuts to snow and a shot of Chief Spence's tipi. Obomsawin's narration follows:

> December 2012. Chief Spence begins a hunger strike. She takes up residence in a tipi on Victoria Island facing Parliament Hill in Ottawa. She is requesting a special meeting with Prime Minister Stephen Harper, the governor general, David Johnston, and all the First Nations leaders in Canada in hope of improving the relationship between the First Nations leaders in Canada and the Canadian government.

The juxtaposition of these opening scenes and voices goes to the heart of Obomsawin's documentary. Framing its attention on the intersections of Indigenous bodies and rights and the discourse that circulated around these at the height of the Idle No More movement, *Trick or Treaty?* calls its viewers to recognize the importance of the embodied Indigenous activism that has occurred and is still occurring in the 110 years between the James Bay Treaty and Idle No More.

Obomsawin narrates Bill C-45's attack on sovereignty through the lens of affective relationships. In particular, she depicts Chief Spence's hunger strike as an embodied political action that has wide-ranging affective consequences for First Nations, Métis, and Inuit peoples. As the Kino-nda-niimi Collective explains in the Introduction to *The Winter We Danced*: "The impact of Chief Theresa Spence's fast on the movement . . . cannot be understated," nor, they continue, can the bodily sacrifice of "the fasting Ogichidaakwe, who went without food for six weeks on Victoria Island in Omàmìwinini (Algonquin) territory, Ottawa, to draw attention to unfulfilled treaties and the consequences on her community."[9] Situating Chief Spence as an "Ogichidaakwe," which translates from Anishinaabemowin to English as "female warrior" or "ceremonial woman" marks her importance for the movement, a connection seen throughout the documentary. In a scene early in the film, for example, Obomsawin's camera lingers on a banner near Chief Spence's encampment as she interviews Joe Red Sky (Roseau River First Nation) and Thundering Woman (Sandy Bay, Manitoba). The two stand in front of a sign that reads "Brave Hearted Women 'Okiijida ikwe' Together Protecting the Land, Water, Peoples." In their interview, they emphasize the history of women in Indigenous activism, saying that the work "done regarding the land, the water, the future of the unborn, has always been the women. Any occupation . . . it has always been the women who stood up and said that we're tired of this." In *Trick or Treaty?*, Obomsawin depicts Chief Spence's hunger strike as a real-world example of just such affective labor—she is an Ogichidaakwe, a powerful Indigenous woman warrior, employing her body in the service of Indigenous community.[10]

Though not directly referenced by Obomsawin, Chief Spence's actions exist within a larger narrative in which the body acts as an instrument of transformation. Fasting has valence across many spiritual traditions. There is an extensive history of Native people fasting, praying, and forgoing food for spiritual, political, and community benefit. Speaking of the Sun Dance, Andrew Soliz (Lakota) describes fasting as a way to empty oneself, to "have room to receive the teachings that the creator has for us." He comments: "I will fast around ceremony. It allows me to really focus on the reason why I'm doing the ceremony. It helps us understand what commitments are. It helps me understand what a commitment *is*."[11] Here we see the body as integral to the spiritual process rather than absent from it or, even worse, as inherently profane, as is so often taught in evangelical Christian traditions. Speaking of the IRA hunger strikes in the early 1980s, Maude Ellmann contends that through the hunger strike, "protesters transform their bodies into the 'quotations' of their forebearers."[12] This concept of the body as citation aligns with my previous arguments about the body as archive. We see such resonances in Leanne Simpson's support of Chief Spence's fast. She says in "Fish Broth and Fasting":

> Ogichidaakwe Spence isn't just on a hunger strike. She is fasting and this also has cultural meaning for Anishinaabeg. She is in ceremony.... We support. We pray.... We take care of all the other things that need to be taken care of, and we live up to our responsibilities in light of the faster. We protect the faster. We do these things because we know that through her physical sacrifice she is closer to the Spiritual world than we are.... This is the most basic building block of Anishinaabeg sovereignty and governance.[13]

Simpson's comments underscore the fact that in Indigenous communities the body has been deployed as a change agent for generations—there is precedent and there is protocol and those knowledges are held in the body as well as in the reciprocal relationship between the faster and her Indigenous community. Importantly, too, here, those embodied methods of prayer and political intervention have direct ties to the enactment of sovereignty.

Critics of Chief Spence, unsurprisingly, often included overt anti-Indigenous sentiments in their attacks in the press, on social media, and in person. Such charges arise briefly in *Trick or Treaty?* when Chief Spence is heckled when she emerges from her tipi to speak to gathered reporters. The shouts invoke the specter of the many bitter attacks on Chief Spence's character and person that arose during the course of her fast.[14] A narrative of corruption, for example, garnered much conservative press in an attempt to transform Chief Spence from Ogichidaakwe to villain. There was, however, a more pervasive critique that proliferated across conservative responses and that involved a focus on the body as a site of shame, an affective response Leanne Simpson calls "an insidious and infectious part" of settler-colonial "cognitive imperialism."[15]

The scrutiny on Chief Spence's body during her fast relied on settler logics that questioned the validity of both her fasting process and her physique. In both cases, these settler critiques turn on the axis of shame—Chief Spence's fish broth fast was not a "real" hunger strike, and her form was too large. (The latter charge, of course, invokes the productive and capacious bodies of big moms discussed in chapter 3.) Chief Spence's body became something of a public obsession; reporters barraged her with questions about what, exactly, she was consuming—lemon water, medicinal tea, and fish broth—and how her body was reacting to the passage of time during her six-week hunger strike. She was not, it seems, wasting away at a pace to meet settler desires. Akwesasne Mohawk theorist Audra Simpson comments:

> A hunger strike under conditions of ongoing death deserve
> more interpretive flexibility than Theresa Spence or any
> Indigenous or racialized woman in Canada would or could be
> afforded in those moments. . . . This was not a hunger strike
> in the "classic" sense—it was rendered a "soft" hunger strike.
> And as such we read in endless newspaper articles, blog posts,
> vicious comments sections, in twitter flame wars and heard on
> TV . . . that her campaign did not compare to . . . other strikes
> [that] nearly ended in death, or in fact, ended in death. . . . Irate
> Canadians "weighed in" continuously on her insincerity, her
> avarice, her body, and, in particular, her fat.[16]

The vicious rhetoric can only be read in the context of ongoing attacks on Indigenous women's bodies. Leanne Simpson explains: "The racism, sexism, and disrespect that has been heaped on Ogichidaakwe Spence . . . have been done so in part because it is acceptable to treat Indigenous women this way."[17] The epidemic of missing and murdered Indigenous women that Chief Atleo references at the start of *Trick or Treaty?* is directly related to the public obsession with Chief Spence's body, and Obomsawin makes that tie directly through the opening sequence, which crafts a through-line from Atleo's commentary to Chief Spence's fast.

By tying women's bodies not to death but instead to sovereignty, Obomsawin's documentary argues that *the body serves as an archive of memory and history with the power to disrupt cycles of trauma.* In this paradigm, Obomsawin depicts Chief Spence's body as a political tactic that challenges and ultimately disorders settler narratives; as Ogichidaakwe Spence smudges, prays, and negotiates during the course of her hunger strike, her body becomes a sacred space that is both a field of contestation and a force for change. And further, as

Audra Simpson argues, in this resistance and "refusal of domination," Theresa Spence adamantly refuses to do "what she is required to do, with or without the starvation," which is to die.[18]

This refusal is catching. Obomsawin's film includes multiple examples of Chief Spence's affective resonance: her hunger strike calls others into action—it is, to return to Blackman and Venn, an enfleshed process, "something that perhaps escapes or remains in excess of the practices of the 'speaking subject.'"[19] Most notably, by choosing to twine the narrative of the Nishiyuu walkers—David Kawapit Jr., age seventeen; Stanley George Jr., seventeen; Travis George, seventeen; Johnny Abraham, nineteen; Raymond Kawapit, twenty; Geordie Rupert, twenty-one; and their guide and relative, Issac Kawapit, forty-nine—with that of Chief Spence, Obomsawin highlights the powerful affective impact of the latter's somatic intervention.[20] As David Kawapit, the young Cree man who initiated the walk, explains in the film:

> I was really tired of what was going on, the government pushing us aside. . . . They continue to let Theresa Spence suffer.
> So, I want[ed] to show my support to what was going on and I want[ed] to go with something *grassroots* from the Cree people. And I remembered stories of our ancestors who went on journeys that lasted for months to trade with fellow First Nations across Canada. They walked with snowshoes. . . . So it's pretty much how the idea came to me. The journey.

The walkers' journey from Whapmagoostui to Ottawa, as Kawapit reminds listeners, springboards off the combined momentum of Idle No More and Chief Spence's hunger strike to offer another form of embodied political action that has a long history in Indigenous communities. In the words of another walker whom Obomsawin interviews, Brock Lewis (Ojibway First Nation), "Walking is medicine." He continues: "You get to feel the land. That's how our ancestors are speaking through us, is through the land. I feel myself now very close to my ancestors and we're doing a lot of the same things that they have always fought for. . . . And as we keep walking through the land, our ancestors will rise through us and we will be together once again." Inspired by the physical acts of their ancestors as well as by the sociosomatic reverberations of the hunger strike, *Trick or Treaty?* shows that Chief Spence and the walkers offer alternate forms of embodied protest.

Considering a like journey, Sam McKegney has written about the importance of the Residential School Walkers' 2,200-kilometer expedition from Cochrane, Ontario, to Halifax, Nova Scotia. In this latter event, six men from the Mushkegowuk Nation, who make up a group that has also been called the Oskapewisk (The Helpers), coordinated their nearly two-month-long trek as an embodied response to Canada's residential school legacies—their walk was timed to enable them to attend the Truth and Reconciliation Commission hearings. McKegney maintains that the Residential School Walkers (also called the Truth and Reconciliation Walkers)

> use the "bodily experience" of agentive (as opposed to forced) "movement" over territory to better "know themselves and their bodies"; in this way, they contest the fiction of Cartesian dualism and resist the colonial pressures of both coerced disembodiment and forced relocation. Through walking and speaking publically, these men strive to enact, embody, and model non-dominative yet empowered subjectivities.[21]

Importantly, then, in thinking of the work done in the last three chapters, these young men enact creative and productive masculinities as modes of intervention and protection for their own and other Indigenous nations. These enactments of gender that are based on models of reciprocity and resurgence. They "honour the capacity to 'feel' and to 'love' while exhibiting physical strength, stamina, and masculine solidarity."[22] Like the somatic labor of Chief Spence, here, too, the body acts as prayer and intercession, interrupting the "insidious and infectious" settler-colonial imperative to offer instead *an affective model of protection arising from Indigenous knowledge systems.*[23]

These politics of embodiment return us to Brian Massumi's reading of affect as a field of emergence that can be linked to "an unleashing of potential."[24] The usefulness of this frame is in its recognition of the power of sensory perspectives that expand, in unruly and powerful ways, beyond the anchor of the body. Massumi writes: "Affect is autonomous to the degree to which it escapes confinement in the particular body whose vitality, or potential for interaction, it is."[25] Obomsawin shows the escape of this vitality to her viewers through the chain of relationships she depicts in which affective interventions ripple out to contemporary Indigenous communities and, simultaneously, invoke Indigenous pasts and work toward productive Indigenous futures. For many viewers, narratives about Aboriginal peoples' geographic journeys would not initially seem tied to a hunger strike; however, Obomsawin teaches her audience how Chief Spence's embodied protest, even though it takes place in a single location, ripples out to unleash the latent political potential of such long-standing journey narratives. In *Trick or Treaty?* the body of Chief Spence and the bodies of the walkers are citations—their contemporary affective responses indelibly wedded with preexisting Indigenous memories and stories in an affective palimpsest. The cartography of the body links to that of the land, and as the walkers multiply throughout the journey, Obomsawin's film suggests the reverberations spiral outward, exponentially increasing an affective potential that builds on existing Indigenous histories even while creating new community and serving as a catalyst for productive change.[26]

Apache 8: Culture, Gender, and Somatic Knowledge in Wildland Firefighting

While the first chapters of *Written by the Body* focused on eighteenth- and nineteenth-century female-identified and gender-variant warriors and their fictional descendants, this chapter extends this genealogy to include contemporary women who follow in the footsteps of their powerful ancestors. To do so I consider *Apache 8,* which depicts a group of strong Apache women who are Lozen's tribal descendants. As the subsequent analysis will show, the members of this all-female wildland firefighting troop—first named Apache 6 and later Apache 8—undertake a process of affective exchange by consciously using their bodies to protect and shield their community just as female-identified and gender-variant warriors and culture bearers like big moms have for centuries.

In *Apache 8,* Sande Zeig, a queer, non-Native filmmaker from New York City who has been making films since the early 1990s, documents the lives and histories of White Mountain Apache women who belong to the eponymously named wildland firefighting crew. A chance 2006 meeting between Zeig and an Apache 8 crew in the

Phoenix airport became the impetus for the documentary, which she began filming the following year.[27] Upon obtaining a meeting with crew boss Cheryl Bones and explaining her hope that she might chronicle the female firefighting unit's story, Zeig was invited to accompany Apache 8 on a forest-thinning project that summer. After interviewing some thirty people, she received permission from the White Mountain Apache Tribal Council to pursue the project officially, which allowed her to bring her research on the history of the unit and the lives of these extraordinary women to the screen.[28] In the tradition of journalistic documentaries, *Apache 8* employs archival photos, news footage, and personal interviews with several generations of female firefighters who were members of Apache 8 and its predecessor, Apache 6, over the units' combined thirty-year history.

Apache 8 explains that more than one hundred White Mountain Apache women served as wildland firefighters from 1974 to 2005. The documentary includes the voices of twenty of these, with the primary focus falling on four: Cheryl Bones, who joined the unit in the mid-1970s, when it was still Apache 6, and became squad boss in 1981;[29] Nita Quintero, who joined Apache 8 in the early 1980s and worked under Bones; Katy Aday, who joined Apache 8 in the mid-1980s when she was a twenty-one-year-old mother of two; and the youngest, Ericka Hinton, who, as part of what the film terms "the next generation of firefighters," trains with Apache 8 and then goes on to work with other established wildland firefighting crews, eventually becoming the first female member of the famed Fort Apache Hot Shots.[30]

While there is much to say about these women, I focus here on how the affective labor of wildland firefighting defines a new generation of warriors and protectors. Zeig's documentary underscores the demanding, embodied service the women of Apache 6 and Apache 8 offer the White Mountain Apache: these firefighters undertake the ongoing material labor of carrying and maintaining heavy equipment, cutting down trees, and removing excess brush from overgrown forests. In addition, when the phone rings to call them into action they move quickly and efficiently toward what most others flee—a potentially devastating combination of smoke, flame, and forest. By deliberately heading *toward* these dangers in an effort to contain and eradicate the threats they represent, the women of Apache 8 literally place their bodies in the line of fire. And, while the crew fights wildfires across the United States, their primary mission is to preserve a specific Indigenous space: the land of the White Mountain Apache Tribe, a nation located in, and predating by thousands of years, what is now eastern Arizona. As one of the crew comments in a voice-over layered atop a map of Arizona and the Fort Apache Reservation: "Our reservation is 1.6 million acres. We have 14,000 tribal members that live here. Our job is to protect *our* land from fires."[31] These female-identified firefighters are, like Chief Spence and the Nishiyuu walkers in *Trick or Treaty?*, represented as powerful figures who share protection, healing, and cultural connection through the bodily interventions they undertake on behalf of their nation.

Though their service does not occur without controversy, the film emphasizes the respect the women are shown by their families, the White Mountain Apache people and government, and the national firefighting community. Firefighting is a particularly esteemed occupation among contemporary Apache, and their crews have been ranked among the elite. *Indian Country Today* notes that "among 26 highly skilled HotShot crews in the United States[,] Apaches are taking the lead nationwide."[32] The *Fort Apache Scout* explains that "the Fort Apache Hotshots are considered the very best firefighting crew in the nation and the reputation they have, has made them the super-heroes of the White Mountain communities."[33] Multiple conversations in the film underscore the standing wildland firefighters garner within their community. As one Apache 8 firefighter says: "My people respect me because I'm putting my life on the line to respect what is ours. The beauty of the reservation." Ronnie Lupe, the White Mountain Apache tribal chairman at the time of the documentary's filming, situates the crew's life-threatening work as undertaken in the service of Indigenous nationhood: "Apache 8, they've traveled all over. And been recognized as one of the top firefighters in the world if you will. And they have been trained to protect our land here on the reservation. Very sacred to us are these mountains. The rivers. The trees. The wind. The clouds. We are one with the land." To underscore this claim, visuals of Chairman Lupe are interspersed with striking vistas of the White Mountain landscape. As Lupe's statement concludes, the shot cuts to a tight focus on a bumper sticker that reads, "I am Apache and I am Proud of It." The film's visual rhetoric further ties land to Apache citizenship and emphasizes Apache 8's place as a crew that protects more than *individual* people or land tracts—their work is overtly tied to the fabric of Apache identity.[34] Through the combination of these commentaries and visuals, *Apache 8* describes a tribal nationalism and landbase maintained and supported by the somatic interventions of Indigenous women.

While the documentary most prominently addresses the community's pride in its all-female firefighting crew, it also depicts the challenges the women encounter when they enter spaces and undertake jobs that in contemporary times are most often coded as masculine. Speaking of such attitudes, Roy and Taylor argue in their analysis of the Shíshál economy and logging in the Pacific Northwest that, in many contexts, people "are surprised to see women . . . out in the woods hauling logs." Such taxing physical work "disrupts the Western dichotomy that separates economy from culture, workplace from domestic sphere, manly from feminine, and—importantly, forest from home."[35] In that enforced settler dichotomy, as this chapter's conversation about the attacks on Chief Spence and the previous chapter's conversations about toxic masculinity show, settler logics of colonial masculinity have actively endeavored to disenfranchise Indigenous women and gender-variant peoples from positions of strength, whether those be aligned with physical labor or leadership within their nations.

The crew of Apache 6 confronted such misogynistic attitudes toward their entrance into a field perceived as the domain of men. In fact, their success is often couched in terms that invoke masculinity as a standard to which they must "rise." Thus, the physical challenges the women of Apache 8 face are repeatedly marked as normatively *outside* the sphere of women's labor and bodily capacity. In opposition to the points Carrie Joe makes in the epigraph to this chapter, the crew's success is therefore crafted not from doing what needs to be done as women but instead as arising from their capacity to act "like men." Multiple interviewees in *Apache 8* employ phrases such as "the same as men," "just like men," "as well as men," and "better than men." These comments invariably reference physical strength and endurance—the ability to lift heavy objects and the sheer will to keep moving (up mountains, through smoke, etc.)—and people identified male at birth, as a bar these female firefighters must meet or exceed. We could consider this rhetoric in light of Achille Membe's claim that colonialism converts its "founding violence," which in this case is the elision of capacious Indigenous gender logics, "into authorizing capacity."[36] Though there have been female warriors and culture bearers among Apache people for centuries, *Apache 8* shows that this first crew of all-female firefighters was not initially viewed in such a positive light. In this respect, the crew's experience aligns with that of other female firefighters. A recent analysis of health and discrimination among female firefighters found that "among tactical professions, which also includes law enforcement and the military, the proportion of women is lowest in the fire service."[37] Furthermore, along with low numbers of female crew members, "a number of studies of women firefighters have documented troubling gender-based discrimination and harassment."[38]

While *Apache 8* focuses on the unit's success in the field, clearly gender discrimination was a significant issue for the first iteration of the all-female crew. In the film, one of the early leaders from the 1970s Apache 6 crew, Marjorie Grimes, comments: "It was an uphill battle. The public was not open to women firefighters. We had to fight for the *right* to fight fires, as women. . . . We did not even know if they were going to issue us the proper equipment." There was a "'Yeah, right, I don't think so' attitude." Robert Lacapa, the forest manager for the BIA Fort Apache Agency, contends:

> This whole concept of having women [serve as firefighters] was rather taboo to this local area. The society here heavily depends on the menfolk, and having the jobs could have really presented a potential issue of strife between the men and the women. But it turned out totally different. From what I could tell, the women were fully accepted as a firefighting crew. They were basically segregated from the men. The men had their own crews and the women had their own crew. They recognized they were out there competing in a man's world. And they actually can come back and say they've outperformed the men.

This sense of the Apache 8 crew outperforming not only gendered expectations of women but also other firefighting units regardless of gender runs throughout the film's interviews. Katy Aday offers this story, which is worth quoting at length as it appears several times across the span of the film:

So here we are working, and in the middle of the day we got this fire call. We grabbed all our tools. And we were walking, and, you know, the man that was leading us was, you know, this big white man. And so we're all walking, we're walking after him. He said, "Now you ladies can rest," and we're all like, "We just got here. What's there to rest about?" You know, let's go! And so, nobody says anything, we're all quiet, we're very respectful. We start going again. We probably go another mile, and he rests us again. And we're like, what is up with the resting bit here? [Aday laughs] You know, I thought we were supposed to be doing a fire. And so, by this time, there's mumbling among us, "What's going on? What's he doing? Why that white man resting?" And all of it is in Apache, of course, because we don't want him to hear what we're saying. Cheryl says, "All right. Let's go!" We bypassed everybody on that crew. Up that mountain. Down. Back up. Then when we got there, everybody was asking, "Who are you? Who are you?" And we're like, "White Mountain Apache. Apache 8. Thank you very much." You know, get out of our way. We've got a job to do here.

While Grimes explains that the women's experiences were by no means easy as they entered the field of wildland firefighting, Lacapa describes an eventual community acceptance: Apache women are provided the same responsibilities and status as men in similar positions. Meanwhile, Aday's story, which becomes a linchpin of the film, suggests the crew understands themselves primarily through a lens of affective labor—they do what needs to be done. They also, notably, function within a particular cultural understanding of self and responsibility as their deployment of Apache language as an alternate form of communication demonstrates. The white male firefighter "leading" them up the hill is entangled in the ideology of colonial masculinity; reading the women through a limiting heteropatriarchal lens, he is as oblivious to the crew's knowledge and abilities as he is to their language. Serving their community more than one hundred years after Lozen, the crew of Apache 8 helps make legible a history of Apache women who place their bodies in danger to fight for their nation. As the above speakers emphasize, their first task was to present a definitive embodied response to settler gender restrictions, barriers that, as we see in Aday's story, exemplify a "founding violence"

rerouted into an "authorizing capacity."[39] Through their perseverance as well as their physical acts of strength and daring, the women
of Apache 6 explode restrictive, non-Apache gender divisions which
imagine women as less competent than their male counterparts.

In the stories Zeig's documentary shares from the early crew
members, there's little question that logics of heteronormativity and
heteropatriarchy are at work. Yet, while colonial masculinity *seems* to
have become ascendant, since "like men" functions as an aspirational
signifier in multiple conversations, the interviewees also repeatedly
cite the strength inherent in Apache womanhood as a coeval reality.
For example, while Chairman Lupe likens the women's success at the
difficult labor of firefighting to that of a "strong man," he also extends
the embodied possibilities of these female-identified firefighters:

> We have handed some of the tools, modern tools, to the women.
> And they can swing a power saw just as well as any strong man
> could. And they can climb the highest mountain and carry the
> heaviest burden on their back. And still put out the fire. And
> we're so proud of that. And we have recognition because of
> that, in this modern day, of our firefighters. And our people,
> White Mountain Apache tribe, our lady folks, young ones,
> just take natural to it. Look what surrounds us—trees, forests,
> mountains, rivers, lakes. We don't want to lose any of that. This
> is a beautiful country, God's country. And that's where our
> firefighters come from.

Here, Chairman Lupe depicts the somatic capacities of the women
in Apache 8 as inherent or "natural," and, even more significantly,
as *emerging from the land itself.* Vice Chair Margaret Naha-Walker
specifically casts such strength as integral to Apache womanhood:
"I know for these ladies, they didn't think about the hot fire. Or the
miles they had to walk up on that mountain to get to that fire. Us
Apache women, you know, we do a lot. We take a lot. And we're very
strong. Strong spiritually. Strong emotionally. And we have very un-
conditional love." Notably, Naha-Walker contends that respect for
these firefighters arises, not from the gendered nature of their work—
they do not garner respect *because* they have entered a male-coded
space—but instead from the larger history of Apache women. These
descriptions of their work for, and their place in, the White Mountain

Apache community emphasize the affective relationship between the women in the crew and the people of the community. While the rhetoric of colonial masculinity is not absent, *the all-female crew's embodied acts of protection and their affective labor are consistently cast in Apache terms—completed for Apache people and arising from Apache land and history.*

In these exchanges, the women of Apache 8 are envisioned as a synecdoche for the strength of the Apache people and a stand-in for the nation. Unlike the exploitative attention to women's bodies so often evidenced in hegemonic cultural exchanges such as those we saw in the settler responses to Chief Spence, the interviewees in *Apache 8* repeatedly claim that the women's physical labor serves the larger interests of their tribal land and community. Markedly affective, that labor is the work of kinship and the manifestation of relational responsibility. The crew members are depicted as emerging from the land they protect and as working *with* rather than against that land as they attempt to eradicate the threat of wildfire. In concert with such beliefs, the land, as the body of the nation, is not separate from them, an object to be subdued and overcome, as it might be in conventional Western contexts. Instead, the documentary offers vignettes in which members of Apache 8 describe themselves and are described by others as conduits for a felt relationship. Following Million, we can understand this felt theory as particularly affective.

To quote Gregory Seigworth and Melissa Gregg, "affect accumulates across both relatedness and interruptions in relatedness, becoming a palimpsest of force-encounters traversing the ebbs and swells of intensities that pass between bodies." They continue: "The real powers of affect, of affect as potential, [lie in] a body's capacity to affect and to be affected. How does a body, marked in its duration by these various encounters with mixed forces, come to shift its affections (its being affected) into action (capacity to affect)?"[40] To make the tie here between Seigworth and Gregg's theory of affect and the visual rhetoric of *Apache 8* more explicit, I suggest that the members of these female-identified wildland firefighting crews can be read through the lens of the women warriors and big moms whose acts of protection, as we have seen, emphasize kinship and tribal responsibility. To place this in Seigworth and Gregg's terms, the women shift from "being affected"—being members of their nation—"into action"—being defenders of their nation. Their affective labor is literally integral to the survival of their people and landbase. As such, *these women's bodies are, in fact, constitutive:* they *enact* protection, *promote* knowledge production, and *forward* cultural renewal. Like the female-identified and gender-variant warriors in chapters 1 and 2, the big moms of chapter 3, and the Indigenous leaders and activists represented in *Trick or Treaty?*, the women of Apache 8 share embodied stories of healing and survivance that are embedded in specific national histories and, as we'll see, in particular Apache cultural practices.

Fire, Protection, and the Space of the Sacred

Nita Quintero's narrative, in particular, highlights the imbricated nature of the body and culture as depicted in *Apache 8*. Her dedication to her work as a wildland firefighter is figured as intimately related to her participation in an Apache rite of passage for young women, the Sunrise Dance, also known as the Sunrise Ceremony or Sunrise Dance Ceremony, which adolescent girls undertake upon the start of their menses. In 1976, when Quintero was fourteen, her participation in those puberty rites was photographed by her in-law Bill Hess, which led to a *National Geographic* feature story titled "Coming of Age the Apache Way." Speaking of Apache culture, Quintero's fellow Apache 8 crew member Katy Aday describes the ceremony this way: "We have a lot of ceremonies in our culture. One of the biggest ceremonies that is open to the public is the Sunrise Dance Ceremony. When your daughter becomes of age, she goes and she tells her parents. And they're taught that from a very young age. You know, we need to know as soon as it happens. You gotta let us know." Zeig includes pictures from Quintero's ceremony in the archival photos in *Apache 8* and also interviews the firefighter about what her participation in this cultural milestone meant to her.

Notably, Quintero describes her experience primarily in Apache. As the first inclusion of the Apache language in the documentary, the transition is striking, marking Quintero's recollection as a grounded cultural practice that, like the Apache language use in Aday's story, is still living and relevant to the lives of contemporary White Mountain Apache people. Quintero explains how, in 1976, she awoke to find herself surrounded by older relatives. When she asked what was happening, her mother explained: "You're going to be dancing for us." "Through this ceremony," Quintero clarifies, a "girl can be blessed with a long life so that one day she can gain wisdom, knowledge, understanding, and prayers." In "Coming of Age the Apache Way" she emphasizes the fact that the ceremony requires significant community participation—her parents, relatives, a medicine man, sponsors, as well as numerous friends and neighbors come to support her transition "from childhood to womanhood."[41] Importantly, in terms of reading an adult Quintero as having an embodied tie to previous female-identified and gender-variant warriors, the Sunrise Dance also requires the sharing of embodied knowledge from generation to generation. She explains, "The most important thing Godmother [Gertrude Foster, Quintero's sponsor] does in the whole ceremony is to massage my body. She is giving me all her knowledge."[42] Quintero's description of this pivotal event in the Sunrise Dance reinforces the importance of sociosomatic bonds and embodied knowledge.

If the body holds Indigenous knowledges, then Quintero presents an important example of exactly *how* this collection of information is accessed, opened, and engaged in powerful affective exchanges between and among Indigenous people. The segment concludes with her connective claim, which links the knowledge gained through ceremony to her current occupation: "The Sunrise Dance helped prepare me for the biggest challenges of my life. Like being a wildland firefighter." We see this connection between ceremony and fire/firefighting recur in a 2018 interview Ericka Hinton gives about her long career with the Hotshots in which she ties her job, and fire itself, to the sacred: "With our tradition we have a sacred ceremony, the Sunrise Dance. It lasts for four days. The Sunrise Dance is for the young lady coming of age. The godmother and father stand by her side. Blessings and Apache songs are for the girl. Once she builds her campfire, the family moves into the camp and the ceremony begins. While building a fire you say a prayer. The fire is sacred."[43] I want to return to my previous argument that land and the other-than-human world is not separate from these firefighters, an object to be subdued and overcome, as it would be in conventional Western contexts. Instead, we see members of Apache 8 in felt relationship, even with fire itself. If previously the Apache 8 crew was depicted as both protecting and emerging from the White Mountain Apache nation, here Quintero and Hinton offer an embodied Indigenous theory in which long-standing Apache cultural practices define their experience of wild-land firefighting.

Quintero's interviews underscore the importance of embodied narratives to Indigenous cosmologies. These exchanges reinforce the fact that, among the Apache, as the Sunrise Dance emphasizes, the female body functions as a source of inspiration and strength. The previous chapters maintained that the body acts as a form of cultural continuity—it archives Indigenous knowledges. In this context, we are reminded that the sharing of such embodied knowledges is a *conscious* act of exchange *between and among* Indigenous people: Quintero's experience at the Sunrise Dance was not just for her, but, as her mother explains, "for us"—for her relatives, her clan, her nation. While Daniel Heath Justice crafts understandings of menstruation as generative practices for his imagined Indigenous people, the Kyn, here we see the Indigenous cultural imperative behind such depictions. And though not every one of the hundred women who served in Apache 6 and Apache 8 crews undertook the Sunrise Dance Ceremony, *Apache 8* depicts their understandings of self and responsibility as arising from just this sort of highly embodied ethic of community relationality. This connection resonates with Leanne Simpson's observations about her Michi Saagiig Nishnaabeg community: "People were expected to figure out their gifts and their responsibilities through ceremony and reflection and self-actualization, and that process was really the most important governing process on an individual level—more important than the gender you were born into."[44]

This emphasis on acts and responsibilities rather than gender roles permeates *Apache 8*. Thus, while the film does not gloss over the contemporary gender barriers faced by Apache women, it presents differences in gender and sexual preference with little fanfare, much as we saw in the gender-variant representations of Justice, Womack, and Erdrich. As a result, along with emphasizing the ties between ceremony and wildland firefighting, the documentary situates Quintero's relationship with her partner, Verda Lupe, as pivotal to her life in the Apache 8 crew. It's notable that the documentary's interview, editing, and production choices present the women's life together matter-of-factly. There is no overt discussion of gender identification or sexuality in the film.

While Quintero and a number of other Apache 8 firefighters present an aesthetic that could be read as butch—cropped hair, jeans, work boots, no makeup—and though Quintero, who identifies in the documentary as a women, has a female-identified partner, *Apache 8* omits terms like "queer," "lesbian," "butch," "femme," or any other explicit markers of the sort. By contrast, the film privileges the sacrifices entailed by the career, which is a larger pattern seen in interviews with family members of wildland firefighters, whatever their gender or marital status. In many ways, this pattern returns us to the points made by Carrie Joe in the chapter epigraph: Indigenous folks do what they need to do to get the job done, even when it's hard.

To offer further context, the segment with Quintero's partner and children immediately follows the film's sequence about the Sunrise Dance. Thus, on-screen is a still of a young Quintero at the ceremony, while the audio is Quintero's previously referenced statement that "the Sunrise Dance helped prepare me for the biggest challenges of my life. Like being a wildland firefighter." The scene cuts to the outside of Quintero and Lupe's home and then moves to a candid shot inside. In it, Quintero hangs up her keys next to a portrait of a Christ figure, which the camera lingers on briefly. As she heads to the shower, Quintero tells the two children to choose a film to occupy themselves and to not open the door for anyone. The normativity of this scene is underscored by the everyday pattern of Quintero's interaction with her and her partner's kids.[45] When one of the children chooses a movie, for example, Quintero queries, "That one again?" Lupe is introduced at this point, as a voice-over in which she says of Quintero: "She's going to be leaving in the morning." Using the dialogue as transition, the scene cuts from the interior of the house to a medium shot of Quintero and Lupe sitting under a tree, leaning close together, hands touching. Lupe continues: "She's got another assignment out in California. It picks up, again, where I'm going to be left home with the kids. Taking care of the kids and being at work. Taking care of what needs to be done at home. [We'll] wait for her phone calls every day. But, you know, she's out there to work and do what she's assigned to do."

They identify Quintero's becoming a crew boss as a shared goal, and both joke that Lupe is Quintero's "'boss' . . . the real boss of the family." The intimacy and ease between the couple is further underscored when they share that they've been together fifteen years and Quintero helped raise Lupe's daughter. The final word goes to Lupe, who says, "We have her. She has us. And that's all that matters."

Through this conscious narrative choice, *Apache 8* both introduces a sort of queer normativity and also subverts any sense of the all-female crew operating in a separate sphere from other firefighters. There is, in fact, no discussion of any barriers that Quintero might face as a female firefighter or that Quintero and Lupe likely faced as a queer couple, which, while admittedly leaving a potential narrative gap, also resonates with Simpson's discussion of a community emphasis on "gifts and their responsibilities."[46] The subsequent sequence includes conversations between another Apache 8 crew member and her husband in which they discuss similar difficulties in the absences required by their careers. Katy Aday addresses this reality, as well, in an earlier segment when she speaks of missing her daughter's birthdays, since the seasonal work of firefighting kept her occupied and away for long stretches each summer. *Apache 8* very deliberately reshapes a settler labor economy—we repeatedly see in the included interviews that labor is divided by responsibilities, not by gender.

I conclude this reading of *Apache 8* with the turn the documentary takes in the penultimate segment of the film to the women's losses. In a chilling juxtaposition, the film moves from Katy Aday and her daughter Jovanna's laughter at friends attributing Jovanna's strength and vision to being "just like" her mother, to Cheryl Bones standing in tears with a picture of her daughter, Martha. Aday narrates the voice-over: "Cheryl didn't get to see her daughter, Martha, become 'just like her.' Martha was murdered by drug dealers who thought she was an informant." Another past Apache 8 crew member, Dean Caldera, explains: "It had to do with meth. There's a lot of meth on the reservation. And my son got involved." Caldera's twenty-one-year-old son, who was one of five people involved in Martha's murder, was sentenced to life without parole. Caldera describes the rift these horrifying events caused her and Cheryl's longtime friendship. In rapid succession, this story is followed by Aday's brief description of losing two sisters, in separate incidents, to drunk drivers. Thus, while the majority of the film narrates embodied relationship, one of the final segments confronts the unraveling of such bonds and the rupture that fragmentation causes.

These scenes return us to the discussions in chapter 3 that addressed how damaging settler logics can infiltrate lives and spread like a cancer. In the brief conversations the film presents about drug use and alcoholism, they speak, in Bones's case in particular, of how lives are shattered when the bonds of kinship and relationship are ignored. Addiction and drug trafficking, the events behind the murder of Bones's daughter, are closely tied to the realities of unemployment on the reservation, which the film references a number of times. These issues are unquestionably part and parcel of a larger narrative of colonial extraction. In it, Indigenous people like the Apache were forbidden from traditional land use and labor practices and forced into an androcentric labor economy that demands gender-specific labor divisions and also privileges individualism. This extractive settler narrative continues to perpetuate a capitalist divide-and-conquer mentality, which is the wellspring of the sort of lateral violence that led to the devastating murder. "Colonialism and capitalism," Leanne Simpson explains, "are based on extracting and assimilating."[47] Indigenous land, bodies, knowledges are all resources for that divisive economy. And as the rift left in the wake of this murder shows, "the art of extraction removes all of the relationships that give whatever is being extracted meaning."[48] It is impossible to argue for a broader reading of gender, and what the inclusion of gender variance produces, without addressing the losses settler legacies have promoted in Indian Country, as it is those continued violences that make such conversations vitally necessary.

If Indigenous knowledges are held within the body, and if, like trauma, survivance narratives are embodied practices that are passed on, then they can chart a path through the chaos of colonial logics and practices. As Simpson explains, "the alternative to extraction is deep reciprocity."[49] The conclusion of *Apache 8* returns such knowledges to front and center in a final sequence with Katy Aday and scenes from an Apache 8 reunion. In it, the bodies and knowledge of Indigenous women are cast as a direct response to the fragmentation introduced by settler practices. Particularly, in a move reminiscent of the discussions that surround the significance of Lori Piestewa's contributions and women service members more broadly, the film brings Katy Aday's military service forward and casts her, simultaneously, as a community change-maker and a strong proponent for Apache culture, values, and futures. After her six years in Apache 8, Aday earned a degree in social work and entered the service. She narrates that story by first alluding to a longer history of settler incursion: "A long, long time ago, the army was in charge of us here. That's why we have Fort Apache. But the army couldn't keep track of all the health problems that we were having that they brought with them. . . . And so the Navy came in and that's what's called the Commissioned Corps." As a member of the Corps, Aday is among some highly trained health professionals who bring "essential health care services to underserved and vulnerable populations."[50] She details her rise through the ranks, her attainment of a master's degree, and her deployment in Desert Storm, explaining that she is a commander in the Navy. While Aday casts her Navy service as an invaluable site of education, she privileges Apache knowledges as preceding and reinforcing that service. She says of her military training: "When the army tried to teach me about loyalty, I was like, no way. This is something the tribe has taught me since the day I was born. Integrity? Something they taught me since the day I was born. We already know that. That's who we are."

Aday and Quintero—and indeed, the majority of the crew whom *Apache 8* depicts—mark their work in Apache 6 and Apache 8 as a vital embodied labor buttressed by Apache knowledges and an Apache way of being in the world. Furthermore, their success is described in terms of strength inherent in Apache women. That strength is, in the end, an embodied understanding, or what this book, building on Million, continues to term felt theory. Such knowledge about who they are in the world, about what they can do, about what their responsibilities are resonates with the stories we've seen of female-identified and gender-variant warriors and big moms. Million might argue here that "the actual affective intensities, powers of transformation lodged within these women's (and some men's) understanding of society are moments of practice that can be glimpsed and reflected on." Speaking of Aboriginal women's activism against the patriarchal provisions of the Indian Act and the Canadian nation-state, she explains: "They worked toward an Indigenous symbolic that does not see the polity organized around a white male subject *or* a female Indigenous one. They moved to transform the order."[51] The final segments of *Apache 8* resonate with such knowledge-making. The documentary argues for the value of and need for embodied processes of protection and responsibility rooted in Apache land and kinship structures. Further, over and over across the course of the documentary, the women of Apache 8 are described, both by members of their community and by their peers in the crew, as upholding such important reciprocal relationships. There are no utopias here—in its unflinching portrayal of the deep losses members of the crew undergo, *Apache 8* acknowledges the human capacity to err, to hurt, to deny and rupture relationality. But in response, just as we saw in the historical and literary accounts of female-identified and gender-variant warriors and big moms, these wildland firefighters offer narratives of embodied possibility, community protection, and cultural continuity that promote dynamic Indigenous futures. When read together, *Trick or Treaty?* and *Apache 8* index affective spaces of potential that exist in, work through, and are written by the body.

CHAPTER 5

HIV/AIDS ACTIVISM AND THE INDIGENOUS EROTIC

Carole laFavor

> The use of erotic imaging in Native lesbian work becomes a
> tool by which we heal ourselves.
> —Beth Brant, *Writing as Witness*

From May 26 to June 30, 1988, the U.S. government attempted a
theretofore unprecedented task—to contact every U.S. citizen via
direct mail about a pressing health crisis: the rise of HIV/AIDS. The
rapid spread of the then untreatable disease, which had first been
identified in 1981, had in less than a decade become a subject of significant concern for the U.S. Secretary of Health and the Centers for
Disease Control (CDC). The May 6, 1988, *Morbidity and Mortality
Weekly Report* of the CDC described one prong of their planned
response:

> Approximately 107 million English-language versions of
> a brochure "Understanding AIDS," will be distributed to
> every home and residential post office box by the U.S. Postal
> Service.... A Spanish-language version will be distributed in
> Puerto Rico and will also be available upon request.[1]

An additional one million advance copies were "sent to doctors,
nurses, dentists, pharmacists, hospitals, and public health officials."[2]
This mass mailing was both preceded and accompanied by intense
publicity that included press conferences and print advertisements,
television PSAs, and accompanying media coverage. The brochure

was also reprinted in national publications with vast reading audiences such as *Time* and *People*. An impact assessment by Niki Hutton Keiser, a CDC AIDS communication specialist, reported that "1,376 articles appeared in general audience publications, 86 in black publications, and 86 in Hispanic media. Reader impressions exceeded 350 million. Television and radio coverage resulted in 144 broadcast stories, generating more than 700 million audience impressions."[3] While this CDC campaign, called "America Responds to AIDS," is widely known and has been highly scrutinized because of its breadth and viewing impact, a lesser-known aspect of the campaign is its relationship to the history of Indigenous HIV/AIDS activism. Surprisingly, if we look more, we find the face and words of an Ojibwe HIV/AIDS activist, novelist, woodworker, and nurse: Carole laFavor (1942–2011).[4]

As laFavor's presence in one of the largest CDC mailing of all time suggests, she has been an important voice not only in queer Native literature but also in the rise of HIV/AIDS education and activism. Her prominence in the late 1980s and early 1990s was recognized at numerous events and by several awards and appointments. To offer one notable example, laFavor was the only Indigenous person among the impressive roster of HIV/AIDs activists to be appointed to the first Presidential Advisory Council on HIV/AIDS (PACHA), formed by President Bill Clinton in 1995.[5] Moreover, because she was an out butch lesbian who identified as Two-Spirit, laFavor's cultural advocacy for Indigenous-specific HIV/AIDS education displays an embodied understanding of "health sovereignty" that existed long before the term was coined.

I came to laFavor's work when writing about her two novels— *Along the Journey River* (1996) and *Evil Dead Center* (1997)—for a special Two-Spirit issue that Sabine Lang edited for the *Journal of Lesbian Studies*. The first books by an Indigenous author to feature a queer Indigenous protagonist since Paula Gunn Allen's *The Woman Who Owned the Shadows* (1983), laFavor's texts offered something entirely new at the time of their publication—a Two-Spirit protagonist who was proud of the intersections of her sexuality and Indigeneity. My biographical research led me to the powerful stories of her activism, which I hope readers find as meaningful as the histories and literary legacies of the warriors, big moms, firefighters, walkers, and leaders highlighted in previous chapters. In the context of this book, the stories of laFavor's political life and creative writing function as a moment of pause, allowing for an in-depth look, a specific case study if you will, of what it means to use felt experience as activism. For this, in the end, is what laFavor did: as both agitator and author throughout the 1980s and 1990s, she used the somatic archive of her experiences to help end the silence on HIV and speak to, for, and about Two-Spirit realities.

Story as Activism, Activism as Story

Dian Million calls the late 1980s and 1990s "years where women developed and honed a profound literature of experience."[6] She further contends that this period, during which laFavor testified, acted, and wrote, "offered individuals new possibilities and language to narrate life experience. . . . Personal narrative and personal testimony empowered individual experience, and 'bearing witness' was a powerful tool."[7] LaFavor's life and writing exemplify exactly this sort of embodied, affective narrative. In many ways, as we'll see, she fits the role of warrior–protector found in previous chapters. A vocal advocate who called for a recognition of, and end to, the pervasive violence against Native women, she spoke out for LGBTQ rights and visibility and called for culturally specific physical, mental, and spiritual support systems for Indigenous people living with HIV/AIDS.

White Earth Anishinaabe writer Marcie R. Rendon, who interviewed laFavor about her novels in the 1990s, commented that "laFavor's life itself is a story of understories. An early AIM activist, she was involved in sending medical supplies to Wounded Knee during the stand-off with federal authorities. She was instrumental in setting up the People's Tribunal where testimony was heard about corruption in law enforcement, and what role that corruption played in the whole Wounded Knee event."[8] According to my December 2016 telephone interview with laFavor's daughter, Theresa LaFavor, her mother, who was born in St. Paul, Minnesota, as Carole Nelson, changed her name in the 1970s as part of a reclamation of her Indigenous heritage that led to this life of activism.[9] Her mother's family was originally from Sault St. Marie, Michigan, and her father, who died when she was twelve, was white. LaFavor, who had a brother and sister, was the only one of the three who was identifiably Native (her daughter called her "the brown sheep of the family"). Theresa explains, "it was a very intentional decision she made to go back and find where she came from." Carole met one of her cousins, Dawn LaFavor, and "found this heritage in Michigan [and] felt it connected that piece of her." However, when Carole told her mother, she refused to talk about it. This rift was compounded, according to Theresa, when Carole later came out as a lesbian and, eventually, as HIV positive. Finally, when, in the 1980s, she "sat down with her full family and said I'm going to be on the television, I'm going to be everywhere. . . . It was another nail in the coffin" that led to their estrangement.

As she did with her birth family, laFavor chose throughout her life to publicly embrace all of who she was, whatever the cost. She was on the first lesbian softball team in Minneapolis, which was, at the time, one of the few in the country, of which she explained in an interview: "It was a very political thing to play lesbian softball. There were dyke softball players *all over,* but to *say* it, to play *as* a lesbian team, was really making statement."[10] When I asked Theresa about how her mother talked about being a queer Indigenous woman, she explained: "She definitely identified as butch, which was funny because in her generation that was kind of taboo or passé. Most of her friends were still into no roles and overly expressive womanhood for lack of a better way to describe it. I would say she described herself as both Two-Spirit and butch as well. She was *proud* of it. She even had a mullet of sorts to go along with it."[11] Though these examples are lighthearted, I want to suggest that laFavor's demand for recognition—of her Indigenous heritage and of her queerness—was a form of bodily witnessing that, as we'll see, can be considered affective labor or care work when we consider how it extended out into the world to make change.

LaFavor's visibility as a Native and queer person did not go unnoticed, and such intersections, as Indigenous people—especially women and queer folks—know all too well, carry with them very real danger in settler society. LaFavor is one of the many Indigenous women who endured sexual assault. According to the American Indian Law Resource Center, currently "more than 4 in 5 American Indian and Alaskan Native women have experienced violence, more than 1 in 2 have experienced sexual violence."[12] I address laFavor's experience here because she chose to take that bodily trauma and share it as public testimony, but I want to highlight that, like all stories of assault, it is a difficult to hear.

In 1983, laFavor used the powerful tool of witnessing: in the Minneapolis proceedings of the Pornography Civil Rights Hearings, she recounted the story of her rape by two white men. While the reverberations of the attack were painful, laFavor explains she spoke because of her responsibility to Theresa—then just four years old—as well for other Indigenous women and children at risk of assault. And though Andrea Dworkin and Catherine A. MacKinnon's proposed anti-pornography legislation was the impetus for these hearings, laFavor notably used the platform to direct attention away from the central concerns of white feminism to the specifics of racialized violence experienced by Indigenous women. LaFavor's hearing transcript begins with her taking the committee to task over its lack of diversity: "First, I want to thank my friends and family for coming to support me today. It's scary to stand before you and talk of something so painful. It helps me having women on the Council. It makes it a little easier. I wish more of you were people of color."[13] Her introductory remarks, then, recognize the importance of representation and also, explicitly, the affective impact bodies have on one another, making the point that bodily absence can say as much as bodily presence.

In her testimony laFavor takes a sociosomatic violence intended to harm and defile and intentionally employs it as an embodied path to change. Her Indigenous feminist focus continues throughout her statement, which turns on the dangerous racialized realties that represent one of the most significant daily health threats experienced by women of color. "I was attacked by two white men," she explains, "and from the beginning they let me know they hated my people, even though it was obvious from their remarks they knew very little about us. And they let me know that the rape of a 'squaw' by white men was practically honored by white society."[14] After sharing the horrific details of her sexual assault, she continues: "It may surprise you to hear stories that connect pornography and white men raping women of color. It doesn't surprise me. I think pornography, racism, and rape are perfect partners. They all rely on hate. They all reduce a living person to an object."[15] The pornography laFavor references is Atari's video game *Custer's Revenge*, first released in 1982, in which the player took the avatar of a naked George Armstrong Custer, whose object was the assault of a captive Native woman. LaFavor's rapists referenced the game during the attack, and her testimony hinges on the felt experience of settler ideologies that sanction such imagined and actual violence toward Native women.

Million notes that "unspeakable acts of violence against Indigenous women effectively police them and their communities, but rarely the perpetrator."[16] Both laFavor's public comments at the hearing and her subsequent activism offer affective interventions into such silences. Brian Massumi discusses this type of bodily/emotional/political intervention as an "ethic of caring, caring for belonging . . . that involves thinking of your local actions as modulating a global state. A very small intervention might get amplified across the web of connections to produce large effects—the famous butterfly effect."[17] Massumi's discussion of the politics of affect reminds us how a conflict or event can affect a large polity, thereby reframing an individual act as a communal intervention. Much as Chief Spence and the Nishiyuu Walkers used their bodies to effect change, so, too, does laFavor use bodily experience—the felt knowledge of her survival and strength—to protect both family and Indigenous women more broadly. She bears witness to "the social violence that was and is colonialism's heart" by sharing a story that is "neither emotionally easy nor communally acceptable."[18] In this light, we can see that laFavor's testimony is an affective intervention that supports Indigenous women and names and refutes settler violence. A long-term visioner, laFavor participates in this essential affective labor when she shares her embodied pain to help maintain and protect Indigenous futures, her daughter's among them.

Carole laFavor, the CDC, and the Minnesota American Indian AIDS Task Force

Another way laFavor's actions rippled out to make change for Native people was in the Indigenous health sovereignty organizing she undertook on the community, national, and international levels after she herself was diagnosed with HIV in 1986.[19] LaFavor spoke at conferences, tribal communities, and universities, ran workshops, and started publications to promote education about HIV/AIDS. In nearly every case, her educational work addressed an Indigenous audience and, particularly, Indigenous women's needs. Ruby Denny notes in a 1990 article for the *Seminole Tribune* that laFavor was "one of the first American Indian people to talk about AIDS at a time when most people thought AIDS only affected white gay men."[20] Just a year after receiving her diagnosis, laFavor cofounded Spirits Alive, an organization created to "[train] people to teach others about acquired immune deficiency syndrome."[21] By August 1988, laFavor had given approximately seventy-five presentations to health organizations and Native communities in the United States and Canada. Despite the rapid spread of the virus during this period, laFavor rightly contends that the "concern was not as intense as it would have been had the illness surfaced amongst heterosexual white people who live in the suburbs."[22] LaFavor not only identified but also addressed the lack of HIV/AIDS education for Indigenous women and other peoples of color, and in the process she became a nationally known figure in the movement to inform people about—and support people with—HIV/AIDS. Her tireless educational efforts were recognized by a 1988 Virginia McKnight Binger Award in Human Service.

In a December 2015 phone interview with Irene Vernon, a Mescalero Apache/Yaqui scholar of Indigenous HIV/AIDS studies, I commented on laFavor's hypervisibility at these key moments in HIV/AIDS education organizing as well as the fact that her work seems to have disappeared from public view. In response, Vernon stated:

> I too think that [laFavor] has been . . . marginalized in the field . . . of HIV/AIDS. She, to me, was one of the first Native American woman to really be addressing and talking about HIV/AIDS. Clearly through her video [*Her Giveaway: A Spiritual Journey with AIDS* (1988)], which I showed for many, many years in my classes. But she's an activist. It wasn't just the video—she was actively engaged in all sorts of different ways in regards to getting that question out about . . . HIV/AIDS, and women, and Native people.[23]

The words of a 1988 Associated Press article underscore Vernon's comment, "Through nationwide radio and TV ads and a mailing to every American household, Carole LaFavor [came] to represent the anguish of people afflicted with AIDS."[24] While the language casts laFavor as an "afflicted" victim, Vernon highlights laFavor's tremendous impact on HIV/AIDS organizing efforts. LaFavor did test positive, yet the story of her subsequent political agency emphasizes the fact that she was no one's passive victim; instead of defining her, her diagnosis brought her to expand the care work she had long undertaken with and for other Indigenous peoples. Just as she did in her testimony about her sexual assault, here, too, laFavor used her embodied knowledge as a direct intervention to support other Native peoples and, most especially and intentionally, to improve the lives of Indigenous women.

We can see, then, the many ways laFavor's life and activist outreach underscore Million's claim that "stories, unlike data, contain the affective legacy of our experiences."[25] While laFavor is not the first to undertake such affective labor, her story *is* a legacy that helps us better understand the larger narrative of Indigenous HIV education from its inception to the present. If there is an urgent contemporary need for an "Indigenous framing of radical love" and "a return to a Two-Spirit cultural ethic of support, intergenerational mentoring, and ceremonial healing" in HIV/AIDS education, as influential public health scholar Andrew J. Jolivette (Creole of Opelousa, Choctaw, Atakapa-Ishak, French, African, and Spanish descent) argues in *Indian Blood: HIV and Trauma in San Francisco's Two-Spirit Community*,[26] then I propose Carole laFavor's life as one of the original models for such important affective labor. The story of her intentionally embodied activism speaks to just the sort of purposeful alliance building Jolivette describes—it is a vital piece of a collaborative narrative created by everyday Indigenous folks who stepped up in the early years of the HIV/AIDS crisis when others—out of fear, ignorance, or simply a misguided sense of disassociation—looked away.

This same key period in HIV education and organizing marked laFavor's involvement in the previously referenced 1988 "America Responds to AIDS" campaign. On the second page of the CDC's "Understanding AIDS" mass-mailed brochure, in a section titled "How Do You Get AIDS?," laFavor is identified by first name. The caption with her accompanying photograph states: "Obviously women can get AIDS. I'm here to witness to that. AIDS is not a 'we,' 'they' disease, it's an 'us' disease."[27] Notably, though laFavor contracted the disease through intravenous drug use and was also an out Indigenous lesbian, the CDC campaign references neither. This decision was undoubtedly part of the CDC's conscious attempt to revise the prevailing public opinion that AIDS was a "plague" visited on homosexuals and drug users. In their 1996 Pulitzer Prize–winning *Wall Street Journal* article, investigative journalists Amanda Bennett and Anita Sharpe detail the rationale behind the CDC's plan: "In the summer and fall of 1987 the CDC team developed the idea of filming people with AIDS and building a series of public-service announcements around what they had to say. Subjects wouldn't be identified as gay, and the dangers of intravenous drug use would get little attention."[28] A key policy concern that drove the CDC's approach was the fear that perceptions about HIV/AIDS would impede funding, a fear that was backed by public polls, focus groups, and the negative response of the Reagan White House to CDC ads that attempted to directly target the highest-risk populations. Bennett and Sharpe note that veteran virologist Walter Dowdle, who "helped create the CDC's anti-AIDS office in the early 1980s," was stonewalled by both the media and the White House. Though he oversaw the creation of "AIDS warnings aimed directly at high-risk groups, TV networks . . . refus[ed] to air" the spots. A draft pamphlet "that mentioned condoms as effective in slowing the spread of AIDS" was similarly rejected. Bennett and Sharpe explain that "at the time, all AIDS material had to be cleared by the president's Domestic Policy Council, and the Reagan White House objected to pro-condom messages on moral grounds. The 1986 brochure went into the White House for review and never came out."[29] On a related note, when answering a question on health care and AIDS in one of her public talks, laFavor first advocated for a national health-care system in the United States and then commented on the silence around HIV/AIDS: "There needs to be more said. . . . It took [Ronald Reagan] eight years to say the word [AIDS] publicly."[30]

Notably, laFavor consistently rejected silence about HIV/AIDS as well as any narrowing of the complexities of her identity. She witnessed as a way to effect change, becoming one of a generation of Indigenous people whom Million describes as having to "balance the necessity to change things with constraints to 'silence' their pain and experience."[31] In interviews, talks, videos, and advocacy work, laFavor was frank about how she contracted HIV, her sexual orientation, and her position as an HIV-positive Native person, thereby subverting the CDC's elision of that information from her narrative. In fact, in the previously referenced Associated Press article, which was part of the media coverage that followed the CDC campaign, laFavor shared a story that was "neither emotionally easy nor communally acceptable" as a form of activism, fully aware that it might bring more condemnation of the sort she received from her family.[32] The reporter explains that laFavor "learned she had AIDS-related complex in the fall of 1986. She says she engaged in a lot of unsafe behavior, including sharing needles with other drug abusers, until she was caught stealing drugs from the hospital where she worked as a registered nurse."[33] Sharon M. Day (Bois Forte Band of Ojibwe),[34] another significant Indigenous activist, facilitated the formal intervention that followed laFavor's spiral into prescription drug use.[35] Their alliance and eventual collaborations to fight the spread of HIV/AIDS, as we'll see, would come to represent a powerful example of an "Indigenous framework of radical love."[36]

During the time she was appearing across the nation in the "America Responds to AIDS" campaign, laFavor was partnering with Indigenous people in her Minneapolis community to promote HIV/AIDS education and create support networks for people living with AIDS. Speaking at the University of Minnesota Duluth in 1990, laFavor argued that "too many of us continue to die in cold, lonely places from this illness because our communities deny us welcome. Or, mistaking unfounded fear as fact, receive us at arm's length or with gloves on."[37] She actively worked to change this reality for Indigenous people. For example, she helped found the U.S. organization Positively Native and subsequently edited their periodical, which she described as "a quarterly newspaper created to develop confidentiality as well as an unobtrusive support mechanism for Native Americans who are HIV-positive or who have AIDS."[38] Perhaps most importantly, though, laFavor was a founding member of the Minnesota American Indian AIDS Task Force (now the Indigenous Peoples Task Force), a landmark organization that began as a volunteer-led effort in 1987.

Sharon Day led the creation of the task force and became executive director in 1990. Day and laFavor were the only out Indigenous lesbians on the board, and their collective embodied knowledge guided the educational materials the organization produced. As Day explained to me in a January 2016 phone interview: "So much of the work then . . . really ignored women and . . . still does to a great extent today. But, our first two clients were Native lesbians and I believe we, the task force, put out the first lesbian brochure in the country." She continued: "We created some posters by Native artists that were targeted to gay and bisexual men. And when we did training, we decided that we weren't going to sort of soft-shoe around the whole issue of sexuality. . . . And so what we did was [to start with] the conversation around sexuality." Day further talks about the inception and impetus behind the task force, which she continues to direct. Her comments are worth citing at length as they describe a small portion of the as-yet-undocumented history of this pivotal educational organization:

> I think it was around 1987, [Carole] called me up. . . . She said she had AIDS and what was I gonna do about it? Because, you know, I worked at the State, for the chemical dependency program division and she had contracted it from using with . . . other Indians on Franklin Avenue. So she wanted to know . . . what was I gonna do about it?
>
> Around that same period of time, my younger brother, who's gay, called me up about six o'clock one morning. . . . He said, "It's the big A, Sis." . . . So it was very close, the time when both of these two people came to me and said they had AIDS and [asked] what was I gonna do.
>
> And being at the state, you know, I had some discretion. . . . I hired a young Native woman [Lori K. Beaulieu] who was getting her master's degree to do a paid internship over the summer to create an eight-hour curriculum and then to deliver that curriculum at three different locations in the state. . . . So she did that and then we . . . pulled together kind of a series of community meetings. And there were probably about half a dozen of us. . . . We held several meetings and by 1988 it was clear. You know, we [had] sort of figured some . . . Indian organization that existed would pick up the work. And they didn't. In the meantime . . . we're finding more [HIV-positive] people and so we created the Minnesota American Indian AIDS Task Force.[39]

There are a number of things of note in this interview, but perhaps the most significant is the emphasis on how Day, laFavor, and their allies on the task force took the lead in Indigenous HIV/AIDs activism as well as in providing health services and educational information for LGBTQ/Two-Spirit Native people. Their story shows them enacting the sort of "radical love" Jolivette calls for in HIV/AIDS support today.[40] In doing so, these activists stepped into the gap left by Reagan-era federal and state governments, whose responses to the health crisis were slow in coming and also often ineffective among Native populations, since they primarily targeted prevention and support efforts at white men. As Day remarked later in our conversation, "Native people were dying," and because of a combination of homophobia and the public perception that AIDS was a white man's disease, not only was no one stepping up to intervene, but no one was talking about HIV/AIDS as a health crisis that affected Indigenous people. The Minnesota American Indian AIDS Task Force arose directly from these realities—the needs of Native people were made visible and subsequently addressed by the affective work of committed Indigenous activists whose visceral experience with HIV/AIDS informed their activism.

Along with creating essential informational materials, holding workshops, and providing one-on-one support for Native people, the Minnesota American Indian AIDS Task Force was important to the educational video movement that arose to stop the spread of HIV/AIDS. This involvement was one of the many ways the reach of the task force extended far beyond Minnesota. According to Vernon's research:

> One AIDs prevention tool developed by Native people is AIDs videos. These videos have been essential for disseminating information in a culturally informative context. . . . They provide access to information in an increasingly technological society. . . . Combined with their techno-messages is the oral tradition of storytelling. The stories in the videos carry messages of hope, information, prevention, survival, and cultural continuance.[41]

The task force was a leader in this educational movement. In 1988, laFavor, Sharon Day, Lee Staples (Ojibwe, cofounder with Day of American Indian Gays and Lesbians), and others appeared in *Her Giveaway: A Spiritual Journey with AIDS* (1988), which would become one of the best-known HIV/AIDS educational resources of the period.[42] The video, which was underwritten by grants the task force received from the Minnesota AIDS Project and the Shakopee Mdewakanton Sioux Community, was directed by noted Sisseton Wahpeton Dakota filmmaker Mona Smith, who was herself involved in HIV/AIDS work.[43]

Smith's film, which is part public service announcement and part biography, focuses on laFavor's experiences as a person living with HIV. The video is thought to be the first on Indigenous people and HIV and is today the text for which laFavor remains best known. Film scholar Gabriel Estrada, a Two-Spirit, HIV+, urban Rarámuri/Chíhéne/Caxcan/Xicanx descendant, situates laFavor's collaborative work in *Her Giveaway* as "part of a break-out generation of post AIDS Native Gay/Lesbian films that were a first step to reclaim traditional Native genders and medicine via innovative Native AIDS/HIV+ media spaces."[44] The film weaves interviews with laFavor, her doctor, her partner, and her daughter together with information about common methods of HIV transmission and effective prevention strategies (the latter shared by Lori K. Beaulieu).[45] Smith explained the impetus for the project in a 2013 interview with Jennifer A. Machiorlatti:

> We made *Her Giveaway* for the eleven reservations in Minnesota. That was quite clearly our market. A prime collaborator on the show really thought that there was a possibility that this might be the only HIV education that reservations would get. But within two months after it was released, it was in Sweden and Brazil and other places around the world. So it found a market because of the AIDS epidemic and because Carole's story was one that people of all kinds could connect with.[46]

The video's international success helped raise funds for the task force and further increased laFavor's profile as a speaker and educator, as well. In the years that followed *Her Giveaway*, laFavor crisscrossed the country speaking on HIV/AIDS.

LaFavor recognized the importance of the medium of film in activist work. In 1990 a presentation she gave at the University of Minnesota Duluth on living with HIV/AIDS was disseminated as a videotape titled *Carole laFavor Talking on AIDS*. She was also the subject of a 1991 educational video that arose from the University of North Dakota Family Leadership Project: *American Indians against HIV/AIDS Leadership Project: Presentation by Carole laFavor.*[47] That same year, Smith produced and directed *An Interruption of the Journey*, which featured laFavor. These videos mark another of laFavor's significant contributions to raising awareness about HIV at a crucial point during the fight against the disease.

These stories of laFavor's fierce activism reminds us that, as we saw in chapter 3, the body is a somatic archive of Indigenous knowledge. Carrying powerful affective force, the body serves both as a vehicle for community protection and as an integral aspect of Indigenous knowledge production and historical memory preservation. As Leanne Simpson writes, "Indigenous bodies, particularly the bodies of 2SQ [Two Spirit/queer] people, children, and women, represented the lived alternative to heteronormative constructions of gender, political systems, and rules of descent. They are political orders."[48] I would argue that we see this knowledge at work in laFavor's conscious *deployment* of her diagnosis as a springboard for change—she uses embodied Two-Spirit experience as activist practice that touched the lives of thousands of Indigenous and non-Indigenous peoples. We see, then, how particular felt, or affective, stories create what Million calls "a focus, a potential for movement" arising from a radical and deeply collaborative Indigenous activism.[49] For laFavor, as I'll show next, that embodied activism turned on a call for Indigenous health sovereignty.

Carole laFavor's Health Sovereignty Advocacy

Though laFavor spoke in both Native and non-Native venues and, of course, appeared in the CDC's "Understanding AIDS" brochure, her educational focus was on the needs of Indigenous people, especially Indigenous women and LGBTQ2 folks. As she states in *Her Giveaway* and in numerous interviews, her subjectivity as a person living with HIV as well as her healing strategies were informed by her identity as a Native person. When she presented at Haskell Indian Nations University in 1988 (then Haskell Junior College), for example, she answered the student interviewer's question about the sorts of prejudice she had encountered since her diagnosis:

[HIV] added a whole new dimension to the racism thing. Because now it's not only, "Oh, you're an Indian," and all the racism that goes with that: now it's "Of course you have AIDS, you're an Indian." It's like they put these two together so that the racism becomes even more enhanced. The hospital where I get treated is white, so I experienced several levels of racism in the hospital among the staff.[50]

Thus, much as she turned the anti-pornography hearings in 1983 toward the concerns of Native women, so, too, did laFavor craft her response to HIV/AIDS around the intersections of Indigeneity and sexuality. As Estrada points out, "Along with ACT UP activists, laFavor broke into the normally private proceedings of the 1989 International AIDS Conference in Montréal and interrogated the lack of Native American HIV/AIDS programming." Once gaining entrance, she asked: "How many Indian people does it take for them to be concerned? A hundred? A thousand? How many Indian people make up one white person?"[51]

Along with publicly questioning U.S. health-care protocols, laFavor spoke passionately about the power of Indigenous cosmologies. In so many ways, then, her story aligns with Jolivette's call for "a Two-Spirit cultural ethic of support, intergenerational mentoring, and ceremonial healing."[52] In interviews, lectures, and documentaries she credited her own healing and longevity to Indigenous ceremony. Day explains that when laFavor's health started to decline after her diagnosis,

> Carole called me up. She was in the hospital again. And her doctor had told her . . . basically, go home and get your stuff together because you probably have about six weeks. And so Carole said to me, "Okay, so I tried Western medicine. Do you know an Indian doctor who can help me?" And I said, "Go visit Amos Owen in Prairie Island reservation, [a] Dakota reservation about forty miles from [Minneapolis]."[53]

LaFavor received a spiritual message after her healing ceremony telling her she would live. Day shares that laFavor "believed that she stayed alive because of all the prayers that were offered to her along with that initial ceremony. I remember being in that ceremony and you know, the medicine people talking. . . . It became so clear to me from what they said and how we all felt that it really was like this collective effort to bring healing to her."[54] LaFavor strongly believed her healing was a call to HIV/AIDS activism. As she says in *Her Giveaway:* "In a sense, my vision is to talk to people about AIDS."[55]

Having found mental and physical restoration in traditional Indigenous health practices, laFavor then argued for health sovereignty on a larger scale. Just as we saw in her testimony at the antipornography hearings and her response to the publicity surrounding the CDC campaign, laFavor used embodied story as argument, in this case contending that health care and healing should remain under Indigenous control. Day, laFavor, Smith, and many other Indigenous people who were a part of early HIV/AIDS organizing sought out and privileged Indigenous methods of health and wellness. Speaking of the process the Minnesota American Indian AIDS Task Force employed as they organized their HIV/AIDS educational outreach during the organization's formative years, Day explains that the board began by researching

> what was, in fact, healthy sexuality among Indigenous people. You know, what are *our* thoughts around death and dying? . . . What did our ceremonies tell us about that and what were our rituals around that? We worked with young people and so we had to learn these things so we could teach them. . . . Nobody else wanted to do our work. You know, there wasn't an Indian organization in Minneapolis that wanted to take on HIV and AIDS. And people were dying.
>
> So we . . . started [talking with] the elders, [asking] what do you think? What kind of ceremonies did there used to be in terms of coming of age? How did people teach about getting pregnant, taking care of your body? What were those teachings? And so the elders told us and we also read everything we could. I became immersed in the Midewiwin religion . . . and started going to ceremonies. There's so much information in our own creation stories. I mean that really informs us as to how we are to be in the world with everything and everyone. So those [teachings] became incorporated into much of what we do.[56]

Day, laFavor, and their allies were calling for a return to traditional knowledges and practices. While they did not dismiss Western medicine altogether, their educational strategies privileged the teachings of elders and traditional healers.[57] Such work aligns with what Jolivette terms "research justice," a radically collaborative practice "that seeks to shift our focus from simple data gathering to relationship building, as a single community formed of scholars, cultural experts, and knowledge keepers."[58]

LaFavor advocated for Indigenous-centered healing practices and research justice, or to use her words, "walking the red road," in videos, interviews, and articles from 1987 and beyond. Her coauthored 1997 piece, "Native Women Living beyond HIV/AIDS Infection," presents perhaps the clearest articulation of what such an approach might look like. Many of the culturally focused programs that essay discusses were supported by, or arose from, a two-year Special Initiatives Project of the National Native American AIDS Prevention Center, which funded twelve projects that began in 1993 and 1994. LaFavor and her coauthors—Linda Burhansstipanov (Western Cherokee), Shirley Hoskins (Kickapoo/Potawatomie), Gloria Bellymule (Cheyenne), and Ron Rowell (Choctaw)—begin with a striking statistic: while Indigenous people with HIV/AIDS often do not return to a non-Native HIV treatment/support center until the end stages of the disease, in "HIV/AIDS programs developed by and for Natives, according to project staff, client participation and retention . . . was approximately 90 percent."[59]

After setting up the imperative for culturally specific HIV/AIDS programs, laFavor and her collaborators address a series of treatment considerations central to an Indigenous-centered approach to HIV/AIDS education and support. They first consider key differences between traditional Indigenous health-care methods and Western medicine, such as the former's affective emphasis on listening, prayer, and a focused attention that is bounded by neither appointment length nor insurance coverage. Much as Day spoke of turning to the Minnesota Native community for advice on spirituality and health practices, so, too, do laFavor and her coauthors advocate for the primacy of embodied Indigenous knowledge: "The CDC is not our leader, or whom we turn to for advice. Our elders and healers are our leaders" (342). In doing so, these writers enact what Leanne Simpson calls "resurgence," an approach that includes "actions that engage in a generative refusal of an aspect of state control, so they don't just refuse, they also embody an Indigenous alternative."[60]

To offer an Indigenous alternative, laFavor and her coauthors specifically identify the needs of HIV/AIDS-positive Native women, calling for gender- and sexual-orientation-specific support services, Indigenous support staff, female case managers, and "culturally relevant and competent support services for Native Americans of both sexes" (343). Moreover, they point to common problems that continue to drive those needs today. Among these are health-care providers unfamiliar with Indigenous ceremonies who often respond negatively and/or inappropriately to such treatment options, and, on the flip side, non-Native people who employ Indigenous healing protocols in decontextualized and troubling ways. Correspondingly, one systemic problem is that mainstream HIV/AIDS assistance programs of the period focused on meeting the needs of men and individuals rather than women and families: "There appear to be either limited or no food programs that address the nutritional needs of women who have children," while "nutritional and vitamin therapy counseling also is usually geared to men's nutritional needs" (347). Additional service needs for Indigenous people include "a protocol to maintain confidentiality within sparsely populated, rural, tightly knit communities," family-structured transportation services, and the provision of clothing, haircuts, and care packages that might include sage, cedar, or related items for prayer or ceremony (347–49). They further argue for attention to spiritual concerns and, relatedly, for a non-Western approach to death and dying—items that laFavor addressed in HIV/AIDS presentations throughout the 1980s and 1990s. On the whole, laFavor and her coauthors make recommendations for what we now would term *health sovereignty:* Native-led, culturally specific, nondirective health-care service programs providing child care, family meals, and spiritual support that might include sweats, talking circles, and traditional songs.

IN HER UNCEASING AFFECTIVE INTERVENTIONS on behalf of Indigenous people, laFavor advocated for education, Native representation, and access to appropriate health-care protocols in the early years of the HIV/AIDS crisis. As she said in *Her Giveaway*, "I think the two highest risk behaviors we engage in are ignorance and hysteria. Out of ignorance we engage in all kinds of high-risk behaviors. Out of hysteria we can alienate people who are sick right now." To combat these problems, laFavor courageously shared not only her lived experiences with sexual violence, drug use, and HIV/AIDS but also the *embodied knowledges* those difficult experiences engendered. This work was enhanced by her collaboration with Two-Spirit partners like Sharon Day and Lee Staples. Together they saw the needs in their communities and responded by deploying "an Indigenous framework of radical love" with its entwined "emphasis on physical, spiritual, and emotional health" as an affective ethic of care that centered the particular concerns of queer and Two-Spirit people.[61] With this in mind, we can better appreciate how felt knowledges undergird the early work in Native-centered HIV/AIDS education and activism, which privileged communal narratives of holistic healing rather than individual, symptom-based treatment plans.

Along the Journey River and the Indigenous Erotic in Carole laFavor's Fiction

Before turning to laFavor's creative writing, it is useful to return to the affective claims that undergird *Written by the Body*. First and foremost, somatic relationships are integral to Indigenous activisms and literature. In these spaces, the body presents a mode of understanding, a vehicle for change, and a space of transformative possibility. As Robert Warrior states, "Bodies are legitimate sites for theorizing and one of the important links between theory and experience."[62] Million's articulations of felt theory align directly with Warrior's claim and more overtly define the particularly *affective* nature of such transformational somatic processes, especially as related to Indigenous women's narratives. Million maintains that such women "create new language for communities to address the real multilayered facets of their histories and concerns by insisting on the inclusion of [their] lived experience, rich with emotional knowledges."[63] Jessica Danforth's previously referenced arguments more explicitly address the place of sexuality in this formulation: "Traditional forms of medicine and health all centre around people's sexuality, which is really their bodies and their bodily rights, their bodily sovereignty.

And autonomy, really, because when we lose control of our bodies, we lose control of our nations. There's a saying that we need land for the people. We need people for the land, as well."[64] Relatedly, in an interview with Marie Laing (Kanyen'kehá:ka), Two-Spirit Opaskwayak Cree educator and activist Alex Wilson explains that "bodily sovereignty is inseparable from sovereignty over our lands and waters. It means that we are reclaiming and returning to traditional understandings of our bodies as connected to land."[65] LaFavor's fiction arises from these lived intersections of bodily sovereignty, felt theory, and land. Just as in her own life, in her novels she represents such embodied knowledges as a path to social justice. Thus the story of affective power told in this chapter includes two entwined threads—one biographical, one literary—that must be read together for the full picture of how laFavor employed felt theory in her activism *and* her art to change—and save—lives.

In her interview with Marcie Rendon, laFavor commented: "Writing fiction was like a therapy to counteract the activism. I am more than HIV. HIV was too much consuming my life. I wanted to do something that wasn't HIV."[66] Never one to do something by half measure, laFavor's "therapy" includes two novels that center a butch Two-Spirit protagonist, *Along the Journey River* and *Evil Dead Center.* These two books, which represent the first lesbian detective fiction published by a Native author, follow the adventures of a Two-Spirit detective, Renee LaRoche, as she solves crimes on the fictional Minnesota Red Earth Reservation in collaboration with tribal authorities. Significantly, there is only one prior novel by an Indigenous writer with an overtly queer Indigenous protagonist—the mixed-blood, haunted Ephanie in Paula Gunn Allen's *The Woman Who Owned the Shadows.* LaFavor offers readers a stark contrast to Ephanie in her depiction of Renee, a queer Ojibwa protagonist who is accepted by her family and culturally integrated into her tribal community.

To date, little critical attention has been paid to laFavor's texts, a fact that ideally will change with the rerelease of her novels by the University of Minnesota Press in 2017. Siobhan Senier offered the first critical essay on laFavor's literary contributions. In "Rehabilitation Reservations: Native Narrations of Disability and Community," Senier, who has been at the forefront of scholarship that connects Indigenous and disability studies, reads laFavor through the lens of Robert McRuer's "rehabilitation contract," arguing that her novels "imply a contract: in exchange for giving up alcohol, Renee gets 'wholeness within her self' (her health), within her family (monogamy), and within her tribe (her cultural re-integration)."[67] Senier's analysis is joined by Estrada's scholarship on laFavor's HIV activism, and particularly on the previously mentioned documentary *Her Giveaway*. Adding to these two pieces is settler scholar James H. Cox's 2019 *The Political Arrays of American Indian Literary History,* in which Cox reads laFavor as part of the larger body of "detective fiction by Native authors [that] rigorously centers the most urgent concerns of Native communities."[68] Outside these three pieces, only a handful of book reviews and a few brief references to laFavor exist in reviews of contemporary mystery/detective fiction or LGBTQ literary histories.

An analysis of laFavor's innovative and understudied creative writing brings to light the powerful ways she crafts affective intersections of the body, sexuality, and the erotic. In *Sister Outsider,* African American scholar, creative writer, and change-maker Audre Lorde, who first theorized the erotic, tells us the erotic is a "power," a "resource," and a potent "creative energy."[69] The erotic forges activist consciousness: "Recognizing the power of the erotic within our lives can give us the energy to pursue genuine change within our world, rather than merely settling for a shift of characters in the same weary drama," and, as we'll see in laFavor's work, reconnects "the spiritual (psychic and emotional)" to "the political."[70] In Indigenous studies, as chapter 2 notes, discussions of the erotic have been taken up by Aboriginal and Native American theorists like Beth Brant, Kateri Akiwenzie-Damm, Qwo-Li Driskill, Deborah Miranda, and Robert Warrior.[71] In her landmark piece "Erotica Indigenous Style," Akiwenzie-Damm writes: "To deny the erotic, to create an absence of erotica, is another weapon in the oppressor's genocidal arsenal. When this part of us is dead, our future survival is in jeopardy."[72] Miranda likewise contends that an Indigenous erotic directly challenges "the violence and domination" of settler culture.[73] Driskill, who theorizes a "sovereign erotic," asserts that, for Indigenous peoples, "relationships with the erotic impact our larger communities. . . . A Sovereign Erotic relates our bodies to our nations, traditions, and histories."[74] Warrior, following Lorde, argues that "the erotic can be a crucial source of power in the struggle for justice."[75] While Akiwenzie-Damm, Miranda, Driskill, and Warrior build off Lorde, they extend her theory by constructing an erotic that focuses on an embodied sense of Native history, land, and sovereignty. Warrior notes that "the connection between the erotic, bodies, and Native survival is vital."[76] Native peoples' relationships with and understandings of land and tribal responsibility therefore play key roles in an Indigenous erotic, as chapter 2's analysis of Daniel Heath Justice's fiction showed us and laFavor's fiction further underlines. *In laFavor's novels, the erotic, in the form of an affective understanding of Two-Spirit identity, joins her central character to family, land, and nation and also provides the impetus for the protagonist's embodied interventions on behalf of her community.*

From the novel's opening scene, readers of *Along the Journey River* are shown that tribal land, family relationships, and Two-Spirit understandings combine: land, family, and desire coalesce in the palimpsest of an Indigenous erotic. We first meet Renee when she pulls her jeep up next to a "giant eastern pine" on the fictional Red Earth Reservation that is her home.[77] Mindful of her surroundings, Renee considers the land around her as she alights from the car, wryly referencing the disjunction between settler and Indigenous perspectives of the ground upon which she stands. The narrator explains: "She looked around the family land that government rhetoric labeled 'without improvements,' land the Coon family left to its natural state. The cabin seemed as if it had grown there right along with the trees and bushes. A wood fire and fresh fry bread smell drifted across the yard" (*Along*, 9). The scene accentuates a marked difference between Renee's perception of her homelands and settler understandings of that same land: the irony of a language of "improvements" being equated with incursions or alterations of the Minnesota landscape is clear. Moreover, along with crafting a particularly Indigenous understanding of that landscape, laFavor's descriptions of place engage all aspects of the body, referencing sight and smell together with the deep contentment Renee experiences in her grandmother's presence. This markedly affective experience relies on a felt connection with land and family.

The matrix of land/family/desire that laFavor creates here is integral to an Indigenous erotic and is what, in the end, distinguishes an Indigenous erotic from Lorde's theory of the erotic. To return to Brant's foundational articulation of an Indigenous erotic: "Land.

Spirit. History, present, future. These are expressed in sensual language."[78] She continues, "Native lesbian writing is not only about sex and/or sexuality. There is a broader cultural definition of sexuality that is at work here. Strong bonds to Earth and Her inhabitants serve as a pivotal edge to our most sensual writing."[79] Akiwenzie-Damm states that "in Indigenous societies, like that of the Anishnaabe, the earth and all who dwell within it contain a 'manitou,' a vibrant energy that is creative and procreative and thus . . . sexual."[80] The sort of deep, embodied peace that Renee experiences when she steps onto her land and, subsequently, into her grandmother's presence suggests that this Indigenous erotic, with its ties to tribal land, lies at the heart of *Along the Journey River.*

Renee's interactions with her ninety-year-old grandmother are permeated with descriptions of family and tribal connections, of an embodied Anishinaabe history on this land that runs long and deep. She is "Renee's role model. The elder's willingness to be called to doctor bruises, pneumonia, or problems brought on by decades of stoop labor, as well as her carefully tended spiritual life, served as an example that Renee tried but consistently failed to measure up to" (*Along*, 10). LaFavor crafts Renee's grandmother as an elder who gives back to her community and thoughtfully follows Anishinaabe traditional practices. This depiction subsequently legitimizes one of laFavor's key arguments in the text—that Two-Spirit people are not only accepted in but also essential to tribal communities. Thus, while land and family are crucial to an Indigenous erotic, as we see in the novel's opening scene, so, too, are sexuality and desire. In fact, all these aspects of Indigenous cosmology are ultimately inseparable: an Indigenous erotic is not a late addition to conversations about sovereignty and Indigeneity, but rather has always already been integral to Native nationhood. While laFavor envisions her Two-Spirit detective well before Driskill theorizes a sovereign erotic, Renee's experiences reflect Driskill's claim that, for Native peoples, "erotic wholeness" must be "rooted in the histories, traditions, and resistance struggles of our nations."[81]

Importantly, in *Along the Journey River,* Renee's lesbian desire, her "erotic wholeness," is *hailed* by her grandmother rather than simply tolerated. In the process, laFavor crafts an Indigenous erotic that carries both historical and contemporary currency. The scene, which occurs in the first pages of the text, introduces the overt ties between Two-Spirit identity and community responsibility that permeate both laFavor's novels:

> Gram was the one she went to at sixteen bursting with her secret. "I've been waiting for you," Gram began quietly, after listening to Renee. She wiped the teen's tears then with her long apron. "You were named Wabanang Ikkwe for a reason. Morning Star stands between—not night or day, but guiding each. You live in the space between women and men. We are Great Spirit's pure thoughts, *nojishe,* all of us. Here to love, so do not be ashamed of who that is. Creator made you and we don't question the work of our Creator." Gran's attitude about her being a lesbian wrapped Renee with the love she needed. "Two-Spirits have always been part of our community, *nojishe.* It's good you are ready to accept it." (*Along,* 11)

LaFavor suggests that the erotic exists *within* the continuum of cultural continuity and also that Two-Spirit people have particular responsibilities in that space of exchange; thus, her descriptions of the erotic include the same sort of affective relational ethos and care work we saw in the lives/representations of warriors and big moms. And likewise, Two-Spirit people exist in a place of continuity; like the female-identified and gender-variant warriors in chapters 1 and 2, in laFavor's fiction, non-cisgender roles have historical precedent. The reciprocal responsibility between gender-variant people and Indigenous communities also recurs. For example, Renee's grandmother makes clear that by inhabiting "the space between," Two-Spirit people serve as guides for their people. While this exchange is a flashback, Renee fulfills that role in time present of the novel through her ongoing informal detective work in which she facilitates the return of sacred objects to the tribe and uncovers racially biased detective work.

Notably, laFavor's explicit construction of an Indigenous erotic presents a familial blessing—Two-Spirit identity is "good"—from the most traditional figure in the text. As a result, the conversation subverts the temporal logic of a Western "coming-out" scene in which an older relative (mother/father/auntie/uncle) accepts or rejects a queer adolescent or young adult when they reveal their same-sex desire. For Renee, there is no closet from which to emerge—no scene of disclosure in which the queer subject is revealed. Instead, when she is "ready," Renee is welcomed into an Indigenous erotic that laFavor depicts as having been there all along. Importantly, that erotic identity ushers Renee, not into a single subject position resting on *individual* lesbian desire or gender identification, but instead into *a web of affective relationships that situates an Indigenous erotic as a site of community connection and reciprocal responsibility.*

The work laFavor undertakes by overtly privileging an Indigenous erotic at this particular historical moment is weighty. While Renee's experience speaks powerfully to the possibilities of ongoing Indigenous traditions that recognize and, at times, celebrate nonbinary gender roles, such experiences were not the case for all queer Native people at the time of the book's publication. Writing five years after *Along the Journey River*'s publication, Akiwenzie-Damm addresses the absence of the erotic in Native literature: "A person could reach puberty, live her entire adult life, go through menopause and still not have stumbled across a single erotic poem or story by a First Nations writer. Or, to make it even more depressing, I realized one could live and die as an Indigenous person and not come across a single erotic poem or story by an Indigenous writer."[82] Speaking to another aspect of that absence, Driskill asks, "How many Two-Spirit people are forced to leave their families and thus their primary connection to their traditions because of homophobia and transphobia?"[83] In a January 12, 2015, interview, the cofounder of the Northeast Two-Spirit society, Beaver Lake Cree Two-Spirit activist Harlan Pruden, likewise addresses the pain that can split Two-Spirit people from a fully realized sense of the erotic:

> When I came out in the mid-'80s, which was the height of the AIDS crisis, there was so much stigma around [being Two-Spirit]. Compounded around that was . . . being gay. And so I lost many friends, family members, when I made that pronouncement of who I was. . . . When I was growing up on the Beaver Lake Reservation, no one talked about "agokwe" or Two-Spirit people.[84]

As we know, laFavor experienced similar stigma and familial rejection. In fact, her daughter suggests that laFavor "healed her own coming out . . . her own family experience" by writing *Along the Journey River*.[85] LaFavor's Indigenous erotic, then, functions as felt theory and, as such, serves as an intervention in Indigenous fiction from this period and beyond.

Both *Along the Journey River* and *Evil Dead Center* craft Renee as having a calling to care for her people—this embodied ethic of community responsibility is inherent to laFavor's Indigenous erotic. Again, we can draw a distinction between an Indigenous erotic and a broader, queer of color understanding of that term. Renee's embrace of a Two-Spirit identity, as her grandmother emphasizes, affords her a very specific obligation to her people. Sociocultural anthropologist Brian Joseph Gilley (Chickasaw/Cherokee) explains in *Becoming Two-Spirit* that gender-variant or Two-Spirit people "did not have to earn the respect of their people through acts of bravery, because they gained their prestige through the obligation to the people that was built into their role." He further notes that Two-Spirit people's "willingness to make sacrifices for the good of the society earned them a considerable amount of prestige and veneration."[86] Two-Spirit Chickasaw scholar Jenny L. Davis found similar distinctions made by participants in the contemporary Two-Spirit /queer Indigenous groups with whom she collaborated, noting that the "responsibility of a Two-Spirit person . . . involves taking on ceremonial and cultural duties, which might include community roles such as being mediators . . . artisans . . . teachers . . . caregivers or medicine people," among other possibilities.[87] Just as we saw this ethic of reciprocal relationship in laFavor's activism, in which she employed what Jolivette calls "an Indigenous framework of radical love" in her collaborations with and for Indigenous women and HIV-positive Indigenous people, so, too, do we see this kind of community-focused emphasis in her writing: the Indigenous erotic is an affective ethic of care that serves as the foundation for laFavor's creative vision.[88]

One example of this embodied responsibility occurs in Renee's role in the investigations that appear in the two books. Each text addresses myriad issues of import to Indigenous communities: in *Along the Journey River*, Renee helps uncovers an international ring of thieves who trade in stolen Indigenous sacred items and human remains; in *Evil Dead Center*, she reveals a cover-up and subsequently solves the murder of an Indigenous women and, in the process, exposes a pornography ring that works together with foster-care workers to target Native children. In each case, Renee is not a paid detective; she is, instead, a part-time teacher, a skilled beadworker and basketmaker, and an avid runner. She works informally, then, for the tribal police and is described as having a spiritual calling to such affective labor. LaFavor thus specifically removes these responsibilities from the system of economic exchange—Renee is not undertaking her protective work to meet job requirements. Instead, the narrator explains: "Gran said it was because the family was Bear Clan, peacekeepers of the tribe. Ren figured it was part that and part her thinking she could fix everything."[89] Though her lover, Samantha Salisbury, a white women's studies professor, disapproves of Renee's keen interest in the investigations because of the potential danger, Renee will not extricate herself from such protective work. Embodying an affective relational ethos, she fulfills the Two-Spirit responsibilities outlined by her grandmother even when doing so is dangerous. Notably, Renee's personal accountability to past and present members of her Red Earth community—which we can read as the sort of deeply collaborative care work of the sort laFavor herself undertook during her lifetime—is established because of her Two-Spirit identity and manifested in embodied Indigenous knowledge. For example, in *Along the Journey River*, Renee dreams of the stolen items:

> She could see the stem and bowl still separated in their red flannel wrap, the way to keep the power suspended until the keeper began the ceremony. . . . The Living Pipe called to Renee. It had witnessed the birth of babies. It had called out their names to the Great Mystery. It had whispered the way in Healing Ceremonies and promised the People's word during the peace signings. Its power was limitless. (*Along* 53; italics in original)

When she awakens from this dream, Renee hears her grandmother saying, "Your gift is also your responsibility" (*Along*, 53). Renee's dreamscapes resonate with chapter 3's discussions. To return to Million: "Dreaming is a communicative sacred activity" and a "way of knowing."[90] Million's definition of this space for Indigenous knowledge aligns with laFavor's Indigenous erotic—as a Two-Spirit person, Renee accesses the sacred through her body and gains knowledge that she subsequently uses to help her community. Further, just as in

Renee's "coming-out" story, laFavor places the erotic outside an *individual* experience of desire or sexuality. *In* Along the Journey River, *to be Two-Spirit is to be enmeshed in a cycle of responsibility that joins an embodied understanding of gender and sexuality to an affective web of relationship between and among land, family, and nation.*

The Indigenous Erotic as Antidote to Settler Violence in *Evil Dead Center*

Both the resurgent possibilities of an Indigenous erotic and the ongoing traumas that radiate out from settler incursions into Indigenous communities are engaged in *Evil Dead Center,* the second of laFavor's two novels. Though first published twenty years ago, *Evil Dead Center* could be written today as it confronts the willful blindness and often purposeful negligence that surrounds cases involving missing and murdered Indigenous women. While this violence has a five-hundred-plus-year history, in the twenty-first century the complicity of the police, justice system, and government in both perpetuating and attempting to erase knowledge about this genocide has prompted multiple reports and inquiries. These include the 2004 *Stolen Sisters* report from Amnesty International and the subsequent campaign to document and foreground the systemic nature of this serious problem. To investigate and address the ongoing patterns that allow such events to continue unchecked, Canada undertook the National Inquiry into Missing and Murdered Indigenous Women and Girls from December 2015 to June 2019. As part of this inquiry, commissioners held investigations, conducted hearings, and guided community dialogues that included over twenty-three hundred participants. They published *Reclaiming Power and Place,* their final two-volume report, on June 3, 2019: "The National Inquiry's Final Report reveals that persistent and deliberate human and Indigenous rights violations and abuses are the root cause behind Canada's staggering rates of violence against Indigenous women, girls and 2SLGBTQQIA people."[91] These rates of violence include that grim fact that "Indigenous women and girls are 12 times more likely to be murdered or missing than any other women in Canada, and *16 times* more likely than Caucasian women."[92]

Speaking of how Indigenous writers engage such weighty issues in their work, Cox notes that detective fiction such as laFavor's "allows for focused commentaries on the legacy of settler colonialism."[93] In fact, according to Marcie Rendon, *Evil Dead Center* arose from laFavor's work with incarcerated women in Minnesota.[94] The novel emphasizes how violence against Native women often goes overlooked and unredressed by the authorities and shows how such state-sanctioned violence continues after their deaths. Much as she called out the Reagan administration's refusal to engage with the realities of HIV/AIDS, in her creative work laFavor again sheds light on government-authorized erasure and what Million terms "colonialism as a *felt*, affective relationship."[95]

Evil Dead Center begins with a grim story of an Indigenous woman's death. Renee's inquiry reveals not only that "little effort" was made to identify her but also that "she was buried two days after being discovered, in an unmarked county pauper's grave" (*Evil*, 11). Renee's initial queries into the case, prompted by a call from an ex-lover, Caroline Beltrain, show that despite taking no blood alcohol readings, the white county coroner ruled the woman intoxicated and attributed her death to hypothermia. From the pictures of the body, Renee and the tribal police captain quickly ascertain that such a ruling does not align with the facts of the death. The novel follows Renee's investigative work as she uncovers the details of the murder and the biased nature of the original investigation.

A second, equally difficult thread in *Evil Dead Center* involves the abuse of children. In Renee's reservation, Ojibwa children in the child welfare system are placed with a supposedly upstanding white professor from the local college, Floyd Neuterbide. Besides being physically and psychologically abusive, Neuterbide is exposed as the kingpin in a ring of men who help place the children with non-Native families and then force them to make pornographic videos. This story line enables laFavor to address the sexual abuse of children in the foster-care system and also to briefly engage the need for enforcement of the 1978 U.S. Indian Child Welfare Act. As these descriptions suggest, the differences in laFavor's description of the sexual encounters in her novel are stark, as she contrasts the Indigenous erotic, which relies on an embodied understanding of self, community, land, and reciprocal relationship, with the pornographic, which relies on disembodiment and fragmentation—here the psychological and sexual abuse of children who are forcibly separated from their people.

Renee and the tribal police chief's discovery of video evidence underscores the especially painful nature of the case, which Renee describes as its own form of embodied trauma. The initial revelation of the details, when shared by one of the adolescents involved, carries an "impact like spray from the bottom of the falls" (*Evil*, 44). As they attempt to play a movie that may potentially be one of the sex tapes,

> everything was suspended for a millisecond, as though the universe was deciding whether the ends justified the means, whether showing this video was worth it to get the people who made it. Then the music started. . . . The children's alphabet song stopped on K, the K expanded to KIDS, then KIDDIES, in a child's handwriting across the screen. . . . The three Ojibwa watched another few minutes before the images on the screen of their young, naked Ojibwa brothers were so disturbing that they turned it off. (*Evil*, 66–67)

The horror of the discovery returns us to Lorde, who differentiates between the erotic and pornography. Lorde argues that "pornography is a direct denial of the power of the erotic, for it represents the suppression of true feeling. Pornography emphasizes sensation without feeling."[96] LaFavor similarly contends in her testimony on her rape, as noted previously, that "pornography, racism, and rape are perfect partners."[97] *Evil Dead Center* aligns with these definitions, drawing distinct separations between a damaging expression of sexuality based on exploitation and the productive aspects of an Indigenous erotic. With this distinction laFavor parses out a difference between the worst aspects of settler sexuality, which uses and defiles bodies, situating them as sites of shame, and an Indigenous approach to sex and sexuality, which values and celebrates bodies, situating them as sites of pleasure and healing.

As a result, while *Evil Dead Center* depicts an ongoing crisis for Indigenous women, it also offers the restorative lens of the Indigenous erotic as an embodied path to social justice and healing through Renee's experiences. And much as we saw in *Along the Journey River,* reciprocal relationship is again the keystone of Renee's work on behalf of her community. Renee's elders—her grandmother and her grandmother's sister Lydia, whom she calls "the living memory of the people"—play a significant role in defining such embodied webs of relationship (*Evil*, 19). This time it is her aunt, rather than Gran, who reminds Renee of her responsibility to her community and marks her detective work as affective labor when Renee embarks on the investigation: "Auntie handed Renee a small yellow bundle. From the smell Renee could tell it was sage and cedar. 'Remember, my girl, you belong to Mukwa Odem, protectin's in Bear Clanner's blood'" (22). The novel suggests, then, that Renee's embodied knowledge arises both from clan knowledge—or what N. Scott Momaday might term "memory in the blood"[98]—and from walking in the Two-Spirit "space between." This powerful affective force moves Renee to and through her investigations in both of laFavor's novels.

Importantly, the protective bundle Renee receives is paired with the restorative power of her relationship with Samantha in the text. While Renee trades security and safety for the good of her people, exhibiting an embodied ethic of care by knowingly putting herself in danger to solve the case, she finds healing in the emotional and sexual rapport she shares with her partner. In his essay on the erotic, Warrior looks to the work of Joy Harjo, writing that "Native theory comes back to the deep embodiment of Harjo's idea of our skin being a map. The map is not a policy, a political strategy, or an ideology. It is . . . the body."[99] Such is the case for the erotic in both of laFavor's novels. Renee fulfills a deeply felt Two-Spirit calling when she goes into the community and off-reservation lands as a protector for her people. At the same time, in laFavor's Indigenous erotic, such responsibility melds with love and lesbian desire to bring her safely back home.

Across both *Along the Journey River* and *Evil Dead Center*, to use Warrior's words, "erotic contact become[s] an act of defiance in the face of power . . . an act of resistance through reclaiming [the] body and that of [one's] lover."[100] Lesbian desire, depicted throughout the text as a place for play and healing, functions as a curative, an antidote for the sexual violence that permeates the narrative. Renee teases her partner, for example, in what becomes a running joke about her hand being "Eve Garden's latest state of the art sex toy," which ends with the two of them on the bed in "gales of laughter" (*Evil*, 36). This instance and others like it show that laFavor's rejection of pornography is not a puritanical stance—she simply depicts the erotic and lesbian desire in starkly different terms from the damaging practices both she and her character call out as abusive. To recall previous arguments in the book, we see laFavor crafting a relationship in which shame is no longer tied to sexuality; both the women's bond and their sexual desire is cast as inherently generative. Further, land remains part of the equation throughout laFavor's representations of the Indigenous erotic. When Samantha thinks of Renee, she recognizes that "the Ojibwa woman didn't just love nature; there was a sensuality in the way she reacted to it, as though the environment enveloped her in the emotions of a lover" (*Evil*, 38). With these somatic intersections, the matrix of land/family/desire arises again as an animating force and a much-needed healing given the particularly difficult nature of the cases Renee works.

I want to conclude my foray into laFavor's fiction by turning to the end of *Evil Dead Center* and marking its call for the visibility and viability of the erotic in tribal contexts. In the last section of the text, Rosa Mae Two Thunder's body is returned to her father, a Cree healer, and Renee and her collaborators capture the leader of the child pornography ring and his accomplices. The final scene finds Renee home with her partner. When they walk out to watch the Northern Lights, Renee says: "I've been thinkin', *saiagi iwed,* how'd you like to have a ceremony? For the two of us" (*Evil*, 220). She expands, "Basically, they wrap us in a quilt, symbolizing our joining together, our partnership. We'd ask Gran to do that. The folks invited to witness the ceremony make a promise to always be there for us to help us remember our promises. Then we promise from then on to be there to share our wisdom with the young ones of the tribe" (220). This conclusion makes the two women's love the definitive statement of the novel. In doing so, it places a healthy lesbian relationship and, with it, an Indigenous erotic at the heart of the Anishinaabe family and traditions imagined by the text. Again, we see an affective network—Two-Spirit desire circulates productively, bringing together Renee, her lover, her family, her community, and a larger Anishinaabe history, both past and future. The skin, then, *is* a map in laFavor's novels: erotic wholeness enables Renee to retain her sanity in the face of the systemic sexual and sociosomatic violence she investigates and therefore, concomitantly, helps her meet the reciprocal responsibilities she carries as a Two-Spirit person. Brant argues that "the use of erotic imagining in

Native lesbian work becomes a tool by which we heal ourselves."[101] Like her HIV/AIDS education, which, as Day explained, *started with sex and sexuality,* laFavor's fictional landscapes puts this healing erotic knowledge into embodied practice.

Carole laFavor's Legacy

While so much more can be said about the significance of laFavor's life and literary legacy, I conclude by reiterating a single claim: laFavor has much to teach us about the power and vast range of Indigenous embodiment. Her testimony, continued witnessing, and health sovereignty activism saved lives in the 1980s and 1990s. Further, like her HIV/AIDS outreach, which employed an "Indigenous framework of radical love," so, too, does the Indigenous erotic in her fiction write relationship and enact a somatic tie to community.[102] In *Along the Journey River* and *Evil Dead Center,* the first novels to represent the breadth and depth of the erotic, laFavor reminds readers that Two-Spirit people exist—and have always existed—in the powerful interstices of land, family, nation, and desire. Such intersections are inherently relational—to be Two-Spirit, she argues, is to be called to recognize, honor, and work for Indigenous people. Like the warrior women and other long-term visioners who came before her, laFavor used her artistic vision, her felt experience, and her tenacious belief in Indigenous knowledges to fight for Native people during her lifetime and light a way forward for those who come after.

CHAPTER 6

AN EROTICS OF RESPONSIBILITY
Non-Cis Identities and Community Accountability

> Who remembers us? Who pulls us, forgotten, from beneath
> melted adobe and groomed golf courses and asphalted freeways,
> asks for our help, rekindles the work of our lives? Who takes up
> the task of weaving soul to body, carrying the dead from one world
> to the next, who bears the two halves of spirit in the whole vessel
> of one body?
>
> Where have you been? Why have you waited so long? How
> did you ever find us, buried under words like *joto*, like *joya*, under
> whips and lies? And what do you call us now?
>
> Never mind, little ones. Never mind. You are here now, at last.
> Come close. Listen. We have so much work to do.
>
> —Deborah A. Miranda, *Bad Indians: A Tribal Memoir*

My work on overt engagements with Indigenous masculinities and
erotics began in my last book, *The Queerness of Native American
Literature,* with a reading of the female masculinity of Celestine
James, a gender-expansive character from Louise Erdrich's 1986
novel *The Beet Queen.*[1] In that work, I fell a bit in love with Celestine's
smoky, strong-boned masculinity. While critics often read Celestine's
gender presentation as a lumbering and/or comic failure of femininity, I saw her disobedience to dominant gender norms as an indica-
tion that "there's something queer in Indian Country." As argued
there and expanded on here, such productive queerness resides in the
unruly bodies of warrior women, big moms, butch dykes, and trans,
Two-Spirit, and other nonbinary, non-cis Indigenous people who

seize, employ, and/or reject the affective demands of cisgender hegemonic masculinities.

In *The Beet Queen*, for example, Erdrich's depiction of Celestine's uncontrollable masculinity revises the text's representations of *both* queerness and normative heterosexuality, showing the transformative possibilities of gender expansiveness. Inhabiting the space of such possibility, Celestine shows the *potential* inherent in the "failure" to meet heteronormative gender imperatives. In *The Queer Art of Failure*, Jack Halberstam defines such failures as "queer struggle," which reflects "the refusal of legibility, and an art of unbecoming."[2] He further contends that "the queer art of failure turns on the impossible, the improbable, the unlikely, and the unremarkable. It quietly loses, and in losing it imagines other goals for life, for love, for art, and for being."[3] The suggestion we can find meaning and value in lack, difference, and the also-rans offers a lens for Celestine's female masculinity and her awkward love scenes with the similarly queer Karl Adare. This gender "failure" that Celestine experiences and, in fact, cultivates from childhood, presents one of the possible alternate paths Halberstam imagines. *A key argument in this book, then, is that, such non-cis masculinities refuse settler terms of being.*

This chapter builds on many of the same questions about noncisgender performances and affective power that spurred those earlier explorations—it looks across examples of the activism, film, literature, and self-representations of folks who overtly claim butch, Two-Spirit, femme, or other non-cisgender articulations in ways that *purposely* engage both hegemonic and Indigenous masculinities. As opposed to warrior women, who acted within a particular masculinized cultural occupation of intertribal combat, or big moms, who use their bodies to archive Indigenous knowledges and effect change in spaces that do not necessarily signify masculinity, these filmmakers, activists, and writers purposely inhabit and/or deliberately interrogate the somatic space and cultural responsibilities of masculinities. As a result, this chapter continues *Written by the Body*'s investigation of embodiment and non-cis potentialities by analyzing how Indigenous film, memoir, fiction, and poetry index the affective power, mobility, and utility of such expansive gender performances.

THESE CONSIDERATIONS begin, then, by reiterating one of this book's essential contentions: When Indigenous peoples (re)claim non-cis spaces, they actively work against settler logics that used Indigenous peoples' gender expansiveness as a rationale for the imposition and extension of settler colonialism. A return to Qwo-Li Driskill's analyses of eighteenth- and nineteenth-century invaders' accounts of Native/non-Native contact recalls that colonists depicted Cherokee men as improperly masculine and that Cherokee women were often "characterized in both masculine and animalistic terms, at once dehumanizing Native women and representing them as gender nonconforming."[4] These depictions framed such women "as a potential threat to masculine colonial power."[5] Likewise, in "Cutting to the Roots of Colonial Masculinity," Scott Morgensen contends that Indigenous peoples "who presented the traditional gender diversity of their nations" and therefore did not conform with hegemonic, binaristic gender norms "significantly informed Indigenous understandings of human potential and differences in ways that colonizers refused to comprehend."[6] While colonists saw non-cis people as a substantial problem, this chapter reads gender-nonconforming women, non-cis men, and Two-Spirit-identified people as intentional change agents who purposefully threaten settler power by continuing to inhabit Indigenous ways of knowing.

Deborah Miranda's work is particularly relevant here. In "Extermination of the *Joyas*," where she discusses the long history of invader/settler suppression of Indigenous knowledges, Miranda deploys the term *gendercide* in a new way. This term, coined by Mary Anne Warren in 1985, has been most often used to discuss attacks on women and girls in which gender is used to as a defining factor in assault and/or murder.[7] Warren defines *gendercide* as "the deliberate extermination of persons of a particular sex (or gender)."[8] Miranda expands this term in her exposé of the mission system and attention to Spanish attacks on third-gender people—later termed *joyas*—in what is currently California. She highlights the imbricated nature of settler genocide and its embedded, relentless, and brutal attacks on Indigenous gender roles and expressions. Through her recovery of often ignored or overlooked historical records and family history, Miranda shows that "the Spaniards made it clear that to tolerate, harbor, or associate with the third gender meant death."[9] Her work demonstrates that the settler histories of genocide and gendercide are therefore inseparable, which points to the necessity of engaging Indigenous histories/present practices of gender expansiveness in any consideration of Indigenous futures.

Such decolonization projects, as Miranda shows, hinge on a return to Two-Spirits and other non-cis people who challenge the boundaries of white masculinity and reassert the primacy of Indigenous knowledges about their own bodies and genders. As the attacks on their existence indicate, non-cis Indigenous people undermine such settler hegemonies from several angles. The first means by which these folks fracture what Sam McKegney calls "socially engineered hypermasculinity" and Brian Klopotek the "perpetually outlandish representations of Indian gender" generated by non-Native popular culture is by highlighting the mobility, and therefore inherent instability, of the very masculine gender performances that settlers used to rationalize and uphold colonization.[10] Masculinity's mobility, as the previous chapters demonstrate, calls into question the practice of reading warrior identities and attendant understandings of power and acts of protection as bound only to the bodies of those identified male at birth. Warriors and protectors inhabit a wide array of bodies and identifications and across historical periods in both life and literature. The art and activism of non-cis Indigenous people illuminates masculinity's mobility and overtly ties their gender performances to an ethic of community care. These transformative and creative interactions produce a relational exchange between non-cis gender and Indigenous community that *Written by the Body* terms an *erotics of responsibility*.

In its analysis of an erotics of responsibility, this chapter approaches the blurred edges of gender. In many ways, the texts and personal narratives examined here changed the face of this book—every time I tried to better understand how these artists, theorists, and activists imagined gender, those definitions and distinctions unraveled. I initially intended to write a chapter on self-identified butch dykes, but across many conversations, performances, films, and texts, those deceptively clear boundaries came undone—butch folks transitioned, Two-Spirits eschewed categorization and/or chose multiple signifiers, and non-cis people's relationships to masculinities constantly shifted, strained, and evolved. One of the things that became evident in this deliberate undoing was how these shifts worked *across and through* non-cis interactions. In many ways, all non-cis folks—be they female-identified, male-identified, nonbinary, Two-Spirit identified, or beyond—confront, effect, and delineate the contours of masculinity as a *structure*, highlighting its fissures and its possibilities. This chapter lingers in that fruitful space of gender's perpetual revision, or at times even in the moment of gender's undoing, precisely because it is *through* these malleable and generative sites of intersection and change that these writers and activists refute gendercide.

In Miranda's tribal memoir, *Bad Indians,* as we see in the epigraph, Two-Spirit ancestors call contemporary queer, Two-Spirit, or gender-variant folks into relationship.[11] The writers in this chapter take up that work: they refute gendercide by embracing non-cis genders and putting aside the "whips and lies" of settler gender norms—or, at more difficult times, bearing that violence alongside their ancestors. This chapter will show how, consequently, these artists and activists painfully, purposefully, and beautifully "weave soul to body" in a world that, for queer, non-cis, and Two-Spirit people in particular, often tries to pull the two asunder. Moreover, the authors considered here use the raw stuff of gender as their creative impetus, assembling films, novels, poetry, and memoir with its fragments. Much as we saw Zitkala-Ša do in "A Warrior's Daughter," these artists use gender performance as a self-defined tool—with it they reclaim Indigenous genders and remake the possibilities for Indigenous futures, fostering narratives in which nonbinary folks survive and thrive.

As we enter the 2020s a fantastic number of Indigenous artists are undertaking this endeavor. I center Thirza Cuthand, Joshua Whitehead, and Carrie House in particular because their creative work engages non-cis representation in three notably different mediums—film, fiction, and memoir. The juxtaposition of their texts also foregrounds the rich diversity of gender expansiveness in Indigenous lives and imaginations as each considers non-cis gender from different subject positions and different cultures. We begin with Cuthand's contemplations on butch, trans, and Two-Spirit masculinities in the short film *Boi Oh Boi,* then turn to Whitehead's creation of a femme Oji-Cree Two-Spirit ideology in his novel *Jonny Appleseed,* and conclude with House's reverie on "female bodied" Diné masculinity in his memoir, short film, and poetry. *In the face of five hundred*

*years of attempted gendercide, these artists reclaim gender expansiveness
and articulate an erotics of responsibility that links expressions of non-cis
gender to the span of Indigenous histories, the realities of Indigenous presents, and the possibilities of Indigenous futures.*

Thirza Cuthand's Two-Spirit Butch Reveries

With the 2012 film *Boi Oh Boi*, Thirza Jean Cuthand constructs a powerful nine-and-a-half-minute experimental film that rearranges gender to present multiple articulations of non-cis masculinity. A Plains
Cree/Scots filmmaker, blogger, and performance artist from the
Little Pine First Nation in Saskatchewan, Cuthand (b. 1978) began
making films at age sixteen. They graduated with a BFA in film and
video from Emily Carr University of Art and Design in 2005 and an
MA in media production from Ryerson University in 2015.[12] Among
their many shorts, they earned accolades for films such as *Lessons in
Baby Dyke Theory* (1995), *Through the Looking Glass* (1999), *Helpless
Maiden Makes an "I" Statement* (2000), *Anhedonia* (2001), *You Are a
Lesbian Vampire* (2008), and a recent favorite, *2 Spirit Introductory
Special $19.99*, commissioned by ImagineNATIVE in 2015. In a
2018 article on *Lessons in Baby Dyke Theory*, Lindsay Nixon maintains that "Cuthand's work is of paramount importance to LGBTQ+
Indigenous art histories, yet it never received the same exposure as
that of her peers."[13] From their earliest films to their latest, Cuthand
interrogates the intersections of and expectations about Indigeneity,
gender, sexuality, and disability.[14] Cuthand furthers their analyses of
these inherently affective junctures through the articulation of non-
cis masculinities in *Boi Oh Boi*.

Thinking particularly about the discourses surrounding Indigenous men and masculinity, McKegney defines *masculinity* "as a
tool for describing the qualities, actions, characteristics, and behaviors that accrue meaning within a given historical context and social
milieu through their association with maleness, as maleness is normalized, idealized, and even demonized *within a web of power-laden
interpenetrating discourses*."[15] Meanwhile, Ty P. Kāwika Tengan considers "the way cultural and gendered formations emerge through *discursive practices*."[16] In *Boi Oh Boi*, Cuthand examines such discursive
understandings of masculinity in relation to their own body. While

the film looks across several periods of Cuthand's life from adolescence to adulthood, it centers on the six months in which they lived as a trans man and considered physically transitioning. Throughout the film, Cuthand layers a spoken rumination on non-cis genders—a running monologue about their shifting identifications as a butch lesbian, a trans man, and a Two-Spirit person—atop quickly changing visuals of the body as they literally and figuratively practice multiple forms of masculinity. In addition to embodying a classic butch visual aesthetic—husky body, short hair, jeans—Cuthand also includes numerous thigh-to-stomach close-ups of themself as they pack—at times inserting a banana into their pants, at times a packing penis. The embodied juxtaposition of Cuthand's frank monologue with an array of sometimes funny, sometimes provocative, and often contradictory rhetorical claims for a non-cis masculinity underscores Halberstam's contention that "masculinity must not and cannot and should not reduce down to the male body and its effects."[17] Yet even while calling for the necessity of more nuanced analyses of queer practices, Halberstam recognizes a "general disbelief in female masculinity," a "failure in [our] collective imagination," given that people assigned female at birth "have been making convincing and powerful assaults on the coherence of male masculinity for well over a hundred years."[18] In *Boi Oh Boi*, Cuthand's embodied, relational constructions of non-cis masculinities not only complicate the imaginative "failures" Halberstam references but also highlight the fact that discourses of gender expansiveness have existed since time immemorial in Indigenous contexts.

Non-Cis Masculinity and the Affective Circuit

From the opening scene of their short film to its final moments, Cuthand represents their non-cis masculinity as a rhetorically produced affective circuit—it is an expressive act that comes into visibility through a discursive relationship with others. In other words, gender is felt/gender is read/gender is affectively interpreted and this interactive cycle occurs within the space of social exchange. In the film's examples, non-cis masculinity gains discernibility through affiliation and association with others.[19] *Boi Oh Boi* comments on this active interplay through its depiction of an affectively engendered butch masculinity in the opening sequence: "When I was in high school, I asked my soon-to-be-one-time lover: Do you think I am butch or femme? I was clearly butch but I hadn't yet identified myself. I really wanted to know. I think she was being polite, because she just said, 'I don't know.'" The audience hears these words while seeing Cuthand in jeans and a black muscle tee looking at themself in a mirror while applying hair product to their short hair and then leaning, arms crossed, against a brick wall—a scene implicitly asking observers how anyone could look at Cuthand and *not* see them performing non-cisgender. Through this interplay of voice-over and visuals, viewers are thus encouraged to interpolate Cuthand into a space indicative of certain forms of non-cis masculinity—the butch body.

In this brief introductory segment, *Boi Oh Boi* casts butch masculinity, at least for this Indigenous filmmaker at this particular historical moment, as an embodied, relational experience. The film argues that Cuthand's masculinity is read and, moreover, *manifested* through the act of discursive exchange—Cuthand's interactions with their friend/later-lover speak particular gender possibilities into being through an exchange of questions. In this remembered interaction, knowledge circulates outside the body and gender performances can exist without one's conscious awareness—as seen in Cuthand's comment "I was clearly butch but I hadn't yet identified myself." Yet, the masculinity that Cuthand had "not yet" recognized and their friend refused to verbalize was an open secret between them, a queer possibility that, to invoke José Esteban Muñoz, hangs in the air like rumor.[20] In rhetorical studies, this sort of felt experience has been described as a form of *embodied knowledge*. The embodied knowledge of Cuthand's butch identity is created in the relay between bodies, in the implied exchange of gazes, and in that which remains unsaid. These politics of recognition hinge on embodied routes of intimate knowledge that we could call *an affective circuit*—that burgeoning, ever-morphing space of possibility within which gender becomes, at least briefly, intelligible. In this particular affective circuit, gender identities become legible through an act of exchange. Non-cis gender then, moves outside the realm of the individual and into the space of the communal, reminding us of the ways Carole laFavor configured Two-Spirit identities and responsibilities in her novels.

In *Boi Oh Boi,* Cuthand describes the butch gender expression their younger self had "not yet" recognized and their friend/soon-to-be-lover refused to verbalize as a secret waiting to be acknowledged and articulated through discursive interaction, an affective circuit. This facet of the film's representations of non-cis masculinity evokes a concept of affect directly tied to understandings of the body. In her theory of embodied rhetoric, which delineates the difference between embodied language, embodied knowledge, and embodied rhetoric, settler scholar A. Abby Knoblauch refers to "gut reaction," or the "sense of knowing something *through* the body," as embodied knowledge.[21] *Boi Oh Boi* represents gender identity as just such embodied knowledge. Cuthand "knows" their butch identity and presents it in a recognizable form to others even before they name it as such. But importantly, for Cuthand that "gut reaction" operates within a circuit of knowledge production, an affective economy, in which Cuthand presents as butch, is perceived as butch, *and then* comes to self-define as a butch lesbian. The process of gender identification here is interactive and communal: embodied knowledge is mobilized through the proximity of bodies. We can see, then, that Cuthand represents non-cis masculinity as engendered by an embodied relational exchange—an affective circuit—in which, to use Knoblauch's distinctions, *a way of knowing becomes a form of knowledge.*[22]

I want to return to a contention made early in this book, namely, that affect offers us a particularly useful language through which to integrate these intersecting spaces of mind, body, and knowledge. In his Foreword to *The Affective Turn*, Michael Hardt looks to the foundational theory of Baruch Spinoza to situate affect in the act of synthesis, which we can understand as the sort of syncretic or intersectional spaces of embodied knowledge that Cuthand depicts in *Boi Oh Boi*. Hardt writes:

> The mind's power to think and its developments are ... parallel to the body's power to act. This does not mean that the mind can determine the body to act, or that the body can determine the mind to think. On the contrary, ... mind and body are autonomous [though] they nonetheless proceed and develop in parallel.... [Additionally,] *the mind's power to think corresponds to its receptivity to external ideas; and the body's power to act corresponds to its sensitivity to other bodies.*[23]

This relational, reciprocal sense of feeling, knowing, acting, and interacting is evident in *Boi Oh Boi's* depictions of non-cis masculinity, which nod to the way embodied knowledge, gender performances, and community interactions coalesce, thereby interrogating *how* such ways of knowing gender become forms of knowledge about gender. Sara Ahmed extends this interaction of bodies and affect by emphasizing that bodies necessarily form in response to others. In *The Cultural Politics of Emotion* she explains: "Bodies take the shape of norms that are repeated over time and with force. . . . How bodies work and are worked upon shapes the surfaces of bodies."[24] Both Hardt and Ahmed, then, suggest that the sort of embodied knowledge that Knoblauch describes and Cuthand depicts in film is necessarily affective; embodied knowledge, even that which we script as "gut reaction," arises from a "sensitivity" to other bodies and, as McKegney and Tengan note as well, to the discursive forces that surround us. We are, Cuthand shows, always already an affective circuit of bodies in relationship, identities in community.

Boi Oh Boi is replete with examples of how this affective circuit informs and produces non-cis genders. I turn here to the pivotal scene during which Cuthand narrates a six-month experience of living as a trans man. Cuthand's exploration of the space of transition—that shifting bridge between and among differing articulations of masculinity, femininity, and gender nonconformity—relies at both its beginning and end on physical and psychic connections, on affective understandings of the self in relation to others. While the first section of the film narrates a butch identity that was always already present—as my reading of the opening scene demonstrates—Cuthand represents their experience of transition as a tentative, experimental foray into manhood. The physical aspects of masculinity—such as testosterone's potential effect on libido—are integral to the experience; however, they're overtly tied to a female-identified body. Cuthand explains: "I felt this tingling in my crotch. And also my body temperature rose. And I swear my clit felt just a little bit bigger. I wanted a bigger clit, being a show-off butch with big breasts and all." This sense of themselves as a "show-off butch," with its implied audience, speaks to the *relay* Cuthand represents between their articulations of masculinity as a butch lesbian and as a trans man.

Though the genders differ, Cuthand depicts the experiences of butch and trans masculinities as both becoming intelligible through a web of relationships. In fact, Cuthand narrates the beginning and end of their six months as a trans man through the lens of conversations with those close to them. The affective circuit I previously identified is further privileged through these acts of interpersonal exchange. Correspondingly, *Boi Oh Boi's* representations of non-cis masculinities enable us to build on Knoblauch's contention that "it is through my body, our bodies, that we know the world."[25] We do understand the world through our bodies; however, Cuthand shows that we develop such embodied knowledges—to return to Hardt's definition of the affective turn—*through* our "sensitivity to *other* bodies."[26] In its depictions of non-cis masculinities, Cuthand's film crafts an affective circuit, suggesting that the visceral experience of gender knowledge—what Knoblauch terms "embodied knowledge"—is produced and supported by intimate relationships.

A specific example of this affective circuit—the interplay between embodied knowledge and non-cis masculinities—lies in Cuthand's description of their first experience with testosterone, which takes place prior to the aforementioned period of transition. Notably, this exploration is marked by attention to relationship. In a scene in which Cuthand describes taking a hormone shot and subsequently informing their friends, they craft an affective circuit, describing a gender exploration framed vis-à-vis the gaze of others. The discursive nature of this affective exchange is accentuated by what Cuthand depicts as a marked need for audience response. They explain: "I'd had a shot of testosterone a few years before the whole trans thing came up in my life. I was curious. . . . I remember going to an opening and sitting on my friend Rebecca's lap and suddenly announcing, 'I had a shot of testosterone!' I remember everyone's head swiveled around to look at me." While the physical body is discussed—it's after this shot that Cuthand notes that their "clit felt just a little bit bigger"— the emphasis in the scene is not on that physicality but instead on the affective circuit formed by the gender exploration, the desire for social interaction, and the attendant audience response. From sitting on their friend's lap to the public announcement of the testosterone shot, Cuthand crafts the non-cis body as a discursive space that incites engagement. In other words, even in that corporeality, the physicality of this moment in which Cuthand's body interacts with a chemical compound, *they construct non-cis masculinity not in the body but in the affective spaces between bodies.*

This affectively produced depiction of non-cis masculinities is privileged through the visuals that run when Cuthand describes their exploration of FTM transition. The sepia-tinged shot begins when Cuthand, wearing a plaid button-down, stands against a white wall as the voiceover describes their brief foray into manhood. They state, "In 2007, when I turned 29, I was considering transitioning to male. I changed my name informally to Sarain, which is what I would have been called if I had been born a boy." At this point in the film, Cuthand raises their hand and reveals the black object they're holding is a decidedly fake mustache, which they don crookedly. The narration continues as Cuthand begins to drape a tie around their neck: "I made a packer out of hair gel, condoms, and a sock, and wore baggy shirts to hide my tits, which didn't really work because I have large breasts. I tried taking up space differently, but I wasn't interested in aping the irritating aspects of men." Finally, while Cuthand clumsily ties the tie, they note, "I talked to my doctor about transitioning and she was looking into where the gender clinic was for me." Throughout this scene, both the visuals and the narration craft Cuthand's FTM transition as a form of play, a narrative that, it should be noted, differs distinctly from classic transgender plotlines.[27] In such stories, which are often told through memoir, the gender assigned at birth is usually at odds with the trans person's embodied knowledge of their gender identity. As a result, many trans narratives describe an experience of gender dysphoria present from childhood to transition. Cuthand experiences "one really clear moment of gender dysphoria when I was 20 and looking at myself naked in a full-length mirror. My body didn't make sense to me. Didn't feel like it was mine. It shook me a bit, but then faded away." Between the playful mustache, the packing penis, and this shared memory, the representation of non-cis masculinity offered here crafts a radically different rhetoric of embodiment than the gut reaction that, for Cuthand, marked their butch identity. Instead of arising from—or being indicative of—embodied knowledge, in *Boi Oh Boi* trans masculinity circulates within a performative narrative that relies on overt, affective exchange with an audience.

While the forms of knowledge and iterations of gender identities function differently in each case, the film posits each example of non-cis masculinity as part of an affective circuit. The interstitial space of relationship engenders these rhetorics of masculinity. This discursivity situates non-cis masculinities as both inherently relational and also contingent. However, in the first sections of *Boi Oh Boi* these contingencies, though moored by the body, do not mesh entirely with an understanding of embodied rhetoric, which requires "a purposeful decision to include embodied knowledge and social positionalities as forms of meaning making within a text itself."[28] Knoblauch contends that while "embodied rhetoric born from embodied knowledge... can rattle loose... privileged white masculinist discourse," such disruptive work requires a recognition that "*knowledge comes from somewhere, from a particular body,*" with a particular history.[29] In this theorization, embodied practices must purposefully address a politics of location, as such "an embodied rhetoric that draws attention to embodied knowledge—specific material conditions, lived experiences, positionalities, and/or standpoints—can highlight difference instead of erasing it in favor of an assumed privileged discourse."[30] Thus, however interactive Cuthand's affective articulations of non-cis masculinities might be in the first two-thirds of the film, it is not until the final segment that such a politics of location is addressed. By shifting the focus from the embodied knowledge that often underpins non-cis genders to a larger commentary on the circulation of gender expansiveness in Indigenous histories and presents, the film constructs an embodied rhetoric with subversive potential.

Two-Spirit Traces

Until the last third of *Boi Oh Boi,* the film's commentary on the affective nature of non-cis masculinities rests upon seemingly deracinated evocations of butch and trans identities that, while clearly classed, don't suggest specifically Indigenous associations. This potentially mainstream queerness fragments when the film engages Two-Spirit ideology and Cuthand reads gender through a decolonial lens, creating a powerful embodied rhetoric that shifts the film's focus and argument about non-cis genders.

The monologue introduces the idea of Two-Spirit identity with an almost academic distance. Cuthand says: "I remember reading about Two-Spirited people when I first came out. About women who lived as men and went hunting and to war and took wives, and rode horses bare chested like men. I didn't know if they were trans or butch. They were from a different time when those labels didn't even exist yet." Interestingly, as first articulated, this knowledge of expansive gender roles in Indigenous communities, rather than being the sort of embodied knowledge Cuthand described previously or laFavor spoke of in her work, comes not from gut reaction but from texts. Moreover, the existence of Two-Spirit gender performances, or what Lakota anthropologist Beatrice Medicine has called "facets of action," is kept at a temporal distance, as well, through the comment that such gender roles and discourses existed at "a different time."[31]

Over the course of the monologue, Cuthand moves away from the academic distance that initially situates Two-Spirit identities at an emotional and temporal remove. Imagining a more expansive gender rhetoric, Cuthand subsequently remarks: "I sometimes think about what my role in my tribe would have been if colonization hadn't happened, if I was dealing with being queer from a position completely uninfluenced by white Western thought." By reflecting on the generative possibilities of Indigenous knowledge, on what it would mean *to make such knowledges their place of departure in understanding gender,* Cuthand revises the troublesome demand that they stand on one side or another of discrete settler binaries between femininity and masculinity, between a male-identified person and a female-identified person, between a butch lesbian and a trans man. Indeed, when Cuthand employs Two-Spirit histories to reconsider non-cis masculinities through a particularly Indigenous lens, they refuse a butch or trans identity that presupposes a racially unmarked body and remind non-Native audiences of the colonial history of the land they inhabit.

Importantly, too, along with privileging Indigenous gender constructions as a space of knowledge production, *Boi Oh Boi* shows Indigenous gender traditions to be not only *still extant* but also *distinctly different from* trans identities. Cuthand explains at one point in the film that, when they were living as a trans man, their mother, the noted artist Ruth Cuthand, "refused to call me by my boy name, or my chosen pronouns. She basically ignored the whole thing." However, while Cuthand's mother might refuse to accept Cuthand as a *trans* man, by contrast, she *invokes* the cultural memory of alternate gender roles in Native communities:

My mom told me I would have been a third gender. . . . I think that's how I own my butch identity now. I like the overlap between man and woman. The blurring of the lines. Becoming something totally different from man or woman. Owning my curves, my hardness, and softness and gentleness. And yes, even for me, that fierceness.

Cuthand's concluding segment again situates gender in an affective circuit, so gender knowledge is produced and supported by intimate relationships, as seen previously. Significantly, though, the relationship cited here arises from not just their mother but also from the embodied archive of Indigenous knowledges to which Cuthand's mother refers. In many ways, this scene changes the direction and function of the film and entirely revises its representation of noncis masculinities by interpolating them into a matrix of Indigenous understanding.

The exchange speaks to the continued circulation of multiple gender roles in Indigenous cultural memory. While Cuthand's mother refuses to acknowledge Cuthand in a *trans*-identified gender performance, she by no means refutes Cuthand's performance of non-cis gender; instead, she makes Cuthand's gender performance legible within a particular Indigenous context. Their affective exchange thus exemplifies the survivance of certain types of cultural knowledges as well as the strength of Indigenous peoples' ideological refusal of settler narratives. To return to previous discussions in this book, we can clearly see Cuthand refuting gendercide through the embodied archive of Indigenous knowledges. Moreover, keeping Knoblauch's definitions of embodiment in mind, we can also see that *Boi Oh Boi* employs a specifically Indigenous form not just of *embodied knowledge* but also of *embodied rhetoric* when, through this representation of their mother's words and actions, Cuthand makes a "purposeful decision to include embodied knowledge and social positionality as forms of meaning making."[32] Indeed, Knoblauch's contention that embodied rhetoric requires one to speak from a politics of location has particular weight when that bodily location challenges damaging settler ideologies and emphasizes the continued existence of Indigenous cosmologies. In this case, when *Boi Oh Boi* presents a scenario in which a mother's words negate a Western definition of her child's gender and desire, Cuthand uses an embodied Two-Spirit rhetoric to subvert a settler narrative of queerness and maintain and support Indigenous ways of knowing and being.

In the Introduction to *Masculindians,* McKegney interrogates the hypermasculine stereotypes of Indigenous men and calls for a more productive understanding of Indigenous masculinities. He contends that scholars like Kim Anderson, Robert Innes, and Jonathan Swift "provide a model of [a] type of balance" in conversations about masculinity. He continues:

> Such investigation and theorization is not strictly *reclamatory* but indeed *creative.* The [focus of such analyses] therefore, is not on the recovery of a mythic "traditional" or "authentic" Indigenous masculinity. . . . Rather, the emphasis must be on exploring sources of wisdom, strength, and possibility within Indigenous cultures, stories, and lived experiences and *creatively mobilizing* that knowledge in processes of empowerment and decolonization.[33]

My brief reading of Cuthand's film demonstrates how the affective, relational expressions of non-cis masculinities in *Boi Oh Boi* exemplify this type of creative decolonial practice. To do so, Cuthand's smart, funny, experimental short places the range and complexity of masculinities at the center of theoretical inquiry. By the conclusion of the film, Cuthand's representations of non-cis masculinities archive more diverse social roles and present essential meaning-making practices through which to produce and organize embodied gender knowledges. Through their reveries on butch, trans, and Two-Spirit masculinities and the relay among them, Cuthand shows how those affective spaces generate embodied knowledge about non-cis masculinities to create an embodied rhetoric of Indigenous survivance.

Joshua Whitehead's Two-Spirit Refusals: Non-Cis Femininity and Two-Spirit Dreaming

Cuthand's turn to a Two-Spirit ideology in *Boi Oh Boi* and depiction of their mother's insistence on Indigenous, rather than hegemonic, iterations of non-cis genders has direct parallels with those seen in this section, which moves to a recent Two-Spirit novel and considers how non-cis *femininity* can help define and challenge the demands and limits of *both* hegemonic and Indigenous iterations of masculinity. Rather than begin with the novel itself, however, I offer a story that sets the stage for this intervention into the gendercidal demands of colonial masculinity. As such, this section furthers this chapter's exploration of the power and creativity of gender expansiveness—the non-cis gender representations forwarded here help us identify the structures of hegemonic masculinity, or recognize the bars of the birdcage, and also to see how, even in the face of oppression and pain, one might learn to open the door and begin to fly.

On March 6, 2018, when the nation's oldest organization dedicated to promoting and recognizing queer literary arts announced their finalists for the Thirtieth Annual Lambda Literary Awards, among them was a brilliant young Indigenous writer and theorist, Joshua Whitehead (Oji-Cree). Whitehead was nominated for his debut book, *Full-Metal Indigiqueer* (2017), an innovative collection of poetry narrated by a hybridized cyber trickster. On March 14, Whitehead withdrew his book from Lammy contention. His nuanced letter to the Lambda organizers, published by TIA House, speaks directly to the difficulties of fitting queer Indigenous people into preexisting Western gender categories, thereby narrating a resistance akin to that of Cuthand's mother.

The diversity of Indigenous gender categories has been referenced in the twentieth and twenty-first centuries by non-Native activists as a way of validating the long-standing existence of identities now deemed queer (but which would not have been queer in Indigenous cultural contexts). Morgensen traces this practice of signification in *Spaces between Us*, which shows how non-Native queer communities in the 1960s and 1970s deployed the term *berdache*—a word missionaries and settler anthropologists used for nonbinary Indigenous peoples—to authorize settler claims to gay rights. That term, which was subsequently rejected by Indigenous activists due to its troubling etymology and deployment, became a way for non-Native people to craft a queer genealogy that was used in equal rights discourses. Morgensen demonstrates that such arguments activate a settler sleight of hand in which queer Indigeneity is invoked to support white queer rights claims and then conveniently disappeared as non-Indigenous folks continue to inhabit tribal lands and often also commodify Native identity markers.

Whitehead's letter, "Why I'm Withdrawing from My Lambda Literary Award Nomination," circulates in the wake of the complicated relationships between the less-than-parallel histories of settler and Indigenous queerness. His explanation of why his poetry can't be categorized as "trans" offers a particularly relevant entrance into a discussion of how and why the gender expansiveness of many Indigenous nations and traditions does not translate neatly to hegemonic gender categories; thus while trans and Two-Spirit folks may both fall under a label of non-cis, they have distinctly different relationships to gender, as Whitehead's forays into non-cis femininities underscore.

In his letter, Whitehead describes himself as "a 2SQ (Two-Spirit, queer Indigenous) person" who inhabits a nehiyaw (Cree) space of 2SQ-ness.[34] This tribally connected Two-Spiritedness informs both his understanding of self and his subsequent rejection of settler categories of queerness. Whitehead's discussion of the disconnect between his Lammy nomination in the category of "trans poetry" and queer Indigeneity as he lives it deserves to be quoted at length:

> I recognize the difficulty of categorizing Two-Spirit (2SQ) within Western conceptualizations of sex, sexuality, and gender. I cling to Two-Spirit because it became an honour song that sung me back into myself as an Indigenous person, a nehiyaw (Cree), an Oji-Cree; I have placed it into my maskih-kîwiwat, my medicine bag, because it has healed and nourished me whenever I needed it. To be Two-Spirit/Indigiqueer, for me, is a celebration of the fluidity of gender, sex, sexuality, and identities, one that is firmly grounded within nehiyawewin (the Cree language) and nehiyaw world-views. I think of myself like I think of my home, manitowapow, the strait that isn't straight, fluid as the water, as vicious as the rapids on my reservation, as vivacious as a pickerel scale. I come from a nation that has survived because of sex and sexuality, as post-contact nations that deploy sex ceremonially. My gender, sexuality, and my identities supersede Western categorizations of LGBTQ+ because Two-Spirit is a home-calling, it is a home-coming. I note that it may be easy from an outside vantage point to read Two-Spirit as a conflation of feminine and masculine spirits and to easily,

although wrongfully, categorize it as trans; I also note the appropriation of Two-Spirit genealogies by settler queerness to mark it as a reminder that Western conceptions of "queerness" have always lived due in part to the stealing of third, fourth, fifth, and fluid genders from many, although not all, Indigenous worldviews.[35]

I would be remiss if I didn't first point to Whitehead's gorgeous prose; he is both a talented creative writer and an incisive gender theorist, as are so many of his contemporaries—such as Billy-Ray Belcourt (Driftpile Cree Nation), Erica Violet Lee (Cree), and Lindsay Nixon (Cree-Métis-Saulteaux)—as well as the influential queer Indigenous writers who came before them, perhaps most notably, in terms of their theoretical work, Paula Gunn Allen, Beth Brant, and Janice Gould (Koyoonk'auwi).[36] Whitehead differentiates between Western and Cree understandings of genders and sexualities in a way that marks how Cree Two-Spirit identities supersede dominant categories of non-cis genders. Thus, while acknowledging the recognition as an honor, Whitehead makes visible how it *simultaneously* functions as an erasure of the specificity of Two-Spirit presents, histories, and identities. His Lammy withdrawal emphasizes, then, how dominant conceptions of LGBTQIA identity can gesture toward Two-Spirit categories even while subsuming Two-Spirit under settler understandings of gender. If we return to Miranda's theory of gendercide, we can see how physical practices of genocide and gender suppression are echoed in this discursive erasure of Indigenous knowledges about, and categories of, non-cis genders.

Though some might see such contemporary differences as simply a matter of semantics in which the expansive nature of trans should be able to stand in for or directly parallel the concept and practice of Two-Spirit identities, Whitehead describes his Two-Spiritness as an embodied knowledge and an embodied rhetorical practice that functions differently from a broader trans sensibility. To consider the facets of this difference, we can first look at the deployment of the term *Two-Spirit* and then turn to Whitehead's fiction to consider how experiences of non-cis femininity and Two-Spiritness can both coalesce and radically diverge in the contexts he imagines.

Two-Spirit Histories

As most folks reading this book likely know, the term *Two-Spirit* did not come into common usage until the late 1980s and early 1990s. After being used informally, it was presented at the third annual intertribal Native American/First Nations gay and lesbian conference in 1990 as a replacement for *berdache*. First seen in Jesuit documents from the late 1600s, the word *berdache* emerged in English from Arabic, Spanish, and French translations of loaded expressions like "kept boy" or "male prostitute," which have negative connotations in their respective cultural contexts.[37] In light of such troubling histories, queer Indigenous people came together at this historic conference to reject not only the problematic anthropological term but also the loaded settler ideologies to which it is so closely allied. Thus, while in recent years *Two-Spirit* has at times been criticized for being pantribal and romanticized—the latter critique aggravated by non-Native people's continued co-option of the term—this term for non-cis gender presentation arises directly from Indigenous activism and the archives of embodied Indigenous knowledges that demarcate and subvert settler gendercide.

To offer further context, non-Native invaders, including the Spanish, French, and English, physically and psychologically attacked gender-expansive—non-cis, nonbinary, nonheteronormative, gender-fluid—Indigenous people at and after contact. In one of the most-cited examples of this genocidal oppression, on his 1513 expedition to Panama, Vasco Núñez de Balboa and his crew seized and murdered some forty Two-Spirit people—whom he identified as men dressed as women—by throwing them to his war dogs to be torn apart. Balboa was by no means alone in such practices. As Miranda notes, "By the time Spaniards had expanded their territory to California, the use of dogs as weapons to kill or eat Indians, particularly *joyas*, was well established."[38] These continued violent attacks on nonbinary peoples also included years of psychological and physical violence perpetrated by priests, missionaries, church and government boarding and residential schools, and Judeo-Christian heterodoxy. Speaking of the psychosocial violence of colonization, Brendan Hokowhitu looks at later historical moments in the genealogy of Indigenous masculinity and settler interpolation to show that "postcolonial construction of 'traditional' Indigenous masculine cultures (e.g. as zealously patriarchal and heterosexual) were invented in part to mirror Victorian masculinity so that settler states could better intervene into, could better assimilate, could better govern Indigenous communities."[39] It is this tightly enforced mimicry, he continues, that normalized the heteropatriarchal family and heterosexuality and "ostracize[d] other sexual ontologies," such as, in the context of this book, non-cis genders. Herein, then, lies the painful irony of later settler populations invoking queer Indigenous people and traditions to authorize white queer identifications and rights. And herein lies a key reason for Whitehead's rejection of any settler definitions for his gender, sexuality, and life.

However, even more than rejecting pejorative connotations and settler ideologies, the term *Two-Spirit* is intended to evoke the particular histories *and* particular presents of Native North America. Most Indigenous nations had names and social and/or ceremonial places for nonbinary peoples. To offer one example, the Diné (Navajo) have third- and fourth-gender positions—*náadleehí*[40] and *dilbaa'*—and gender shifts play a part in their creation narratives.[41] While the contemporary term *Two-Spirit* was never intended to be translated into Indigenous languages, it emerges from the Ojibwe phrase *niizh manidoowag. Niizh manidoowag, náadleehí, dilbaa', badé* (Crow), *hwame* (Mohave), *winkte* (Lakota), *tainne-wa'ippe* (Shoshone), and so many more such names/gender positions are linguistic traces of Two-Spirit histories and roles within Indigenous nations. In some cases, such roles are extant, in some cases not, and in some cases they are being resurrected by present-day Indigenous people. Just as genders and sexualities are fluid and, for many, changeable over a lifetime, so, too, are Indigenous traditions active and vibrant constructs.

In contrast to hegemonic categories of gender and sexuality, non-cis gender roles among Indigenous nations have been more often identified with occupation than sexual object choice. As Diné anthropologist Wesley Thomas has noted, "a true *nádleeh* or traditional *nádleeh* is somebody who is one hundred percent . . . a woman, who was born as a man but is a woman in Navajo society, not in their sexual preferences or sexual persuasion, but as an occupational preference."[42] There is not, then, a one-to-one correlation between lesbian, gay, bi, trans, intersex, queer, and Two-Spirit. While the hypothesis from oral tradition and extant archival evidence in existing photographs

and written accounts is that Two-Spirit people sometimes had partners who seem to be what Western eyes would perceive as "same sex,"
these third- and fourth-gender positions operate outside such binaries. This is one of the distinctions to which Whitehead refers when
he states that "it may be easy from an outside vantage point to read
Two-Spirit as a conflation of feminine and masculine spirits and to
easily, although wrongfully, categorize it as trans."[43]

To build off Whitehead, the "two" in "Two-Spirit" often misleads
non-Two-Spirit folks into reifying an existing binary in which "male"
and "female" and/or "masculine" and "feminine" are two preexisting
roles that somehow meld together in this Indigenous understanding
of gender. However, such reliance on hegemonic dualisms entirely
misses the point that while Two-Spirit is a contemporary pantribal
term, it references peoples who inhabit/inhabited *different, tribally
specific* gender positions operating within and through Indigenous
knowledge systems. Evidence suggests, for example, that unlike men
who identify as gay and seek same-sex partners as objects of desire,
historically Two-Spirit people would not have been in romantic
and/or sexual relationships with one another: Two-Spirit people inhabiting third- or fourth-gender positions would take partners from
other genders. Sabine Lang explains: "Regardless of whether they are
of the same sex or not—the partners in such relationships are never
of the same gender. Within such systems of multiple genders, Native
classifications of sexual partner choice are based on the gender rather
than the physical sex of those involved in a relationship."[44] While
Two-Spirit people subvert current dominant norms around gender
and sexuality, thereby fitting the category of queer as it is now under-
stood, within their home cultures they would not necessarily have
been perceived as subverting norms or having same-sex/same-gender
relationships. And, as Whitehead emphasizes, Two-Spirit roles do not
neatly translate to contemporary understandings of trans identities.

Non-Cis Narratives and Heteropatriarchal Resistance

Whitehead's creative work addresses both how these understandings
of Two-Spirit circulate in contemporary Cree culture and how such
folks, in the form of his fictional and poetic avatars/characters, run up
against very real barriers of homophobia, transphobia, misogyny, and

settler hegemony that cause a non-cis person be perceived as performing male femininity rather than a tribally recognized third or fourth gender. While Two-Spirit roles and identities have at times been simplified and romanticized, the worlds Whitehead creates extend no such trite or easy answers; thus, his readers encounter twenty-first-century Two-Spirit realities, which are named and highly valued, *and* they simultaneously see the infiltration and violent ramifications of Judeo-Christian prohibitions against queerness.

In *Jonny Appleseed* (2018), Whitehead's first novel, the titular character has moved to Winnipeg from the Peguis First Nation Reserve, which has a population of Ojibway and Cree descent located in what is currently the province of Manitoba, Canada. The novel opens with the narrator's explanation: "I figured out that I was gay when I was eight. I liked to stay up late after everyone went to bed and watch *Queer as Folk* on my kokum's [grandmother's] tv."[45] The story subsequently moves between several days of the narrator's life during which he's raising money to return home for his stepfather's funeral and flashbacks to his coming of age on the reserve.

Despite the fact that he's a Two-Spirit person, Jonny, the compelling central character who narrates the book, in many ways fits into a paradigm of a gay man who inhabits a non-cis space of femininity. Reminiscing about his early years as a "brown gay boy on the rez," Jonny notes that though he wasn't out, "the others at school knew I was different. They called me fag, homo, queer—all the fun stuff" (8, 9). Jonny's self-identifications and gender role-playing situate him as non-cis, and particularly, femme, throughout the text. To offer just a few examples, as he prepares to move from Peguis to Winnipeg he feels "like Elle from *Stranger Things* holding weights much too heavy for little girly-boys" (22). Likewise, after his move he calls himself "an urban NDN, Two-Spirit femmeboy" and trades on this identification in his sex work, where non-Natives' romanticized visions of Indigeneity become Jonny's capital (45).[46] A self-identified "bad girl," Jonny regularly meditates on both the boundaries and possibilities of gender, noting in a memory of being refused entry to a sweat lodge because he wore a skirt that "when I think of masculinity, I think of femininity" (89, 79). When taken together, his descriptions suggest Johnny views his non-cis femininity as part inexorable force—or what we've previously termed *embodied knowledge*—and part finely honed craft—or what we might look at as a highly conscious gender performance that Whitehead, like Cuthand, anchors in an *affective circuit*.

To consider exactly how Jonny *crafts* rather than simply inhabits a non-cis gender requires a turn to how and where he takes up femininity. A key marker in these gender performances can be found in his experiences around makeup and the rituals connected with it. One of Jonny's early encounters with cosmetics is with his best friend/lover Tias's babysitter, who would give them "makeovers" in which she painted their nails and faces. This was, he explains, "a tradition we wholeheartedly signed up for" (73). The boys' joy in this play is met with violence when Tias's adoptive father discovers the nail polish and viciously cuts Tias's nails to a bloody mess as punishment. This is not, then, an uncomplicated narrative of acceptance where, because Jonny is Indigenous, his coming-of-age as a Two-Spirit person is inherently easy. Instead, *Jonny Appleseed* presents a world in which the titular character faces a sharp divide between the violence of male responses to his non-cis gender presentation and the acceptance of his close female relatives, particularly his mother and kokum, who acknowledge his Two-Spirit identity with warmth and support.

As noted, Whitehead, like Cuthand, situates non-cis gender in an affective circuit, repeatedly marking the importance of audience as well as of the relations between bodies and the affective impact of those relations. Keeping in mind Hardt's argument that though "mind and body are autonomous . . . the mind's power to think corresponds to its receptivity to external ideas; and the body's power to act corresponds to its sensitivity to other bodies," we can again see the relationality present in these representations of non-cis gender.[47] When Jonny is a prepubescent boy in a bath with his mother, for example, he describes her approval for his gender play, saying: "I built myself a pair of breasts just like my mother's using the soap from my head. 'Momma, you think I'm pretty?' I'd ask and she'd reply, 'M'boy, ain't no one ever looked better'" (67). His mother consistently reacts to Jonny's femme gender performances with complete equanimity. As opposed to the aforementioned trauma Tias and Jonny experience when Tias's father confronts them upon seeing their nail polish— which is clearly marked in his eyes as an accoutrement of femininity and, by association, of the boys' potential queerness—Jonny remembers loving reactions to his displays of non-cis attire and behaviors from his female relatives. As in this example, he often calls those gender performances to his mother's attention as he seeks and finds approval for his femininity in a warmly recalled affective circuit.

Embodied familial ties and affective exchange also undergird Jonny's interactions with his kokum, who, like his mother, accepts his femininity with little fanfare. His earliest experience with makeup is, in fact, with his kokum. He describes this memory, which is captured in a laughing photo of the two, with deep emotion:

> She would apply her powders and lotions to my face with such grace and softness that I would fall asleep, smelling of talc and lilac. She would push back my hair with her hand and tickle my widow's peak with her fingers, applying concealer to the scar there. I like thinking that she is impressed on my forehead even now—that the stories in her body are written on mine. (105)

Read comparatively, this scene shows the radical difference between Jonny's experiences with Tias's father and later his own stepfather, two men who police settler gender norms and threaten Jonny and Tias if they fail to perform cishet masculinity. Here, with his kokum, we see Jonny *invited* into a non-cis space as he is ushered into a ritual marked as feminine. Moreover, he is not just grudgingly allowed to inhabit practices marked female; he is, rather, welcomed into the fold of femininity with love and, to use his words, "grace," by the women in his family.

Importantly, Jonny particularly highlights the somatic exchange he shares with his kokum as an affective engagement he holds in his physical body as well as his memory. This bodily memory becomes part of an archive of Indigenous knowledge that Jonny carries with him. Speaking of such embodied practices, Dian Million discusses affective exchange in Indigenous writing, explaining that "earlier First Nations and Métis women's affective personal narrative explored the racialized, gendered, and sexual nature of their colonization."[48] As noted in previous chapters, Million considers the impact of Native women's narratives that transform "an old social control, *shame,* into a social change agent" and points to "the importance of felt experiences as community knowledges that interactively inform our positions as Native [writers and] scholars."[49] I would argue that Jonny's exchange with his grandmother demonstrates Indigenous women's affective power—Jonny's kokum fosters his incipient femininity by literally stroking her approval into his body in a scene reminiscent of Nita Quintero's experience with her Sunrise Dance Ceremony sponsor in chapter 4. To return to Jonny's claim that "the stories in her body are written on mine," we see his kokum offer an embodied tale of gender expansiveness through her caress (105). That story, which not only allows for but also *cultivates* non-cis gender, is shared through a felt experience that subsequently nurtures and sustains him after he leaves the reserve for Winnipeg.

Jonny's mother, like his kokum, invites Jonny into the rituals that surround the construction of certain forms of femininity. When Jonny watches her getting ready to go out at night, his mother offers him makeup tips coupled with advice on men. As she puts on makeup that "border[s] more on drag than natural," she tells Jonny, "this is eyeshadow, but you can also use it to color your lips if you're out of lipstick, remember that. . . . You want to snag yourself a man? Then you best slather this shit around your eyes. . . . Smoke your eyes and they'll be begging to smudge you. That's a fact" (124). Her invitation to him suggests her realization that gender is, after all, just drag, as Judith Butler noted nearly thirty years ago and Indigenous people have known for millennia. Like his kokum, Jonny's mother invites him into a femininity that, while bounded by particular rules and rites, is an expansive space in which there is room and grace enough for all. Through repeated stories like these about his mother and kokum, Jonny makes clear that in these women's eyes he is welcome to follow his own desires about his gender presentation and sexual preference.

His mother's and grandmother's acceptance of Jonny's non-cis femininity and their related—if unspoken—recognition that gender is a construct he can rightfully inhabit is decidedly absent in the attitudes of some of the men he depicts in his memories of the reserve (as the previous example with Tias's father suggests). If femininity is something Jonny can be taught, heteronormative masculinity is something that is expected by the authority figures in his life regardless of the existence of Two-Spirit roles in Ojibway and Cree cultures. Jonny comments: "The men in my life liked to pressure me to butch myself up and ridicule me for my feminine ways" (172). As with his memories of his mother and grandmother, Jonny again highlights his complete understanding that gender acts and expectations are per-formance, as seen in the phrase "butch myself up." Furthermore, the "practical skills" the men pressure Johnny to perform include "how to use tools, start a fire, hunt, and skin animals," all futile exercises for Jonny, who has "no aptitude" for such training (172). However, his aptitude—or lack thereof—is clearly not the point of the pressure to adhere to normative masculinity, which demands that he maintain at least the appearance of cisgender conformity. Speaking of the pressures of colonial masculinity in the Introduction to *Indigenous Men and Masculinities*, Innes and Anderson note:

> The ways in which hegemonic masculinity has acted to subordi-nate Indigenous men encourages them to similarly assert power and control by subordinating Indigenous women and women of color, as well as white women (where circumstances allow), other Indigenous men who are considered physically and intel-lectually weak, and those who do not express a heteronormative identity.[50]

The experiences Jonny describes adhere to Innes and Anderson's observation. As a non-cis boy, Jonny becomes the focus of such at-tempts to "assert power and control." Further, Jonny's experiences suggest that, for the majority of the boys and men he encounters, the possibilities of gender expansiveness are either unknown or rejected entirely.

Significantly, Jonny's commentary on this memory challenges romanticized concepts of Two-Spirit identity. Instead of the easy acceptance we see in his maternal line, Whitehead here depicts the lack of understanding that can exist for gay, queer, nonbinary, and/or Two-Spirit roles and peoples in some Indigenous contexts. As a result, while the "masculine" practices he references relate to Native subsis-tence practices, they are also, as noted, firmly situated in a dominant gender binary by the men who demand them. *Jonny Appleseed* sug-gests, then, that straying from cishet gender practices can have very real consequences for a boy assigned male at birth, no matter how they might experience their gender. In fact, Jonny says that "'Man up' was the mantra of [his] childhood and teenage years" (79). To offer just one of a number of examples, when Jonny comes home from a fourth grade dance and excitedly tells his family he waltzed with a boy, his mother and kokum laugh and "[pat] him on the arm" (173). In stark contrast, his stepfather, Roger, takes his belt and beats Johnny until he bleeds, yelling emphatically all the while: "'Boys don't'—*smack*—'dance with'—*smack*—'boys'—*smack*" (173). The divide between male and female responses in this scene could not be more evident, and it illustrates the heteropatriarchal settler imperative that, when in the company of men who identify as straight and cis, Jonny should act "butch" no matter what or whom he feels himself to be. Furthermore, given that Roger is emphatically defining masculinity with each blow, "manning up" would mean to recognize and perpetuate an ideological link between cishet masculinity and violence.

Roger's words and violence signify his investment in contemporary cisgender expectations that align with a paradigm of colonial masculinity. Such tensions are frequently the subject of Indigenous masculinity studies. Innes and Anderson note that "the performance of Indigenous masculinities has been profoundly impacted by colonization and the imposition of a white supremacist heteronormative patriarchy."[51] Likewise in *Masculindians*, McKegney comments that "affirmations of biological maleness and celebrations of masculine power always risk trading in biological essentialisms and being conscripted into chauvinism and misogyny, especially when masculinity becomes conflated with strength and dominance," as it is in settler configurations of gender.[52] This conflation has undoubtedly occurred among the male authority figures in Tias's and Jonny's lives, who—in marked contrast to Jonny's mother and kokum—place a settler paradigm of masculinity above the physical and psychological well-being of their children and families.

Two-Spirit Futures

The counter to these harmful iterations of cis masculinity comes in the aforementioned female approval and also in the text's turn to a Two-Spirit ideology that affirms and supports non-cis identifications. In Whitehead's novel, powerful dreams of Two-Spirit people promote healing and integrate genders and sexualities that now might be perceived as queer into the Oji-Cree context of the novel. Much as Whitehead himself rejects the term *trans*, so too does Jonny, who explains to a self-proclaimed "tranny chaser" client that he is "Two-

Spirit, not transgender" (99). Though *femme* might delineate a particular gender performance, *Two-Spirit* marks the person Jonny is and whom the future *Jonny Appleseed* envisions. It's useful here, then, to return to Whitehead's definition of *Two-Spirit* to consider what this means in the world of his novel:

> I cling to Two-Spirit because it became an honour song that sung me back into myself as an Indigenous person, a nehiyaw (Cree), an Oji-Cree; I have placed it into my maskihkîwiwat, my medicine bag, because it has healed and nourished me whenever I needed it. To be Two-Spirit/Indigiqueer, for me, is a celebration of the fluidity of gender, sex, sexuality, and identities, one that is firmly grounded within nehiyawewin (the Cree language) and nehiyaw world-views.[53]

Whitehead's character experiences this same homecoming when he is welcomed into the space of Two-Spiritness by his female relatives. What to dominant culture would be the gender-nonconforming behavior of non-cis femininity is simply who he is and how they relate to him from their nehiyaw worldview. When Jonny is eight and beading a thunderbird as a gift for a crush, his mother comments: "Don't be thinking I don't know who this is for—you like that Walker boy. I'm fine with that, son, Creator, he made you for a reason—you girl and you boy and that's fine with me, but what's not fine is you selling yourself short" (63). In this scene, Jonny's gender identity and desires are a non-issue for his mother; what counts instead is his self-worth and personal sovereignty—she is appalled that Jonny could give something of himself away to someone who "don't give two hoots about" him (63). His kokum has the same nonchalant reaction to his gender identity when, crying, he comes out to her (he thinks) in a phone call after he's moved to Winnipeg. Entirely unsurprised, she comments, "Jonny, m'boy, your kokum old but she ain't dull. You's napéwiskwewisehot, m'boy, Two-Spirit. You still my beautiful baby grandkid no matter what you want to look like or who you want to like" (48). When she gets off the phone to make frybread she tells Jonny "Kisâkihitin"—she loves him—or more accurately, "You are loved by me" (48).[54] Just as when she stroked her love into his body while she put makeup on him, here, too, the affirmation of Jonny as simultaneously Two-Spirit and loved comes to him as medicine, a healing he remembers, holds, and treasures in a world that too often offers him pain rather than approbation.

Notable, too, in Jonny's interaction with his grandmother is how closely it parallels Cuthand's conversation with their mother as depicted in *Boi Oh Boi* and laFavor's depiction of Renee's interaction with her grandmother. In each case, an important female relative names and values Indigenous gender traditions in relation to their younger loved one. Here, Jonny's kokum teaches him about Cree gender expansiveness. He approaches the conversation with her through the lens of a crippling fear that has been fostered by the practices of gendercide. Like Cuthand's mother, Jonny's kokum establishes that such gendercide, though unquestionably damaging, was not successful. She holds and shares an archive of Indigenous knowledge, offered here as an exchange of language, the very bedrock of Cree culture: "You's napéwiskwewisehot, m'boy, Two-Spirit." With this statement, Jonny's kokum interpolates him into Cree ideology, showing him that what is now perceived as a non-cis gender performance has a Cree name, which serves as a linguistic trace of his place in Cree cosmology. Notably, she shares this healing and generative knowledge in the face of Jonny's pain and tears, which arise from a fear that his "failure" to meet cishet gender imperatives, his "failure" to perform settler masculinity and desires, might somehow sever the ties between them and reduce her love for him. But her response rewrites this gender "failure" as the survivance of embodied Indigenous memory archived in, by, and through the body. Thus, Jonny's embodied gender knowledge and place in both his kokum's heart and in Cree society is affirmed. "Kisâkihitin," she says; "kisâkihitin."

To a reader unaware of this cultural specificity, Jonny's story may seem to simply parallel the experiences of any non-cis gay boy coming out to his family, but, as we see throughout *Jonny Appleseed*, Whitehead is as careful to distinguish these roles and beliefs in his fiction as he is in his life. While Jonny performs a non-cis femininity, he *is* Two-Spirit, and the novel emphasizes the fact that such an identification is tied to particular cultural affiliations that are named by Jonny's kokum and also seen in the dreamscapes we encounter throughout the text. In one example, Jonny dreams of and makes a jingle "dress that had the colours of the medicine wheel: black, yellow, and red" (79). His acknowledgment that he would not have been able to wear such regalia on the reserve today due to the infiltration of the sort of colonial heteropatriarchy already discussed doesn't temper the productive effects of sewing his dream into reality. Like his memories of his kokum, Jonny's realized dream in which he wears regalia usually reserved for women assigned female at birth has the power to heal. Jonny recognizes and values this power as seen in his comment after making the dress: "I am my own best medicine" (80).

As noted in my discussion of *Drowning in Fire* and *Along the Journey River,* Million theorizes that such "intense dreaming" is an Indigenous practice of transformation. Among culturally connected Indigenous people, dreaming, she explains, "is the effort to make sense of relations in the worlds we live, dreaming and empathizing intensely our relations with past and present and the future without the boundaries of linear time. Dreaming is a communicative sacred activity."[55] There are two dreams, in particular, in *Jonny Appleseed* that bring this truth home for Jonny and the reader. The first is Jonny's dream of a regenerating and fecund world in which "treaty land has awakened" (69). This world, which he traverses naked, is animated by the erotic: the "buds drip" and the "berries are thick with juice" (69). As he hears a round dance song, Jonny voices his love for the land in Cree and is mounted by Maskwa, a bear, who recognizes him as an Oji-Cree feminine man. As a result, Jonny comes on—or more appropriately, into—the land, saying, "All of this treaty land is filled with me" (71). At the scene's conclusion, Maskwa recognizes and names Jonny's Two-Spirit identity and also reiterates his love, much like his kokum did, not only seeing Jonny for who he is but also telling Jonny he is loved, always: "Kâkike, he huffs, kisákihitin kâkike" (71).

This imaginative world, with its integral tie to the land, is entirely informed by an Indigenous cosmology. And we could also argue that this Cree dreamscape is created through a nuanced understanding of gender and sexuality, of the Indigenous erotic that Brant would tell us includes "strong bonds to the Earth and Her inhabitants serve as a pivotal edge to our most sensual writing."[56] Jessica Danforth furthers this point, arguing for exactly the sort of intersections between sexuality and land that Brant describes and Whitehead creates:

> To place sexual health over here and land rights over there is a very colonial, imperial way of thinking. Environmental justice

is over here, reproductive justice is over there. We have really paid the price for that. [We must make] full cycles tangible so that people can directly see the violence against the land and the violence against our bodies and the different roles we have to play. Which is why the area of Indigenous masculinities is so important because everybody has a specific role to play, and when we lose one area or one person or one gender in the gendered universe it creates a problem for other things.[57]

Whitehead is making these cycles—these connections between healthy sexuality, gender, and land—visible in *Jonny Appleseed*. The sacred dream space Jonny describes joins him with a specifically Cree spiritual world in which the generative power of Two-Spirit desire calls forth erotic sovereignty: spirituality, land, and Two-Spirit desire are acknowledged and recognized as unified.

If "dreaming is a communicative sacred activity," then we can recognize the final dream in the text, which Jonny's mother shares with him when he returns to the reserve, as a powerful message from the creator in which non-cis gender becomes the source of an erotics of responsibility. In it, Jonny and his mother are pushed away from a riverbank where "big-ass Native men in regalia" line the banks, spearfishing unsuccessfully for salmon (205). His mother explains that when Jonny finally penetrates this male-dominated dream space he is mocked as a "girlboy" until he spears the first fish (206). In the aftermath of his success, Jonny gains respect and it is he, in the end, who teaches the men to fish and feed the people. This scene—which shows how the erotic is infused with personal, familial, and tribal responsibility—is reminiscent of laFavor's Two-Spirit protagonist, who also dreams her responsibilities to her people. The third dream in Whitehead's novel ends with Jonny's kokum smiling and telling his mother: "That boy of yours, Karen, he is his own best thing" (207). This particular dream is perhaps the weightiest in the text, since it is predicted by his kokum, who tells Jonny's mother to watch for and share with him an important dream that she'll have about him. Like Jonny's dream of his jingle dress and his dream of Maskwa and the animate treaty land, Jonny's Two-Spirit identity again becomes medicine. In his first dream of the dress, that medicine nourishes him; in the second, his Two-Spiritness feeds both him and the land itself; in this final dream, Jonny sustains the people who make up his nation by not just feeding them but also by teaching them subsistence practices that will sustain them. *This is the epitome of an erotics of responsibility in which Two-Spirit people take on generative, culturally specific roles that augment Indigenous nationhood.*

Million writes that "to 'decolonize' means to understand as fully as possible the forms colonialism takes in our own times."[58] Whitehead's novel underscores this point—his readers are not offered an easy celebration of non-cis gender and/or Two-Spiritness that romanticizes Indigeneity and simplifies the contemporary realities of Two-Spirit people. Jonny has no choice but to face the insistent mandates of a settler-identified masculinity that has invaded even his home life; in the process of confronting the demands and damage perpetuated by that violent and punitive hegemonic masculinity, he experiences the physical and psychological pain caused by a cis heteropatriarchy that tries to erase his very existence. By concretely depicting the dangers of these encounters, Whitehead demands a rejection of settler imaginaries, and particularly of settler masculinity, a form of colonialism that still wields a vicious power today. But while he acknowledges such ongoing colonial infiltrations into Indigenous worldviews, they define neither Whitehead, as we see in his Lammy rejection, nor his protagonist, as we see in his novel. The dreamscapes of *Jonny Appleseed* allow Whitehead to imagine better, to imagine differently, to see Jonny, in all his femme glory, as medicine.[59] Thus, even as Jonny claims a non-cis identity, he narrates his life in a way that defines and privileges an Oji-Cree Two-Spirit ideology. As a Two-Spirit person, Jonny is "his own best thing" and, moreover, his mother's dream argues, the best thing for the nation. Whitehead's embodied dreamscapes ultimately claim the productive possibilities of an erotics of responsibility in which non-cis Indigenous people tenderly and fully inhabiting their genders, desires, and nations is the very best medicine of all.

Carrie House, Diné Masculinity, and an Erotics of Responsibility

I turn to the essay and poetry of Diné/Oneida writer and filmmaker Carrie House to extend my contention that the affective performances of non-cisgender identities often rest on a deeply embodied tie to clan, family, and nation.[60] House, who in his 2013 short film

Shi' Life identifies as a "born-again sheepherder, farmer, and rancher," lives on his family farm within the Navajo Nation in Oak Springs, Arizona. Along with the aforementioned occupations, House is also a poet, essayist, and filmmaker with work in the landmark critical collection *Two-Spirit People* and the acclaimed creative collection *Sovereign Erotics*. Gabriel Estrada, who has written on House and interviewed him at length, situates House as part of the rise of 1990s New Queer Cinema. Focusing on House's experimental 1997 short, *I Am*, Estrada notes the "unapologetic rawness" of a film that focuses on "butch lesbians/two-spirit/genderqueer people transgressing the work boundaries of cis-gender male occupations."[61] While *I Am* looks at queer Indigenous peoples from across tribal backgrounds, the majority of House's work focuses on Diné cultural contexts and his life as a non-cis man within those contexts. Here I focus on that body of work, offering a reading of his autobiographical essay "Blessed by the Holy People," published in a special Two-Spirit issue of the *Journal of Lesbian Studies,* before touching briefly on his autobiographical poetry from *Sovereign Erotics.*

House begins "Blessed by the Holy People" with a personal genealogy detailing clan affiliation before defining his gender identity:

> I am of Diné (Navajo) and Oneida Iroquois descent. In Diné culture, where clans play an important role in many spheres of life, it is customary to introduce oneself to others by giving one's clan affiliations. They reveal who we are and where we come from. I am born of the *Kin Yaa'áanii* (Towering Rock House People Clan, Diné) on my mother's maternal side, and born to the Turtle Clan (Oneida) on my father's maternal side; my maternal grandfather is *Tsenjikini* (Honeycomb People Clan), and my paternal (matriarchal) grandfather is *Tł'ízí lání* (Many Goat People Clan).[62]

Diné scholar Yolynda Begay explains the importance of this type of self-identification: "For the Diné peoples, identity goes beyond a Certificate of Degree of Indian Blood (CDIB) and tribal enrollment. Identity is based in kinship, or *k'é.* This is how we relate ourselves to one another and our surroundings. Our clans are the one string that ties all our generations of people together."[63] It is only after presenting readers with just such foundational kinship knowledge that House then continues: "I am of a male gender, though accepting of my female-bodied status. Both my parents and the endearing traditional community of my ancestral relatives have encouraged my gender and male abilities" (324). Gender is therefore immediately couched in terms of family and cultural connections, a pattern that permeates House's work and is, as we've seen, echoed in Whitehead's. For example, House notes later in the essay that "Mother, [my brother] Conrad, and [my] maternal ancestral relatives have seen my growth and have always been accepting and nurturing; of me being a boy and now a man, although they understand my biological make-up as a woman" (327). House introduces and affirms his masculinity, then, with references to kinship and to his acceptance by culturally knowledgeable Diné people: "I am considered male by my Native medicine people and most relatives, although some who have known me throughout life acknowledge me as a Navajo woman, which is a respected status within my traditional matrilineal culture" (324). Through this accretion of descriptions, which privilege family and clan and therefore emphasize kinship or *k'é* throughout, House signals that in traditional Diné culture his gender identity functions outside dominant binaries and within a very specific cultural context. Thus, from the opening of this autobiographical essay House demands that the audience read non-cis masculinity through a Diné lens. To do this, he crafts masculinity as enmeshed in and informed by the matrix of family and nation.

This pattern can also be identified in House's first published essay, "Navajo Warrior Women." Here, just as in "Blessed by the Holy People," he refutes the logic of gendercide by sharing the entwined narratives of his present-day status as a non-cis Diné person and the cultural histories of gender diversity among Diné people.[64] Citing Diné cultural beliefs and origin stories, House values non-cisgender people as "those who hold in balance the male and female, female and male aspects of themselves and the universe" for the Navajo Nation, calling them "among the greatest contributors to the well-being and advancement of their communities."[65] By stressing the importance of multiple genders in Diné culture, House refuses a story of elimination. We will see this pattern again in "Blessed by the Holy People" when House explains that his sibling, "Conrad was a 'two-spirit'/*nádleeh* who would groom my mother's and grandmother's hair; who helped cook for us nine children, ten other cousins, and relatives; who gained Diné knowledge of *nádleeh* and acceptance" (328). In each case, by tracing a connection between Diné peoples' nonbinary gender traditions and he and his family's *present-day* life, House insists that such knowledges are not just remembered but are also still extant and deployed in the late twentieth and early twenty-first centuries. Together, his two essays, written nearly twenty years apart, chart the path of his life as one in which his embodied gender knowledge and cultural practices are a continuation of Diné beliefs and lifeways. These survivance narratives stem from long-standing and deeply rooted Indigenous knowledges that are archived in his body and articulated through anecdotes of his childhood and present life.

Examples of such narratives recur in "Blessed by the Holy People," especially in House's stories of "growing up as a boy in the context of Diné culture, of being a female-bodied man in that culture" (325). In these stories, House's Diné masculinity is embedded in an affective cycle within which kinship ties, familial affirmation, and community responsibility inevitably intersect, situating non-cis gender within an erotics of responsibility. In his depiction of this interactive cycle, House offers a litany of everyday experiences that illustrate a range of masculine gender performances to underscore how his male gender was accepted, and often encouraged, by his family. "My mom would sometimes get me toy cars, toy guns, and blue-color-like clothing," he notes. "She eventually taught me how to shoot a real rifle" (326). His list of boyhood and adolescent activities, which, given the title of this section—"Born a Girl, Growing Up a Boy"—is undoubtedly intended to underscore a masculine gender performance, includes

> sheepherding, farming, ranching, fishing, trapping, traveling, adventure and learning by observation. My favorite activities include riding and bucking horses and mules; standing in the bed of a moving truck as I threw rocks and hit telephone poles, glass bottles, or cans that were on the side of roads while travel- ing over 30–50 mph; driving motorcycles and trucks . . . helping with barb wire fencing and digging irrigation canals. (326)

Though none of these activities is by any means the sole purview of men in Diné culture, the accretion of physical occupations and feats of daring, such as climbing windmills and then diving into stock tanks, are unquestionably *intended* to mark the space of the masculine. But, despite what a casual reader might intuit from these descriptions, House presents a Diné masculinity that is not defined by physical prowess alone: alongside the rough-and-tumble rhetoric in "Blessed by the Holy People" exists a deeply embedded narrative of cultural exchange. House thus emphasizes that the masculine activities of his childhood and adolescence were bound to corresponding acts of familial and community assistance.

In many ways such an erotics of responsibility mirrors exchanges previously discussed in this chapter. Like Cuthand, House depicts a non-cis masculinity that becomes legible through the act of relationship. And, as with both Cuthand and Whitehead, we can identify an affective circuit at work in such exchanges. For House, that means that his masculinity, in addition to being performed for/approved by spiritual leaders and Diné community, is tied to kinship needs and responsibilities. Thus in "Blessed by the Holy People," House tells of chopping wood and "collecting certain wild plants" for his grandmother and helping his mother "haul the *Navajo Times* from Cortez, CO or from Albuquerque, NM to Window Rock, the capitol of the Navajo Nation in Arizona before a printing press was purchased by the tribe" (326). Likewise, when he speaks of spending time with his father, it is most often in the context of offering assistance. House writes that his father "allowed me to help him weld my tricycle several times; I helped him with plumbing repairs, painting, and household repairs" (326). Diné education scholar Vincent Werito describes a similar experience, tying these sorts of responsibilities to Diné belief systems: "I remember cleaning up and fixing things around our family homestead with my fathers and brothers. In retrospect, I learned that we did all that work in order to maintain the appearance of our home and family life, which is reflective of our life goals, outlook on life, and values" as Navajo people.[66] Werito emphasizes the fact that even seemingly everyday tasks were embedded in and purposely teaching Diné cultural values. In each iteration—as underscored by Werito and emphasized by House—the construction of a particularly Diné masculine gender performance hinges on deploying masculinity in the service of the family and nation.[67]

In *Diné Masculinities*, Diné scholar Lloyd L. Lee explains that key aspects of Diné masculinities arise from Navajo origin stories of First Man, Changing Woman, and her twin sons. Lee comments that "the principles [First Man] lived by are what Diné men strive towards. The life principles taught from the stories of First Man include sustenance, courage, responsibility, respect, hospitality, knowledge, and wellness."[68] House's descriptions of his actions with and for his family, as seen in his two essays and his short educational film, *Shi' Life*, align closely with these values and practices. In fact, in "Blessed by the Holy People" he states that "First Man and First Woman, Changing Woman, her twins Born for Water and Monster Slayer, numerous Holy People, numerous colors of corn, and numerous worlds have always been with me" (329). Emphasizing the importance of these aspects of Diné belief systems, Lee notes that origin story cycles such as those of Changing Woman and her twin sons model masculine behaviors that emphasize responsibilities to family and the larger community. These responsibilities include occupations such as sheepherding, which Lee describes as "the main mechanism to teach the characteristics and values of Diné thought."[69] As mentioned at the beginning of this section, House defines himself as a "born-again sheepherder." And while caring for sheep is not a specifically male-identified activity among Navajo people, House ties it to his performance of a culturally responsible masculinity.

This family history of sheep ownership, with its deep ties to ancestral lands, practices, and responsibilities, grounds House's life and his representations of manhood. The investment necessitates preserving land and familial/national traditions, a fact underlined in both "Blessed by the Holy People" and *Shi' Life*. In fact, the film focuses on the economy, cultural significance, and present-day consumption of sheep on the Navajo Nation in relation to House's experience raising sheep today. House's masculinity is therefore enmeshed in an erotics of responsibility; by this I mean that he purposefully ties his gender to cultural beliefs and practices that privilege a narrative of familial and tribal accountability. It is exactly this connection to a Diné worldview that moves his representations out of an individual account of non-cis gender presentation into an articulation of a particular Indigenous erotic. To further buttress this representation of a specifically Navajo masculinity, House shows how his current life is inflected by Diné origin stories, familial histories, and present-day responsibilities. For example, in "Blessed by the Holy People" his reveries on hunting and ranching, which he locates as masculine practices, are linked to a larger Diné narrative:

> Some of the traditional Diné men's roles still exist (for those not coerced by colonialism) while others have been impacted by assimilation, Christianity, and Indian Relocation Programs. . . . Men adhering to traditional Diné culture acknowledge cultural practices pertaining to hunting and the preservation of their Diné maternal areas (land, economy, family), such as I have, although traditionally the women had voice over land, wealth, livestock, and family. (326)

As part of just such acknowledgments, House names hereditary sheep camps—"At Pine Springs, AZ are our five old summer sheep camps, about a five-mile radius of grazing area" (327)—and foregrounds the place of sheep and hunting in his family and in Diné culture geographically, historically, and spiritually.[70] We can see this in *Shi' Life*, as well, which argues for the importance of retaining and returning to traditional sustenance practices. In the film, House shares how his family's history with Navajo churro sheep and land connects with traditional Navajo cosmology and also how Diné practices of raising and harvesting sheep promote a healthy lifestyle in mind and body. To return to Lee, we can see here how this emphasis reiterates aspects of the "life principles taught from the stories of First Man," which "include sustenance, courage, responsibility, respect, hospitality, knowledge, and wellness."

Thinking again of Million, we can read House's stories of Diné masculinity as felt theory: he crafts gender as an embodied belief system informed by Indigenous cultural knowledges, augmented by kinship relations, and in service to community. Diné scholar Melanie K. Yazzie comments that "felt theory may be useful for describing the micropolitics of any number of colonial situations in which Diné peoples practice culture, experience subject formation, and/or feel their way through multiple sites of power negotiation and brokerage."[71] There is no doubt that these negotiations with culture, subject formation, and power are at work in House's autobiographical essay, film, and, as we will see in the next section, poetry. Collectively, House's self-descriptions reveal that when viewed through the lens of his cultural responsibilities, masculinity is a *process*, a continual becoming rather than a destination or a fixed site of knowledge—he must work to maintain these lands, these practices, and the cultural histories and beliefs that frame him as a Diné man. Masculinity therefore exists at the embodied fulcrum of these actions, histories, and intentions. His depictions of these physical and psychological movements ultimately echo Million's statement that Indigenous people "*feel* [their] histories, as well as think them."[72]

Importantly, such felt knowledges occur for House within a culturally specific familial context that instantiates reciprocity. Within these felt exchanges, masculinity and cultural and familial responsibilities form a palimpsest. These layered expectations are evidenced in House's decision to keep his given name:

> Both my family and the Diné medicine people have always held a positive attitude toward my being a boy/man. My maternal side of the family has been most accepting, including my late mother, Carolyn Taliman House, her mother, Carrie Taliman, and their matriarchal and clan lineages. I am keeping my name "Carrie" because of my deep respect for my grandmother, Carrie Taliman. I have many responsibilities within my culture and family that are tied to my name. My middle name is Henri after my late grandfather Henry Taliman, Sr. I am not interested in changing my name like other transmen, who may no longer want any attachment or connection to history, place, location, culture, gender, and family. (328)

House's overtly articulated sense of accountability is signaled here by his respect for familial inheritance and clan relation. This felt knowledge marks exactly the sort of affiliative and affective sense of gender that I term an erotics of responsibility. To use House's words, such an erotics moves beyond gender identification and/or sexual preference, necessitating a simultaneous "attachment or connection to history, place, location, culture, gender, and family." The layered contours of this structure therefore show how non-cis masculinity differs radically from both hegemonic versions of heteromasculinity and homonormative iterations of butchness. The latter two forms of masculinity most often rely on narratives of individualism and personal power that underpin settler ideologies situating the self at the center of identity formation. Thus, rather than presenting a depiction of *individual* masculine power, House describes masculinity as a communal, dynamic affair. Engendered by an affective cycle of reciprocity, House's non-cis masculinity necessitates, and in fact rests on, the lived memory of specific familial histories and the fulfillment of specific familial obligations such as those he here ties to names and heritage.

While marking the *communal* weight of masculinity, House also affirms *the centrality of women* to Diné cosmology, his gender identity, and his life. A return to Begay is useful to understanding how House's commentary about names and naming underscores this connection:

> Diné identity, in its true form, is centered on the principle of k'é, a system that establishes kinship. Kinship is based on the bilateral inheritance of maternal and paternal clans and maternal and paternal grandfather clans.... The legacy of k'é further establishes the matriarch as the pivotal inherent marker for identity.[73]

Similarly, Diné historian Jennifer Nez Denetdale notes that "Diné stories connect the land to women in several ways to show how identity is central to women's places in Navajo society."[74] In keeping with these Diné kinship traditions, House refuses any articulation of gender that would cast men and masculinity as more valuable cultural commodities than women and femininity, even as he claims a masculine gender himself. In fact, he comments, "As in the Diné matriarchal sense, I'm empowered by my past and present female relatives who have names ending with -ah, -bah, -dah, suffixes that imply 'warrior woman.' The Holy People gave me a female body and a male embodiment: as mother earth and father sky" (330). In "Blessed by the Holy People," ancestral responsibilities tie the writer to particular clan obligations and to matrilineal inheritance. Moreover, to return again to his commentary, we see how House explicitly privileges familial/clan obligations over non-cisgender identification: "I am not interested in changing my name like other transmen, *who may no longer want any attachment or connection to history, place, location, culture, gender, and family*" (328; emphasis added). In this context, the name "Carrie" marks House's "attachment" and "connection" to his Diné ancestral lineage and his land, which are passed down to him through his mother's family.[75]

Thinking back on this chapter's previous discussion of embodied rhetoric and its politics of location, we can see that from his stress on clan lineage and naming to his attention to particular Diné geospacial and kinship networks, House makes what Knoblauch describes as "a purposeful decision to include embodied knowledge and social positionalities as forms of meaning making."[76] With his emphasis on embodied gender knowledge, social positionality, and familial responsibilities, *House constructs an erotics of responsibility in which masculinity comes to meaning through the lens of matrilineal inheritance and Diné cosmology.*

The Space of the Sacred: Non-Cis Masculinity in Carrie House's Poetry

To extend our understanding of House's writing and film, this section turns to the autobiographical poems House published in *Sovereign Erotics*, which was the first edited collection of queer Indigenous literature published since the Gay American Indians and Will Roscoe's 1988 *Living the Spirit*. In these two poems—"Kid" and "Sweet Grass"—House reaffirms many of the themes we've seen in his autobiographical essays and film and further underscores how his coming of age as a Diné man is wedded to both family and Diné cosmology.

In "Kid," the narrator, who is male (though assigned female at birth), begins by describing a childhood trip for a haircut. In a story that clearly signals a conscious move toward boyhood, House explains: "I saw my brothers at the barber shop / My dad gave my mom my pigtails, with marble-looking hair ties."[77] The poem then depicts the non-cis narrator's playground fights with boys, citing report cards that pejoratively state "boys feel intimidated" and "should play with girls more often." These comments point to the coercive expectations of hegemonic gender norms in public spaces and recall the experiences of Whitehead's Jonny, who, because of his non-cis femininity, encountered incessant demands that he "man up."

In the same vein, in House's "Kid," teachers' and administrators' reactions to non-cis gender identity reveal the instability and fears surrounding gender performance and the body. When actual gender does not conform to cishet expectations, authority figures insist on cohesion: a "girl," their comments on school documents explicitly argue, should not pick—much less win—physical altercations with boys. However, "Kid" celebrates the power and physicality of this non-cis boy. Thus, while these authoritarian demands for a gender binary are shared with readers, they do not define the child in "Kid"—he refuses to be misgendered.

In stories that align with those House will later share in "Blessed by the Holy People," "Kid" describes a non-cis boyhood in which the narrator's parents and brothers recognize the speaker's male gender. For example, just as in the previously discussed essay, in the poem the narrator explains, "My dad let me work with him / Hoist vehicles, weld steel, and move railroad ties," while "My mom bought me a toy Colt 44 gun / it seemed like the real deal." However, in "Kid" these memories of his parents' acceptance of his gender performance are paralleled in the poem by his brothers' initial resistance to his joining in their activities. House notes, somewhat comically, "My brothers would tie me up / I would free myself and track them down." The child in the poem is teased, tied up, and left behind by his siblings, though it's unclear from the short piece whether this is due to a difference in age or the differences between their genders assigned at birth. But such divisions are short-lived, since we're subsequently told: "Us guys would hold secret mini-rodeos / We roped, flanked, and bucked sheep, ponies, and horses." We see again, then, the threads of familial acknowledgment, the repetition further emphasizing its importance, and also the way gender and House's boyhood are read *through* relationship—meeting the brothers at the barbershop, their resistance, and then House's eventual integration into their work and play. And in his poetry, as in his essays, House shows the reciprocity inherent in this affective circuit—just as he works for his family, he is also sustained and supported by them. As House's poem shows, then, when outside forces push against his gender affiliation, House's mother, father, and brothers allow for and recognize not only his gender but also his desire to work with and for familial needs in masculine occupations.[78] In "Kid," the non-cis narrator, while chided by school officials for transgressing colonial gender expectations, is the "real deal" at home—a boy in word and action.

While more could be said about the affective circuits at work in House's texts, I want to turn here to a final way in which his work exceeds the logics of gendercide. As discussed throughout this book, along with their murder of nonbinary Indigenous people, conquistadors, missionaries, and settlers attempted—and often still attempt—to erase the complexities and specificities of Indigenous gender systems. House refuses such erasure, as we have seen throughout this section, both by overtly referencing Diné histories of gender and by foregrounding how, when, and where he inhabits such Indigenous knowledges in the current moment. His poem "Sweet Grass" brings us to yet another way in which his work incorporates the complexity of such gender knowledges. In his poetry and essay, House highlights how non-cis Indigenous masculinities differ markedly from non-Native iterations of female and hegemonic masculinities: in their acknowledgment of the importance of spirituality to gender.

In her Introduction to the special Two-Spirit issue of the *Journal of Lesbian Studies,* Sabine Lang addresses how spirituality relates to multiple gender traditions:

> [A] recurrent aspect of being two-spirit is spirituality; the very term/concept of "two-*spirit*" expresses a connection of contemporary Native American LGBTQ to indigenous spirituality in the broadest sense. As has been observed by Lüder Tietz with regard to Canada, "For some *two-spirited people,* the word *spirit* seems to be the core of the use of the term 'Two-Spirited.'"[79]

Such a tie, as well, is seen in Whitehead's previously referenced response to his Lammy nomination: "I cling to Two-Spirit because it became an honour song that sung me back into myself as an Indigenous person, a nehiyaw (Cree), an Oji-Cree; I have placed it into my maskihkîwiwat, my medicine bag, because it has healed and nourished me whenever I needed it." In House's work, we can similarly see an embodied emphasis on the relationship between spirituality and gender throughout his work. In fact, in House's autobiographical writing, non-cis masculinity exists in what I have elsewhere called "the inherently queer space of the sacred."[80]

One example of how gender and spirituality coalesce in House's work is found in his poem "Sweet Grass," in which a female-identified Navajo narrator is called upon to butcher a buffalo. The poem begins with intertribal rivalries and masculine bravado as the narrator states: "One morning, I, Navajo, wake up in Tiwa country / Friend from Taos Pueblo tells me they just killed a buffalo / We drive up the hillside and see a tractor hoisting the buffalo / Ten people are stand-ing around, looking at each other."[81] House clearly ties the ability to butcher with tribal identity as becomes apparent in the following lines when, after the gathered Pueblo seem perplexed, "Someone asks 'Who here can butcher?' / 'She can, she's Navajo!'" This comment of-fers more than a narrative of Diné pride (though it unquestionably does that work, as well); it also resonates with the body of House's commentaries on sheepherding, traditional ranching and animal har-vesting practices, and the ties between those practices and produc-tive tribal identity and community responsibilities. The speaker has the skills necessary to feed those gathered, a valuable commodity. But while the speaker explains with a swagger, "My pocket knife is the sharpest knife in the group," the encounter moves beyond a mere it-eration of strength and skill.

As the act of butchering occurs, the poem enters the realm of the sacred and shifts away from masculine bravado. The narrator de-scribes the scene this way:

> Two men open the cavity and I put my head and arms in
> Steam from the inside smells of sweet grass
>> I close my eyes and am overwhelmed by the sensation of being
>> in a mother's womb.

The allusion to sweet grass turns the previously comic moment into prayer, invoking an affective experience of cleansing and healing, since the plant is often smudged, the smoke purifying people and spaces while also serving as a vehicle for devotions and entreaties to rise to the Creator. Here, House weds the actions of animal harvest-ing to sustenance, to motherhood, and to blessing. Furthermore, the emphasized reference to birth, which is offset from the rest of the poem, returns us to images of Changing Woman and, as previously discussed, the cultural traditions that underpin the existence of mul-tiple sexes and genders in Diné cosmology. In House's allusions, then, we see a non-cis masculinity enmeshed in the affective space of the sacred.

In both autobiographical essay and poetry, House explicitly situ-ates non-cis masculinity as part of embodied spiritual tradition. He writes these connections as central to him since childhood, saying,

"I was a tot when I began experiencing my relationship with the Holy People (the Diné deities) and supernatural occurrences" (329). While he has more to say about these embodied interactions, he concludes "Blessed by the Holy People" by stating, "The Holy People have created me to be, I'm blessed. Among other things, they bestowed me with the gift and foresight to help others" (329). Melanie Yazzie's explanation of particular kinds of power in Diné cosmology can help us better understand House's rhetoric of benediction: "Blessings become a part of us and how we are supposed to take daily responsibility for their presence.... Moreover, we have a keen sense of how these forms of power work on us and how their diffuse and capillary nature conditions our continued negotiation with the world."[82] Through this rhetoric of blessing seen in both his poetry and essay, House insists on the rightness of his masculinity, marks masculinity as a space of radical reciprocity and affective exchange, and describes the way spiritual power begets and infuses both masculinity and gender diversity. As a result, we are again reminded that non-cis masculinities and alternate gender traditions are deeply enmeshed in Diné tradition, serving not as static identities but instead as relational, creative *processes* working in and for the network of family, clan, and nation. In this way, House articulates an erotics of responsibility that disrupts non-Native understandings of gender while simultaneously expanding and complicating current conversations about how, where, and why masculinity circulates in Indigenous contexts.

Beyond a Text: Non-Cis Masculinity in the Everyday

I have spent most of this section detailing the ways in which House offers powerful and positive depictions of non-cis gender in embodied relationship to Diné culture; however, as seen previously in this book, the historical existence of gender-expansive traditions in Indigenous communities does not equate to a romantic present in which nonbinary people exist in their nations in total acceptance and harmony. A testament to the complicated realities lived by folks like House can be found in *The Status of Navajo Women and Gender Violence: Conversations with Diné Traditional Medicine People and a Dialogue with the People,* an important report arising from 2016 public hearings of the Navajo Nation Human Rights Commission, which was the result of innumerable conversations, three public forums, and a two-day workshop with Navajo traditional practitioners. On one hand, the report affirms the expansive nature of the Diné gender perspectives that ground House's understanding of self, citing the existence of three sexes and four genders in Diné cosmology. But on the other hand, while *The Status of Navajo Women and Gender Violence* conveys the multiplicity and transformative possibilities of sex and gender in Diné origin stories, the testimonies and findings make painfully clear that acceptance of the sort House describes from his family is not universal for contemporary nádleehi, LGBTIQ, non-cis, and/or Two-Spirit peoples in Diné contexts.

The report begins with a preface by Chairperson Steven A. Darden, who notes that he learned from "four traditional practitioners who were engaged to provide teachings . . . regarding the Diné journey stories of the separation of the sexes, and the nádleehi who is purported to have brought the reunification of the sexes."[83] He continues: "An interesting perspective shared by one of the female practitioners was that all other Diné persons who identify themselves as nádleehi are pretenders (nádleehi idili'h)," adding, "As the moderator of the Ft. Defiance presentations and hearings, I was personally at a loss as to how to address a person of the LGBTQ community who I perceived as male but presenting themselves as feminine."[84] Darden likely refers to linguistic kinship terms here, since he expands, "Their name as listed was certainly male, but still even from a Diné k'é perspective how do I address someone who may have been born male yet identifies as female?"[85] Chairman Darden ends his statement by urging the Navajo Nation Council to address the modern-day monster of gender violence, his final words alluding to Diné origin stories about the transformative power of non-cis people: "Perhaps, once again, a nádleehi will be the hero for our Diné Nation."[86] As these opening words signal, gender, and non-cis gender in particular, was clearly a linchpin of the conversations and, as Chairman Darden's openly stated discomfort indicates, also a site of concern and some differences in interpretation. Like the chairman, the other four commissioners, too, offer prefatory statements, each asserting the importance of women and LGBTIQ people, several stating some version of "We are all relatives in the Diné way," reaffirming the centrality of k'é and the value of every Diné person regardless of gender or sexual preference. All five commissioners reference the difficulty of the stories they encountered during the course of the hearings, many of which addressed the violence these populations experience in response to their lived articulations of gender and/or sexuality. At the same time, a preponderance of the commissioners also reiterated their belief that same-sex marriage counters Diné tradition, which was a majority finding of the report.[87]

House was present at the public hearings, and the report briefly describes the exchange:

> During the two day session, an audience member Carrie House who identifies as a genderqueer shared her [sic] anger concerning some Navajo sentiments that the story of the Separation of the Sexes is interpreted as a lesson that people should not engage in unnatural sex acts because it leads to the birth of "monsters," whom some take as those who identify outside of the normative gender binaries. Chair Darden marks this exchange with House as a point to clarify K'é as the traditional principle by which we related to each other and that such implications are not intended.[88]

As the description explains, House spoke against interpretations of Diné origin stories that read nonheteronormative people as engendering "monsters," challenging the implication that nádleehi and/or LGBTQIA/Two-Spirit people might be anything other than a productive part of Diné lives, histories, and present-day worldviews.[89] The fact that House felt the need to offer this rebuttal suggests that although cultural memory of multiple gender traditions is extant, interpretations of origin stories and gender practices vary broadly much as we saw in Whitehead's work.

Denetdale recognizes the importance of complex Diné gender traditions and supports current gender-expansive practices in her prefatory comments as a commissioner and in the larger body of her scholarship.[90] In "Carving Navajo National Boundaries," a landmark essay in Indigenous studies/Indigenous feminisms, Denetdale points to the passage of a Navajo Nation law that restricts marriage to heterosexual couples, the Diné Marriage Act of 2005, as an example of how the "conflation of American and Navajo nationalism is complemented by the similar conflation of Western gender ideology and notions of traditional Navajo values."[91] Denetdale concludes: "Asking how we came to equate Navajo concerns and priorities with U.S. foreign policy objectives and oppressive sex-gender systems represents an important first step toward recovering traditional principles of governance that were in place prior to 1863 when the Diné were in charge of their own destiny."[92] Denetdale's work and the Navajo Nation Human Rights Commission's investigations speak to the challenges faced by contemporary nádleehi and LGBTQIA/Two-Spirit people within the everyday world of Dinétah. But rather than undermining House's embodied narrative, the difficult stories shared by Diné people at the hearings and the dissent over the historic and contemporary place of non-cis genders within the Navajo Nation emphasize the necessity of House's speaking and writing publicly about his experiences.

Jack Halberstam's theory of female masculinity envisions an inherent potential in nonwhite masculinities, arguing that "minority masculinities" not only "can undo the hierarchized relations between dominant and minority sexualities" but also "have the power to reorganize masculinity itself."[93] In House's construction of non-cis masculinity we see how such a reorganization pushes at the limits of hegemonic white masculinity by enmeshing masculine performance within layers of accountability and relationship rather than individuality. This understanding of masculinity, which braids manhood together with ethical responsibility to family and nation, is invoked repeatedly in conversations on/scholarship in Indigenous masculinities studies. In their essay "Indigenous Masculinities: Carrying the Bones of Our Ancestors," Kim Anderson, Robert Alexander Innes, and John Swift discuss such ties. While their study focuses on Aboriginal people in what is currently Canada, their findings resonate with House's texts, as well:

> In Indigenous land-based and collective-focused societies, "who you are" is often defined by "what it is that you have to do." . . . Community members carry responsibilities that contribute to the collective and nourish relationships with all of creation. . . . [This ties to] Indigenous men's roles, identities, and the responsibilities that define them.[94]

These affective engagements are, on one hand, practices that always were, as Anderson, Innes, and Swift suggest. At the same time, as their work and House's texts demonstrate, such active, relational practices are the ways to which Indigenous people intentionally return when seeking restorative models of healthy masculinity in the aftermath of colonial incursions and attempted gendercide. Finally, such embodied practices or "who you are" are felt theory, archived in the body, nurtured by cultural memory, and, for culturally connected non-cis men like House, carried out in a daily practice that we might term an erotics of responsibility.

More than a Gender Role: An Erotics of Responsibility as Witness, Healing, and Medicine

At the conclusion of *Diné Masculinities,* looking to the future, Lee says that "Diné communities will need men who can help and plan for family stability, community sustainability, and a nation's wellness.... In the past, Diné men were responsible to the community. Diné men can apply responsibility to community and family to help sustain the Navajo Nation."[95] Lee is explicitly concerned with cis- and hetero-identified men, yet House fulfills these parameters as well, presenting a narrative in which, from childhood to adulthood, he cultivates a masculinity that privileges family, community, and nation. But, as this chapter has shown, House is not alone in choosing to reflect on the parameters of non-cis genders.

Although they work in different genres and engage different identities, Thirza Cuthand, Joshua Whitehead, and Carrie House construct film, fiction, and memoir that speak to the importance of embodied theory as well as to the prevalence of relational, rather than individual, modes of gender identification. In each case, we see the author craft an affective circuit within which non-cis identities function as an embrace of Indigenous ways of knowing and being. Through their references to the embodied memories of Indigenous gender knowledges and their representations of the everyday lives of non-cis Native peoples, these texts present an active refusal of settler terms of being. Moreover, Cuthand, Whitehead, and House deploy such gender knowledges intentionally in film, literature, and life, crafting the terms of their own existence in the face of more than five centuries of attempted gendercide.

Importantly, as well, gendercide is not just a flip, academic term.

It traffics in real bodies and real lives and threatens the psychological and physical well-being of present-day, as well as historical, Indigenous people. Thus, looking across the texts engaged in this chapter, as well as their possibilities, we also see the difficulties encountered by folks who inhabit gender outside dominant binaries. We see bullies and beatings, attempted erasures and painful encounters in which colonial masculinity becomes a weapon. By telling these stories, these non-cis writers speak their truths and, in the process, serve as change agents, unveiling the ways in which gender-expansive traditions are under attack even as they film, write, and make art.

Finally, at the heart of this chapter is the fact that Cuthand, Whitehead, and House not only refuse to be silenced but also move beyond merely saying "we exist." (Though that statement is, in itself, a refutation of gendercidal demands that nonbinary gender traditions disappear.) Throughout their work, these artists stake larger claims for the relevance and connectedness of non-cis people as they tease out the parameters and uses of an erotics of responsibility tied to non-cis gender expressions. Whitehead and House in particular wed non-cis gender expression to nation-specific responsibility. Thus, as opposed to non-Indigenous or non-culturally connected articulations of non-cis gender expressions, an erotics of responsibility includes references to specific landbases, to particular sustenance practices, and to generational knowledges. In other words, this is not a personal or individual erotics. While, as Audre Lorde has told us, the erotic is power, here we see it as an embodied power that moves (at least) two ways, necessitating reciprocity as it upholds Indigenous belief systems. In Cuthand's film that movement occurs in the push and pull between she and her mother, an exchange that causes her to deploy Indigenous knowledge in the form of a Two-Spirit ideology to interpret gender. For Whitehead that exchange occurs through Jonny's relationship with his mother and kokum and, as well, through the powerful world of Indigenous dreamscapes, which enable him to imagine differently, seeing Two-Spirit knowledge as a sustaining practice. Finally, in House's essay, film, and poetry we see multiple interactions with family and community, each of which is enmeshed in Diné cosmology, working in service of Diné community, and explicitly advocating the maintenance of cultural memory. It is in these spaces of exchange, then, that possibilities blossom. Overall, in this chapter we see a growing body of literature that represents the twenty-first-century experiences of non-cis Indigenous people. Created by and for them, each story can bear witness. Each story can provide healing. Each story can be medicine.

WRITTEN BY THE BODY
**Felt Theory, New Worlds, and
Transformative Possibilities**

> The knowledge of how to create a new world is etched into my
>   bones in a language
> that has mostly been forgotten. . . .
> . . . It will not be knowable in advance
> what shape the new world will take. If she will take form framed in
>   fire, or
> arise out of the waves, like the last world. Pronouns are not a
>   given.
>
> ——Kai Minosh Pyle, "The Creation Story Is a Spaceship"

I turn here, as I head to conclusion, to the intersections of gender, the
body, and transformation. In one way or another, these threads have
run through each chapter of *Written by the Body*. From the *affective
shifts in masculinities* that female-identified and gender-variant warriors create on the battlefield and Indigenous authors later depict in
fiction, to the active interventions of the protectors and culture bearers I call big moms, we see evidence that *the body is a somatic archive of
Indigenous knowledge*. These embodied knowledges inform the words
and actions of warriors and writers, fasters and firefighters. In their
affective models of protection, Indigenous peoples use their bodies as
shield and shelter for their nations, a fact shown by *Trick or Treaty?*'s
depiction of Ogichidaakwe Theresa Spence and the Nishiyuu walkers
and *Apache 8*'s chronicle of Apache 6 and Apache 8's all-female wildland firefighting crews. Such somatic interventions are found, too, in
the collaborative *health sovereignty* work Carole laFavor undertook in

HIV/AIDS education and in her centering of Two-Spirit identities and the *Indigenous erotic* in her novels. Finally, transformative possibilities continue to be animated today by the intersections of land, family, nation, and non-cis embodiment, or the *erotics of responsibility*, that exist in Thirza Cuthand's, Joshua Whitehead's, and Carrie House's art and lived experiences.

In every case, in the texts, films, and interviews in this book, Indigenous gender articulations are expansive; held in variously gendered bodies rather than tethered to settler binaries, they shift in mode and meaning and hold real creative potential. Sometimes that potential is met with colonial violence perpetrated in the name of prescriptive cishet gender expectations, because, as Alex Wilson explains in an interview with Marie Laing, "Indigenous women and two-spirit people bear the brunt of colonial hierarchies and processes and we also bear the brunt of whiplash that occurs when colonial frameworks invade our own cosmology and are presented as 'natural,' as something that has always been a part of our traditional teachings."[1] In response, as Wilson's own activism and LGBTQIA+ youth education work shows, and as we saw in laFavor's and House's testimony and Whitehead's fiction, Indigenous people imagine differently and insist on other ways of being. In that resurgent work, "they don't just refuse, they also embody an Indigenous alternative."[2] Thus, somatic knowledge becomes a lived route to protection, strength, and healing. To return to Whitehead's words, felt knowledges serve as "medicine."

These felt theories are found in the expansive bodily possibilities that exist throughout Indigenous art, literatures, films, and lives. They live in the fierce gazes of Diné, Comanche, and White Mountain Apache artist Jolene Nenibah Yazzie's *Sisters of War* on the cover of this book. In this piece, Yazzie uses bold red, black, and white contrasts to "embody . . . Indigenous alternative." Pushing back on the normative gender demands she's confronted throughout her life, Yazzie crafts a story of powerful Indigenous women absent from the comic books of her childhood. These sister warriors, who wear Diné war hats most commonly associated with men, "are the inner spirits from the women in her life depicted as superheroes."[3] In conversation with me and in interviews for the *Native Feminisms* exhibit, Yazzie speaks to how these figures represent the strength and perseverance of her mother, her sister, her wife, and her wife's sisters, all of

whom have experienced, but are not defined by, embodied trauma.[4]
Likewise, Yazzie, who dances in the Northern traditional men's category at powwows, is particularly interested in reclaiming and re-
animating the gender expansive stories of female-identified warriors.
Yazzie's overt representations of these complex relationships reflect
the struggle and embodied transformations that ground this book.

Sisters of War thus serves as a powerful visual representation of the
expansive possibilities imagined over one hundred years earlier by
Zitkála-Šá when her Dakota warrior woman, Tusee, deployed gender
as both weapon and saving grace in one of the earliest fictional depictions of a female-identified warrior. Yazzie's art resonates, too, with
Anna Lee Walters's Pawnee sisters and their recognition that they,
too, are warriors who can take up responsibilities and cultural teachings previously tied to those identified male at birth. We find like possibilities in Tarsa's deployment of the healing power of the erotic and
in Nita Quintero's description of how her Sunrise Dance Ceremony
informs her role as a wildland firefighter and White Mountain Apache
land protector. Again and again, the artists, writers, and filmmakers
discussed here depict affective, embodied, gender-expansive possibilities as transformative conduit: they show how Indigenous people create and extend survivance practices through somatic encounter—in
singing, in drumming, in praying, in fishing, in fasting, in walking, in
writing, in dreaming, in hunting, in dancing, in making films, in making art, in making out, in making love, and *in the felt theory that arises
from those embodied avenues of intellectual exchange.*

The ever-present *possibility* of transformation and *the act* of transformation itself (thus *both* potential *and* action) have always been endemic to Indigenous knowledge systems. So many origin stories rest
on such acts—movements between worlds, from sky to earth, into or
up from water, and through multiple incarnations of bodies and genders. With these connections in mind, we can begin to see how transformation is both inherently affective and inherently significant to
Indigenous cosmologies. These points of embodied exchange are affective circuits that can move both the self and others. Furthermore,
transformation, though it can be narrated, exists outside and beyond
language—something Craig Womack's Lucy shows us when, as an assault survivor, she turns her pain and power into a music that speaks
her truth and healing (however imperfect or conditional that healing

may be). Moreover, in bodily contexts, affective temporalities point to the inevitability and immutability of change, as seen, for example, in the fluid movement between and among genders that both Zitkála-Šá and Thirza Cuthand represent and in the physical transformation we all take part in as we daily shed these skins. Welcomed or not, change is the only constant, as most of us know all too well. Transformation is thus an aspect of all our lives, but it is, I would argue, perhaps most effectively seen in embodied Indigenous knowledge systems because they allow for and often enact transformation, rather than situate origin and ideology in static, singular norms.

Names, roles, responsibilities, status, and ceremony all carry with them the possibility of change. This change may come with the varying shifts in age, season, or ability and through individual or collective acts. Take, for example, the physical and spiritual transitions marked by puberty ceremonies, the seasonal movement of camps, the taking up of a new name, the move from reserve to city (and back again), or the decision to come out (to self, to friends, to family, to strangers). Each of these is a path to, or perhaps more aptly, a marker of, a type of change, a route to transformation. I imagine here something like egg to caterpillar to chrysalis to butterfly, with each aspect of the next seemingly remarkable change already existing, *already encoded in the body.*

Importantly, in terms of the concerns of the writers, artists, and activists at the heart of this book, such transformative possibilities—or what Kai Pyle in this coda's epigraph aptly terms "the knowledge of how to create a new world"—reside in the constellation of practices deployed and represented by Indigenous people who maintain gender expansiveness. These expansive understandings elude the settler ideologies that attempt to erase them, and consequently they become a bodily archive of Indigenous knowledge. As Lindsay Nixon contends in her discussion of the #MeToo movement in Indigenous contexts, transformation occurs "at the relational level."[5] And further, within what she calls the "queer ethics"[6] of such relationship, "the Indigenous revolution is done, enacted, and felt, not said, performed, and speculated."[7] But, as Nixon also carefully reminds us, not all embodied knowledge is transformative, not every gender performance is revolutionary. The readings in this book underscore that truth: to name just a few, we saw such difficult realities addressed by Alexie's predatory actions as opposed to Big Mom's possibilities, by the misogyny and fragmenting settler legacies experienced by the women of Apache 6 and 8, by laFavor's lived knowledge of assault and fictionalized representations of abuse, by Jonny's violent experiences with homophobia and toxic masculinity in Whitehead's fiction, and by the resistances to House's male gender from a cis-normative world.

In light of such realities, I want to conclude by suggesting that the felt theories in this book hold revolutionary potential: the transformative possibility to counter such violence and imagine differently. For example, if recognizing Native masculinities as not only multiple but also mobile requires a paradigm shift, what might that shift bring with it? The answer, I think, is weighty. The non-cis folks and powerful female-identified leaders and inspired young male-identified walkers held up here model an ethic of care that provides an agentive model of change—an embodied revolution that is, to recall Nixon, "done, enacted, and felt, not said, performed, and speculated."[8] If the body is a map, they are wayfinders whose somatic interventions mark a route forward, a route past or through toxic colonial masculinities and toward radical love. Their survival knowledges construct a twenty-first-century gender theory written by Indigenous people and theorized through and by the body

Thus, to follow their lead, if there is to be masculinity, let it arise from the reciprocal relationships inherent in an erotics of responsibility. And if there's no longer a need for masculinities, maybe there's something else, something more, an expansive affective potential before and beyond it—as so many of the accounts in *Written by the Body* suggest. Ultimately, let these brave, often queer, sometimes larger-than-life (or at least more than the current arbitrators of life want to allow) folks tear this androcentric, homophobic, cis-normative colonial castle down now. Burn it to the fucking ground and build something new. Let them remind everyone how it always was done, how it can be done, or perhaps, more aptly, through their energies, bodily knowledges, and the felt theory of their lives, how it can be made what they want it to be.

NOTES

Introduction

1. Lowry, "Republicans Use Sharice Davids' Own Words."
2. Lowry.
3. Vizenor, *Manifest Manners*, vii.
4. Miles, *Ties That Bind*, 36.
5. Driskill, *Asegi Stories*, 94.
6. Hokowhitu, "Taxonomies of Indigeneity," 85.
7. W. L. Williams, *Spirit and the Flesh*, 179.
8. Lang, "Native American Men-Women," 300.
9. Pedro Fages qtd. in Miranda, "Extermination of the *Joyas*," 257.
10. See the Introduction to Sam McKegney's *Carrying the Burden of Peace* for a nuanced overview of these issues and responses.
11. Belcourt, "Can the Other of Native Studies Speak?"
12. Belcourt.
13. Million, "Felt Theory," 61.
14. As Million notes, Bill C-31 was not a cure-all—while those who had been disenfranchised because of the Indian Act provisions about gender and marriage did regain status, in a bizarre twist deemed the "Second-Generation Cut Off," they were not legally able to pass that status on to their descendants if they married a non-status partner.
15. Belcourt, "Can the Other of Native Studies Speak?"
16. Belcourt and Nixon, "What Do We Mean by Queer Indigenous Ethics?"
17. Halberstam, *Female Masculinity*, 1. While I focus here on Halberstam, he is by no means the sole theorist of female masculinity. See, to name only a few, Butler, *Bodies That Matter*; Gardiner, "Female Masculinity and Phallic Women"; Nguyen, "Patriarchy, Power, and Female Masculinity"; Noble, *Masculinities without Men*; Stoller, *Splitting*.

18. Halberstam, 1.

19. Noble, *Masculinities without Men*, xiii.

20. Driskill, *Asegi Stories*.

21. Halberstam, *Female Masculinity*, 276.

22. Anderson, *A Recognition of Being*, 59.

23. Innes and Anderson, Introduction, 4.

24. Tengan, *Native Men Remade*, 5.

25. Tengan, 8.

26. Klopotek, "'I Guess Your Warrior Look Doesn't Work Every Time,'" 251.

27. Tengan, *Native Men Remade*, 10.

28. Tengan, 15.

29. McKegney, *Masculindians*, 3.

30. Bender, "Glimpses of Local Masculinities," 12.

31. Stimson and Houle, "Deeper than a Blood Tie," 149.

32. Sinclair and McKegney, "After and Towards," 225.

33. Hokowhitu, "Taxonomies of Indigeneity"; Byrd *The Transit of Empire*; Coulthard, *Red Skins, White Masks*.

34. Teaiwa, "The Ancestors We Get to Choose," 46.

35. Byrd, *The Transit of Empire*, 11–21.

36. Million, "Felt Theory," 54.

37. Million, 61.

38. Million, 61.

39. Million, 64.

40. Million, 64.

41. Million, 72.

42. Another example of this felt theory is addressed in the powerful Introduction to *Arts of Engagement*, in which Stó:lō scholar Dylan Robinson and settler scholar Keavy Martin consider "the ways in which public spaces and national discourses privilege certain bodies and contribute to the ongoing oppression of others" (Robinson and Martin, "The Body Is a Resonant Chamber," 3).

43. Brant, *Writing as Witness*, 36.

44. Hemmings, "Invoking Affect," 552; emphasis added.

45. My thinking here is influenced by Sedgwick's *Touching Feeling*.

46. Lang, "Native American Men-Women," 303.

47. C. Allen, *Trans-Indigenous*, xxii.

48. Million, *Therapeutic Nations*, 180.

1. Warrior Women in History and Early Indigenous Literatures

1. "Lori Piestewa: The Story of a Brave Soldier."

2. B. House and Shafer, "Mom, Hopi, Hero."

3. King, "Honoring, Remembering, and Praying," 1.

4. Qtd. in Begay, "Piestewa Renamed 'Lady Warrior,'" A1.

5. Wayne, "Lori Died a True Hopi Warrior," A3.

6. Wayne, A3.

7. Though not the focus of this chapter, another place where the complexities of identity become apparent is in tribal identification and cultural traditions. Piestewa's father is Hopi and her mother is Latinx; because the Hopi are matrilineal, Piestewa would be considered Latinx, not Hopi, in traditional Hopi clan structure. *High Country News* editor Jodi Peterson, describing a visit to a group of Hopis who were conscientious objectors in World War II, states, "the traditional Hopi we talked to did not claim her. We are pacifists, they said: we do not go to war. Furthermore, they explained, the tribe traces its descent through the woman's side." Peterson, "Who Is an Indian?," 2. There are other Hopi, however, who do claim her as one of their tribe, as the tribal chairman's comments demonstrate.

8. Film has been a particularly significant place where such narratives have been relentlessly forwarded. See Hearne's *Native Recognitions* for a discussion of such tropes in Westerns and also how the work of Indigenous filmmakers have "alter[ed] the frame through which viewers see 'images of Indians' actualizing dynamic visual processes of political and genealogical recognition" (3).

9. Wayne, "Lori Died a True Hopi Warrior," A3. At the same time, Carroll cites Delfred Leslie, "a Hopi nation judge and religious leader, [who] describes women as being part of Hopi warrior traditions and points to a warrior society, the Kalatakayum or Sword Swallowers, which still exists and has both male and female members" (*Medicine Bags and Dog Tags,* 200).

10. Kraker, "The Tangled Message," 5.

11. McLeod, "Tending the Fire," 210–11. See McKegney, *Carrying the Burden of Peace,* for a sustained discussion of McLeod's problematic history of abuse.

12. Anderson, Swift, and Innes, "'To Arrive Speaking,'" 283–84.

13. Tengan, *Native Men Remade.*

14. Lee, *Diné Masculinities.*

15. Two notable exceptions here are Anderson, Innes, and Swift's interviews with Two-Spirit men in their three-year Bidwewidam Indigenous Masculinities Project ("'To Arrive Speaking'") and McKegney's many interviews with queer and Two-Spirit folks in *Masculindians.*

16. While there are historical accounts *published* in the twentieth century, they look back at the nineteenth century.

17. Lang, "Native American Men-Women," 303.

18. Lang, 303.

19. Lang, 303.

20. Lafitau, *Customs of the American Indians,* 100.

21. St-Onge, "He Was Neither a Soldier nor a Slave," 3.

22. Importantly, despite such settler simulation of Indigenous masculinity, productive models of warriorhood that center familial responsibilities continue to exist among Indigenous people—male, female, and gender-variant or nonbinary—to this day, as will be discussed in later chapters.

23. Morgensen, "Cutting to the Roots."

24. Justice, *Why Indigenous Literatures Matter,* 41.

25. Scudeler, "This Show Won't Mean Anything."

26. See Grumet, "Sunksquaws, Shamans, and Tradeswomen"; Martino-Trutor, "As Potent a Prince as Any Round about Her"; McCartney, "Cockacoeske, Queen of Pamunkey"; Schmidt, "Cockacoeske, Weroansqua of the Pamunkeys."

27. Muñoz, *Cruising Utopia.*

28. Denig, *Of the Crow Nation,* 65.

29. Denig, 66.

30. Denig, 67.

31. Denig, 67.

32. Halberstam, *The Queer Art of Failure,* 88.

33. Halberstam, 88.

34. Medicine, "'Warrior Women,'" 273.

35. R. G. Thomas, "Daughters of the Lance," 148.

36. See Vandervort, *Indian Wars,* 81; Niethammer, *Daughters of the Earth,* 168; R. G. Thomas, "Daughters of the Lance," 147–49.

37. Grinnell, *The Cheyenne Indians,* 47.

38. R. G. Thomas, "Daughters of the Lance," 149. For more, see Grinnell, *The Fighting Cheyenne* and *The Cheyenne Indians;* Powell, *People of the Sacred Mountain.*

39. See Rifkin, *When Did Indians Become Straight?*

40. McKegney, "Pain, Pleasure, Shame. Shame," 13.

41. See Ball and Kaywaykla, *In the Days of Victorio,* 15; and Ball and Sánchez, "Legendary Apache Women," 9–10.

42. Ball and Kaywaykla's *In the Days of Victorio* is novelistic, as seen especially in the direct quotes attributed to the Apache people she represents. At the same time, she worked closely with James Kaywaykla, who read and

commented on a draft of the text before his death. For more see S. Robinson, *Apache Voices,* xi–xiv, 3–4.

43. Qtd. in S. Robinson, *Apache Voices,* 4.

44. Ball and Kaywaykla, *In the Days of Victorio,* 115.

45. Qtd. in Stockel, *Women of the Apache Nation,* 46.

46. For more on Lozen see Ball and Kaywaykla, *In the Days of Victorio*; Ball and Sánchez, "Legendary Apache Women"; Moore, "Lozen"; Roberts, *Once They Moved Like the Wind*; and S. Robinson, "Lozen."

47. Identified, too, as Buffalo Calf Robe Woman and Buffalo Calf Road Woman.

48. See Grinnell, *The Cheyenne Indians,* 44.

49. See also Grinnell, *The Fighting Cheyennes,* 323–24.

50. See Kidston, "Northern Cheyenne Break Vow of Silence."

51. Million, "Felt Theory," 31.

52. Moving Robe is also identified as Tashenamini, She Walks with Her Shawl, and Mary Crawler.

53. She Walks with Her Shawl, "The Battle of the Little Big Horn, June 25–26, 1876," 42–43. The original account can be found in the Walter S. Campbell Collection, Western History Collection at the University of Oklahoma Libraries, Item 5 E, Box 111.

54. See Waggoner, "Itéomagážu," for more on Rain in the Face.

55. Eastman, "Rain-in-the-Face," 511.

56. Cummings, "Jamaican Female Masculinities," 130–31.

57. Eastman, "Rain-in-the-Face," 511.

58. Pyle, "Ozaawindib."

59. Justice, *Why Indigenous Literatures Matter,* 186.

60. Justice, 187.

61. Callahan, *Wynema.* All subsequent citations in text.

62. Womack, *Red on Red,* 116.

63. Callahan's sentimental novel seems to neatly conclude with chapter 17, "Another Visit to Keithly College," in which "Gerald Keithly [wins] his heart's desire," Genevieve Weir (*Wynema,* 70). Chapters 18–24 abruptly turn to the Wounded Knee Massacre, which would have been front-page news across the country in the months immediately prior to the novel's publication.

64. Justice, *Why Indigenous Literatures Matter,* 186.

65. Justice, 187.

66. Medicine, "'Warrior Women,'" 275.

67. Powers, *Oglala Women,* 25.

68. See Du Bois, *The Souls of Black Folks.*

69. Rifkin, *When Did Indians Become Straight?*

70. Bernardin, "On the Meeting Grounds of Sentiment," 219.

71. Bernardin, 211.

72. Bernardin, 212.

73. Tomkins, *Shame and Its Sisters*, 134.

74. McLeod, *Cree Narrative Memory*, 18.

75. For more biographical detail, see Hafen's (Taos Pueblo) Introduction to her collection of Zitkala-Ša's work, *Dreams and Thunder*; Fisher, "Zitkala-Ša"; and Spack, "Dis/engagement."

76. Ruoff, "Editor's Introduction," xv.

77. Zitkala-Ša, *American Indian Stories*, 8.

78. I'm specifically thinking here of the contrast between Zitkala-Ša's letters to her fiancé Carlos Montezuma and the letters from Callahan that Ruoff cites in her Introduction to *Wynema*. Likewise, Callahan seems to have consistently espoused Christianity, while Zitkala-Ša's beliefs shifted over time, as demonstrated most famously by her then scandalizing 1902 essay "Why I Am a Pagan." This piece is the most widely anthologized expression of Zitkala-Ša's spiritual beliefs; she also identified as a Catholic and possibly a Mormon. See Hafen, *Dreams and Thunder*.

79. Zitkala-Ša, "A Warrior's Daughter," 137. All subsequent references in text.

80. Landes, "Dakota Warfare," 242.

81. For more on the history of the periodical, see Mott, "Everybody's Magazine."

82. Though settler audiences often connected the practice of scalping to a perceived "primitive" Indigeneity, the practice has occurred across continents and cultures. In what is now the United States, bounties were put on Indigenous people's scalps, which were collected by colonists and, later, the U.S. government. In 1641, for example, New Netherland governor Willem Kieft offered to pay for the scalps of Hackensack people after a disagreement over reparations for the deaths of two Dutch farmers (Sonneborn 1641). There are innumerable examples of Indigenous people's scalps being collected by settlers for published fees or for battle trophies throughout the nineteenth century.

83. According to Paul Fees, in 1899, just three years before the publication of "A Warrior's Daughter," "Buffalo Bill's Wild West covered over 11,000 miles in 200 days, giving 341 performances in 132 cities and towns across the United States" ("Wild West Shows").

84. Hollrah, *The Old Lady Trill*, 36.

85. Speaking of the primacy of kinship in "A Warrior's Daughter," Rifkin argues: "The story at the text's heart, then, is constructed out of reassembled elements of what can be described as the kinship plot with which it opens.

Rather than serving as a process of breaking away from her family and tribe to create an independent household, as in the romance plot of federal policy, Tusee's reunion with her lover reaffirms her identity as Dakota and the fact that expansive notions of family suffuse all Dakota relationships, providing a shared conceptual and political basis for individual and collective action" (*When Did Indians Become Straight?*, 163).

86. Such images of female strength are analogous to Zitkala-Ša's beliefs about her own identity. In letters that would have been written at the same time as "The Warrior's Daughter" to then fiancé Carlos Montezuma, Zitkala-Ša "declares her independence repeatedly" (Spack, "Dis/engagement," 181).

87. M. W. Smith, "The War Complex of the Plains Indian," 429.

88. P. G. Allen, "The Warriors," 29.

89. Massumi, *Parables of the Virtual*, 30.

90. Massumi argues: "When a body is in motion, it does not coincide with itself. It coincides with its own transition: its own variation.... In motion, a body is in an immediate, unfolding relation to its own nonpresent potential to vary" (*Parables for the Virtual*, 4).

91. Spinoza, *Ethic*, 108, 109.

92. Zitkala-Ša chafed against the rigid hegemonic beliefs she faced regarding the gender expectations placed on both single women and wives in her lifetime. Spack's work is especially useful in showing Zitkala-Ša's quest for independence. A prime example of Zitkala-Ša's sense of Native women's historical power can be found in an editorial she wrote for *The Suffragist*, in which she says: "In the ancient councils, the Indian woman's voice was heard and heeded. In the Iroquois Confederacy, she nominated the chiefs, later confirmed by popular vote. Descent was traced on the mother's side.... When Columbus stumbled upon this continent, a paradoxical thing happened. He spotted the home of world democracy, but for a time upset the equal suffrage of the Indian. Not only did the Indian woman lose caste, but her better half was swept off his feet also" (Zitkala-Ša, "The Indian Woman," 7).

Critics have noted that Zitkala-Ša's literary publication slowed after her 1902 marriage to Raymond Bonnin. Hafen's *Dreams and Thunder*, a collection of Zitkala-Ša's unpublished writings, illustrates that the author continued to write regularly. Zitkala-Ša also remained politically active and, along with her best-known text, *American Indian Stories*, in which she republished her early autobiography and fictions, produced two more major texts, one literary, one political. She wrote *The Sun Dance Opera* in collaboration with William F. Hanson (though for some time he attempted to claim a majority of the credit for the work) and coauthored *Oklahoma's Poor Rich Indians: An Orgy of Graft and Exploitation of the Five Civilized Tribes—Legalized Robbery*

(1924) with Charles H. Fabens and Matthew K. Sniffen. The latter text arose from her many years of reform work and served as an important political report on the corruption and fraud perpetrated by the U.S. government against Indian nations in Oklahoma. So, while Zitkala-Ša did not overtly craft another warrior woman, she continued to occupy that position herself until her 1938 death.

93. Justice, *Why Indigenous Literatures Matter*, 186.

2. Warriors, Indigenous Futures, and the Erotic

1. There is one narrative moment in Mourning Dove's novel—when Stemtemmä tells Cogewea "The Story of Green Blanket Feet" in which the protagonist takes up arms to facilitate her escape—that could be loosely interpreted as a fitting within the literary tradition of warrior women.

2. Kellogg (1880–1947) was a founding member of the Society of American Indians, a staunch critic of the Bureau of Indian Affairs, and an Oneida activist who fought for Indigenous autonomy. Her 1920 book, *Our Democracy and the American Indian,* outlines her plan for Indigenous land, industry, and planned communities. Bronson (1897–1982) was president of the National Council of American Indians from 1944 to 1948, returning again for one year in 1951. She published in 1947 a treatise aimed at white readers titled *Indians Are People, Too.* While this list focuses on female writers, there are also no images of women warriors in the texts of male writers from the turn of the century to the midcentury period such as Charles Eastman, D'Arcy McNichol, Lynn Riggs, or Todd Downing.

3. Justice first published his work as a trilogy with Kateri Akiwenzie-Damm's Kegedonce Press, which included *Kynship* (2005), *Wyrwood* (2006), and *Dreyd* (2007). University of New Mexico Press published *The Way of Thorn and Thunder* as an omnibus edition in 2011.

4. Qtd. in Belcourt, "Can the Other of Native Studies Speak?" I was also in attendance at the panel.

5. Walters, "The Warriors," 112. All subsequent citations in text.

6. See Steinberg's "Myth, Folk Tale, and Ritual" for more on the history and function of Pahukatawa in "The Warriors."

7. The narrator references a series of gray photographs from her uncle's stint in the Korean War: "In only one picture did he smile" (118). Our contemporary knowledge of veterans' postwar struggles suggests this experience may well combine with Uncle Ralph's sense of cultural loss to lead him toward the addiction that strains his family relationships.

8. I gesture toward Toni Morrison's *Beloved* here and the haunting power of repressed trauma and history.

9. P. J. Deloria, *Indians in Unexpected Places,* 6.

10. P. J. Deloria, 4.

11. Halberstam, *Female Masculinity,* 1.

12. Justice, "Notes toward a Theory of Anomaly," 221.

13. Berlant, "Nearly Utopian, Nearly Normal," 274.

14. Massumi, *Parables for the Virtual,* 30.

15. R. Williams, *Marxism and Literature,* 128.

16. Brant, *Writing as Witness,* 17.

17. Brant, 17.

18. See Womack, *Red on Red;* Driskill, "Stolen from Our Bodies"; Miranda, "Dildos, Hummingbirds, and Driving Her Crazy" and *The Zen of La Llorona;* Akiwenzie-Damm, "Erotica, Indigenous Style"; Warrior, "Your Skin Is the Map"; Rifkin, *When Did Indians Become Straight?* and *The Erotics of Sovereignty;* Tatonetti, *The Queerness of Native American Literature.*

19. While I focus here on Tarsa, there is much to say, as well, about Denarra and the erotic, especially in light of Justice's wonderful reveal in his short story "Ander's Awakening" that Denarra is trans.

20. Justice, *The Way of Thorn and Thunder,* 6–7. All subsequent citations in text.

21. For example, Beatrice Medicine explains Lakota understandings of women's power during menses: "The wakan (sacredness or power) of a female's menstrual period could weaken the wakan (power) components of such male things as medicine bundles, war bundles, shields, and other paraphernalia, which belonged to the men in the tipi (dwelling). Thus, at the menarche, an emergent woman was placed in a small shelter outside the tipi. This act of isolation was called ishna ti ('to live alone'). In her menstrual dwelling, she was visited by women who were post-menopausal. The isolation was an opportunity for learning excellence in crafts, such as quilting, and tanning hides. Other womanly knowledge involved sexuality and child care was also dispensed. At this time, according to the Lakota view, a woman embodied power and sacredness" ("Indian Women," 68).

22. Qtd. in Lavender, "Ethnoscapes," 187.

23. Lavender, 189.

24. Dillon, Introduction, xx.

25. Whitehead, Introduction, 5.

26. Nixon, "Making Space in Indigenous Art."

27. See Tatonetti, "Indigenous Fantasies and Sovereign Erotics."

28. Danforth, "Our Nations, Our Bodies," 119.

29. Million, "Felt Theory," 54.

30. Stoler, *Race and the Education of Desire,* 7.

31. Driskill, "Stolen from Our Bodies," 53.

32. Justice, *Why Indigenous Literatures Matter*, 43.

33. Justice, 43.

34. Spinoza, *Ethic*, 109.

35. Million, "Felt Theory," 54.

36. Justice, "Fighting Shame through Love," 142.

37. Hunt, "'In Search of Our Better Selves,'" 74.

38. Nixon, "Making Space in Indigenous Art."

3. Big Moms, or The Body as Archive

1. Million, *Therapeutic Nations*, 132.

2. In reviewing Charles Mingus lyrics, I was unable to find a song that contains this quote. It may be a case of Alexie fictionalizing Mingus to offer something Mingus would have written had he known Big Mom.

3. Alexie, *Reservation Blues*, 6. All subsequent citations in text.

4. Bird, "The Exaggeration of Despair," 49.

5. Bird, 50.

6. Justice, "Fighting Shame through Love," 142.

7. Dias and Ressler, "Parental Olfactory Experiences," 95.

8. Qtd. in Gray, "Phobias May Be Memories Passed Down."

9. Gallagher, "Memories Pass between Generations."

10. Douglas Ford argues that Junior's suicide is the result of "the collective weight of many painful experiences from parental abandonment to a tragic affair with a white woman" who aborts their child (198). Ultimately, Ford points out, "Junior's death makes up only a small part of a larger, more disturbing pattern of eradication" ("Sherman Alexie's Indigenous Blues," 199).

11. Kleinman and Kleinman, "How Bodies Remember," 711.

12. Pettit, "Slaughter of Horses Leaves Lasting Mark."

13. Pettit. See also Ruby and Brown, *The Spokane Indians*, 136–37.

14. Wilkinson, "Wild Horses."

15. Kleinman and Kleinman, "How Bodies Remember," 716–17.

16. Massumi, *Parables for the Virtual*, 30.

17. Million, "Felt Theory," 61.

18. Such exchanges occur within specifically bounded cultural parameters. As Thomas J. Csordas notes, "For Navajo people, sacred knowledge is powerful and potentially dangerous (báhádzid) and it must be treated with a respect that requires circumspection and even secrecy. Spreading knowledge too far could weaken its spiritual power, abuse its power, or turn its power destructively against the original knowledge holder" ("Ritual Healing," 10).

19. Murrock and Higgens, "The Theory of Music," 2250.

20. Murrock and Higgens, 2251.

21. Child, "When Art Is Medicine."

22. Skånland, "Music, Health, and Well-being."

23. Richardson, "Magic and Memory," 42.

24. Child, "When Art Is Medicine."

25. Skånland, "Music, Health, and Well-being."

26. Ford suggests these connections hinge on a combination of an Indigenous oral tradition and an African American blues musical tradition. See Ford, "Sherman Alexie's Indigenous Blues," 201.

27. Morgensen, "Cutting to the Roots," 39.

28. Innes and Anderson, Introduction, 11.

29. Scott Andrews argues that "Big Mom's guitar is made up of the tools at hand for the American Indian—made from the memory of military oppression, genocidal government policies, and from a material plenitude made possible in part by that conquest and the empire it created; her guitar is a memorial to a tragedy in American Indian history, but it is also a celebration of the symbol of the American Dream, of power, excess, and freedom" ("A New Road and a Dead End," 141).

30. Skånland, "Music, Health, and Well-being."

31. Johnston, "Young Men of Good Will," 45.

32. Johnston, 45–46.

33. McKegney, "Into the Full Grace," 4.

34. Anderson, *A Recognition of Being*, 13.

35. Anderson, 56.

36. McKegney, "Pain, Pleasure, Shame. Shame," 13. Notably, though, Thomas, who does not take up a colonial masculinity and respects Big Mom's authority, offers an entirely different way of being.

37. Tengan, "Re-membering Panalā'au," 27–28.

38. Tengan, 29. Tengan shows how the discourse of empire demanded that Kanaka men reframe their gender investments. Thus, King Kamehameha became an icon of a Western militarized masculinity supposedly patterned after an Indigenous leader and Kanaka traditions. In this context a warrior masculinity begins to mean differently.

39. Kiley and Shapiro, "Sherman Alexie Addresses the Sexual-Misconduct Allegations"; Himmelstein, "Children's Publishing Reckons with Sexual Harassment."

40. Some subsequent articles made much of the fact that Dremousis and Alexie had previously carried on an affair. In fact, Alexie's public response to the accusations against him spends as much time on Dremousis as it does on forwarding an apology. Alexie comments: "I reject the accusations, insinuations, and outright falsehoods made by Litsa Dremousis, who has led

charges against me" ("For Immediate Release"). As I write, Dremousis has a detailed public statement on her website in which she refutes Alexie's version of events and offers extensive information about the timeline and events of both their brief affair/longtime friendship and of the development of the NPR story in which Jeanine Walker, Erika Wurth, and Elissa Washuta went on record about his sexual harassment.

41. Neary, "'It Just Felt Very Wrong.'"

42. Alexie, "For Immediate Release."

43. L. B. Simpson, *Dancing on Our Turtle's Back,* 23.

44. Keene, "The Native Harvey Weinsteins."

45. I want to reiterate here that speaking out is not a choice every survivor can make.

46. To be clear about my own position, I no longer teach books by Alexie, nor will I, in light of the income that assigning such work produces. But I have the freedom to make such a decision. Given the cost of books and the complicated process of having texts approved and purchased by school boards, many high school teachers have more limited options.

47. The first novel with a queer Indigenous protagonist was Paula Gunn Allen's 1983 *The Woman Who Owned the Shadows.*

48. At this time the official appellation is the "Muscogee (Creek) Nation." Within national documents and some written venues, many citizens and tribal officials now employ the spelling: "Mvskoke." The term "Creek" is still heard most frequently in conversations/colloquial contexts and is employed throughout *Drowning in Fire,* though Womack also references "Muskogalki" and "Mvskokvalke," the Creek nation. Following contemporary usage, I use Mvskoke and Creek interchangeably in this analysis.

49. Womack, *Drowning in Fire,* 3. All subsequent citations in text.

50. The point of passing is for bodies to slip unnoticed into spaces marked as culturally outside their purview—mixed-background Native or Black folks, for example, moving into predominantly white venues to take part in the privileges of whiteness, which would be otherwise unavailable to them. Since Lucy's community is well aware of her time in jazz clubs, the question arises of for whom Lucy is supposedly passing. The implication seems to be that only non-Creek audiences are unaware of the band's subterfuge.

51. Rustin, "'Mary Lou Plays Like a Man!,'"445.

52. Rustin, 450.

53. Morgensen, "Cutting to the Roots," 48.

54. For discussions of Indian–Black histories and theories, see, among many others, Brooks, *Confounding the Color Line* and *Captives and Cousins;* Lethabo-King, *The Black Shoals;* Miles, *Ties That Bind* and *The House on Dia-*

mond Hill; Miles and Holland, *Crossing Waters, Crossing Worlds*; Porter, *The Black Seminoles*; and Snyder "Conquered Enemies."

55. Kleinman and Kleinman, "How Bodies Remember," 716–17.

56. Million, "Felt Theory," 58.

57. Recent research underscores the effectiveness of music for healing. In a special issue of *Music and Medicine,* the editors note that "survivors of trauma and children coming from families at-risk for abuse . . . link music to a down-regulation of the sympathetic nervous system involved in mobilization behaviors (e.g. fight/flight) and an up-regulation of a component of the parasympathetic nervous system" (Porges and Rosetti, "Music, Music Therapy, and Trauma," 117).

58. Danforth, "Our Bodies, Our Nations," 119.

59. Ellison, "Richard Wright's Blues," 264.

60. Million, *Therapeutic Nations,* 76.

61. Blackman and Venn, "Affect," 9.

62. Million, "Intense Dreaming," 314–15.

63. Desseilles et al., "Cognitive and Emotional Processes during Dreaming," 1001.

64. Desseilles et al., 1001.

65. Rasch and Born, "Reactivation and Consolidation of Memory during Sleep."

66. L. B. Simpson, *Dancing on Our Turtle's Back,* 34–35.

67. Henry, "Canonizing Craig Womack," 38.

68. Henry, 38.

69. Blackman and Venn, "Affect," 9.

70. Kleinman and Kleinman, "How Bodies Remember," 708.

71. Erdrich, *The Birchbark House,* 19–20. All subsequent citations in text.

72. Among the Ojibwe, "hunting and trapping, for example, were ideally the male domain. . . . Gathering wild plant foods and gardening, on the other hand, belonged to the female domain" (Buffalohead, "Farmers, Warriors, Traders," 238). Young women would be instructed "on the duties and responsibilities as Ojibwe women," including motherhood, beading, spinning, making "birch-bark rolls for wigwams," and were expected "to engage in food production and cooking, to attend to the orderliness of the household, to care for children and soothe them" (Denial, "Mother of All the Living," 449).

73. Latham, "'Manly Hearted Women,'" 138.

74. Erdrich, *The Porcupine Year,* 119.

75. Johnston, "Young Men of Good Will," 45.

76. For further discussion on Erdrich and female masculinity see Tatonetti, *The Queerness of Native American Literature,* 73–81.

4. Body as Shield and Shelter

1. Cited in Roy and Taylor, "'We Were Real Skookum Women,'" 104. Bouncing off this quote, which is part of a display in the Sechelt First Nation's tems swiya Museum, Roy and Taylor offer a nuanced reading of how labor and gender among the Shíshálh people subvert dominant expectations of industry, Indigeneity, and gender normativity.

2. P. Wilson, "Indigenous Documentary Media," 90.

3. Million, *Therapeutic Nations*, 62.

4. Million, 62.

5. Pamela Wilson explains that, historically, "Indigenous documentaries have most often served practical, generally collective, needs. These have included cultural knowledge preservation and documentation/archiving—for a culturally internal audience or to share with neighboring villages. Indigenous groups have frequently used visual and audio recording technologies to capture and freeze moments in time, which might then be replayed for later generations (in cases such as the archiving of rituals and oral traditions) or which can be shared externally to galvanize global political support in opposing settler states or corporations" ("Indigenous Documentary Media," 90).

6. Importantly, many men do such productive, community-centered work as well.

7. Zeig is a writer, director, and the founder of the New York City–based distribution company, Artistic License Films. As previously mentioned, she worked with producer Heather Rae as well as Vicky Westover.

8. With this work, Obomsawin's documentary speaks to Haudenosaunee scholar Jolene Rickard's contention that "understand[ing] Indigenous visual culture" necessitates "acknowledging the discourse around decolonization and the unique legal position Indigenous nations occupy in relation to settler colonial nations" ("Diversifying Sovereignty," 83).

9. The Kino-nda-niimi Collective, *The Winter We Danced*, 25.

10. Here and throughout the film, we see Obomsawin exemplify what Michele Raheja has called "visual sovereignty," which privileges "Native-centered articulations of self-representation and autonomy that engage the powerful ideology of mass media but do not rely solely on texts and contexts of Western jurisprudence" (*Reservation Reelism*, 197). Obomsawin works within a film genre with a long colonial history; however, here and throughout all her films she uses documentary as an Indigenous lens for Indigenous ends.

11. Soliz, "Every Step That I Take Becomes a Prayer."

12. Ellmann, *The Hunger Artists*, 14.

13. L. B. Simpson, "Fish Broth and Fasting," 155.

14. Conservatives used the accusation of fiscal misconduct to discredit

Chief Spence and shift the discourse to an attack of Indigenous leadership. Chelsea Vowel (Métis) offers a detailed corrective to the recurring right-wing claims that Chief Spence "squandered" some $90 million in government funds that were "given" to the band council. See Vowel, "Attawapiskat."

15. L. B. Simpson, *Dancing on Our Turtle's Back*, 14.

16. A. Simpson, "The State Is a Man."

17. L. B. Simpson, "Fish Broth and Fasting," 156.

18. A. Simpson, "The State Is a Man."

19. Blackman and Venn, "Affect," 9.

20. Filice, "The Journey of Nishiyuu."

21. McKegney, "Pain, Pleasure, Shame. Shame," 27.

22. McKegney, 27.

23. L. B. Simpson, *Dancing on Our Turtle's Back*, 14.

24. Massumi, *Parables for the Virtual*, 33.

25. Massumi, 35.

26. This claim is echoed at one of the Idle No More rallies Obomsawin highlights: "The circle has not stopped. It will continue and continue and continue and make sure that it does."

27. Wendy Miller maintains that Zeig "knew she had to make a movie about the Native American women before she even spoke to them. She was walking through Phoenix's Sky Harbor International Airport in 2006 when the bright yellow shirts in which they were all clad caught her eye. But it was the vibe they cast that drew her in." Zeig explains, "This was clearly a powerful group of women, and they stopped me in my tracks. The feeling I got being in the area where they were gathered was very powerful, and I got the message there was something there" (see Miller, "Native Eyes Film Festival"). Elsewhere, Zeig comments that "the atmosphere around them was palpable. It was like walking through a vibration" (see Leiby, "*Apache 8* Debuts Sunday").

28. Zeig, "Producer's Notes"; Leiby, "*Apache 8* Debuts Sunday."

29. In *Apache 8*, Bones notes that she joined the wildland firefighting crew at the suggestion of her sister, saying, "the summer of '74 I think it was." She became crew boss for Apache 6 in 1981 and also identifies that as the point at which the crew name changed to Apache 8.

30. See "A Living Thing" for more on Hinton.

31. Zeig, *Apache 8*. All subsequent citations are from the film.

32. Norrell, "Fort Apache Hotshots Battling Blazes."

33. C. Bennett, "Fort Apache Hotshots."

34. Notably, Obomsawin does likewise. Numerous aerial shots of water, caribou migration, and land are woven throughout *Trick or Treaty?* to serve a similar function.

35. Roy and Taylor, "'We Were Real Skookum Women,'" 105.

36. Mbembe, *On the Postcolony*, 2.

37. Jahnke et al., "The Prevalence and Health Impacts of Frequent Work Discrimination."

38. Jahnke et al.

39. Mbembe, *On the Postcolony*, 2.

40. Seigworth and Gregg, "An Inventory of Shimmers," 2.

41. Quintero, "Coming of Age the Apache Way," 262.

42. Quintero, 263.

43. "A Living Thing."

44. L. B. Simpson, *As We Have Always Done*, 4.

45. As with the absence of any overt reference to queerness in and of itself, there's also no reference to this Christian iconography. I attempted to contact Quintero and Zeig in the hopes of finding out more about their decisions in the film's construction but was unsuccessful.

46. L. B. Simpson, *As We Have Always Done*, 4.

47. Simpson, 75.

48. Simpson, 75.

49. Simpson, 75.

50. "Commissioned Corp of the U.S. Public Health Services," usphs.gov.

51. Million, *Therapeutic Nations*, 132.

5. HIV/AIDS Activism and the Indigenous Erotic

1. CDC, "Perspectives in Disease Prevention and Health Promotion," 261.

2. CDC, 262.

3. Keiser, "Strategies of Media Marketing," 625.

4. Carole laFavor did not capitalize the "L" in her last name on her book covers and in official PACHA documents, while her daughter, Theresa LaFavor, does. I follow their usage.

5. According to the organization's charter, PACHA provided "advice, information, and recommendations to the Secretary regarding programs and policies to promote effective prevention and cure of HIV disease and AIDS" (Secretary of Health and Human Services, *Charter: Presidential Advisory Council on HIV/AIDS*, 1). LaFavor commented that, as the only Indigenous person on the committee, hers was a "token" appointment.

6. Million, *Therapeutic Nations*, 61.

7. Million, 59.

8. Rendon, "Mystery Activist," 12.

9. Theresa LaFavor, telephone interview with the author, December 2,

2016. Theresa LaFavor received a doctorate in developmental psychopathology and clinical science. Her research focus is child clinical psychology.

10. Qtd. in Enke, "Locating Feminist Activism," 117–18.

11. Theresa laFavor, email to the author, May 24, 2017.

12. American Indian Law Resource Center, "Ending Violence against Native Women."

13. MacKinnon and Dworkin, *In Harm's Way*, 147. I recognize that not all pornography does violence.

14. MacKinnon and Dworkin, 148.

15. MacKinnon and Dworkin, 148.

16. Million, *Therapeutic Nations*, 23.

17. Massumi, *Politics of Affect*, 43.

18. Million, *Therapeutic Nations*, 59.

19. In several interviews laFavor noted that she initially had ARC (AIDS-related complex), not AIDS. She speaks in multiple interviews about using that distinction to help her daughter cope with her diagnosis. LaFavor lived for twenty-five years after her diagnosis and did not take HIV/AIDS drug cocktails or ultimately die of AIDS-related causes. As I'll discuss, laFavor attributed her longevity to Indigenous healing practices.

20. Denny, "Carole LaFavor," 4.

21. Associated Press, "Woman Gives AIDS A Face."

22. *Carole laFavor Talking on AIDS.*

23. Irene Vernon, telephone interview with the author, December 30, 2015.

24. Associated Press, "Woman Gives AIDS a Face."

25. Million, "Felt Theory," 31.

26. Jolivette, *Indian Blood*, 5, 32.

27. CDC, "Perspectives in Disease Prevention and Health Promotion."

28. Bennett and Sharpe, "Medicine."

29. Bennett and Sharpe.

30. *Carole laFavor Talking on AIDS.*

31. Million, *Therapeutic Nations*, 59.

32. Million, 59.

33. Associated Press, "Woman Gives AIDS a Face."

34. Day continues to undertake important social justice work to this day as discussed later in this chapter.

35. Sharon Day, telephone interview with the author, January 5, 2016. Based on laFavor's comments in *Her Giveaway* (1987), this intervention occurred in early 1984. LaFavor was in treatment for addiction by February of that year.

36. Jolivette, *Indian Blood*, 5.

37. *Carole laFavor Talking on AIDS.*

38. Burhansstipanov et al., "Native Women Living beyond HIV/AIDS Infection," 337.

39. Day interview.

40. Jolivette, *Indian Blood.*

41. Vernon, "AIDS," 244.

42. For more on queer Indigenous organizing in Minneapolis, see MacDonald, "Two-Spirit Identity."

43. From 1989 to 1995 Smith served as program coordinator for the National Indian AIDS Media Consortium. Smith's films "focused on health, wellness, history and Native identity as it is linked to the sense of place or original Indigenous lands. She produced work for the Minnesota American Indian AIDS Taskforce and National Indian AIDS Media Consortium" (Machiorlatti, "Indigenous Women in Film and Video," 13).

44. Estrada, "Ojibwe Lesbian Visual AIDS," 389.

45. See Estrada (394–98) for a nuanced reading of laFavor's theological sovereignty in *Her Giveaway.*

46. Machiorlatti, "Video as Community Ally," 324.

47. I was unable to find an extant version of this videocassette.

48. L. B. Simpson, *As We Have Always Done,* 41.

49. Million, "There Is a River in Me," 31–32.

50. "AIDS Changes Woman's View of Life," 10.

51. Estrada, "Ojibwe Lesbian Visual AIDS," 390. NB: I love this story so much.

52. Jolivette, *Indian Blood,* 32.

53. Day interview.

54. Day interview.

55. In her 1990 presentation at the University of Minnesota Duluth, laFavor pinpoints this progression of her illness and her change of diagnosis from ARC to AIDS as occurring in November 1988: "I felt I needed the healing ceremony. If I was gonna die and go on to the spirit world, I needed help making that transition. And if I was gonna stay alive, clearly I needed help. So I had the healing ceremony. . . . By the end of the week it was clear to me that I wasn't going to die. There was something more for me yet to do. And one of the things that it became clear that I was yet to do was to talk to people about AIDS, especially Indian people and women. I've spent a lot of my effort talking to Indian people and women about the illness because they're closest to my heart" (*Carole laFavor Talking on AIDS*).

56. Day interview.

57. In *Carole laFavor Talking on AIDS,* laFavor explains: "I'm not using AZT and I decided not to use it . . . from my perspective, it's like putting a

major poison into my body in the hopes that's going to make me feel better. And spiritually, I couldn't do it. So that's why I chose Native healing. And you know what they say, when it works, don't fix it." Day noted that her brother, who is still living with HIV more than twenty-five years after his diagnosis, also decided against taking AZT.

58. Jolivette, *Indian Blood*, 5.

59. Burhansstipanov et al., "Native Women Living beyond HIV/AIDS Infection," 339. Subsequent citations in text.

60. L. B. Simpson, *As We Have Always Done*, 35.

61. Jolivette, *Indian Blood*, 5.

62. Warrior, "Your Skin Is the Map," 350.

63. Million, *Therapeutic Nations*, 57.

64. Danforth, "Our Bodies, Our Nations," 119.

65. A. Wilson and Laing, "Queering Indigenous Education," 135.

66. Rendon, "Mystery Activist," 12.

67. Senier, "Rehabilitation Reservations." While Senier finds productive possibilities in laFavor's novels, she also notes that such "rehabilitation comes with an evident cost, insofar as the books ironically revert to distinctions among the 'good' disabled and the bad. The villain of *Evil Dead Center* is a child pornographer who is crippled (not 'cripped') by polio."

68. Cox, *Political Arrays*, 205.

69. Lorde, *Sister Outsider*, 53, 55.

70. Lorde, 59, 56.

71. See Brant, *Writing as Witness*; Akiwenzie-Damm, "Erotica, Indigenous Style"; Driskill, "Stolen from Our Bodies"; Miranda, "Dildos, Hummingbirds, and Driving Her Crazy" and *The Zen of La Llorona*; Warrior, "Your Skin Is the Map"; Rifkin, *The Erotics of Sovereignty*.

72. Akiwenzie-Damm, "Erotica, Indigenous Style," 143.

73. Miranda, *The Zen of La Llorona*, 4.

74. Driskill, "Stolen from Our Bodies," 52.

75. Warrior, "Your Skin Is the Map," 341.

76. Warrior, 343.

77. LaFavor, *Along the Journey River*, 9. All subsequent references in text as *Along*.

78. Brant, *Writing as Witness*, 8.

79. Brant, 17.

80. Akiwenzie-Damm, "Erotica, Indigenous Style," 144.

81. Driskill, "Stolen from Our Bodies," 51.

82. Akiwenzie-Damm, "Erotica, Indigenous Style," 143.

83. Driskill, "Stolen from Our Bodies," 54.

84. Pruden, "Celebrating Two Spirit."

85. Theresa LaFavor, telephone interview.

86. Gilley, *Becoming Two-Spirit*, 10.

87. Davis, "More than Just 'Gay' Indians," 76.

88. Jolivette, *Indian Blood*, 5.

89. LaFavor, *Evil Dead Center*, 30. All subsequent references in text as *Evil*.

90. Million, "Intense Dreaming," 314–15.

91. *Reclaiming Power and Place.*

92. *Reclaiming Power and Place*, 55.

93. Cox, *Political Arrays*, 197.

94. Rendon, "Mystery Activist," 12. In her conversation with Rendon, laFavor is likely referring to her work in the Native American Women's Healthy Lifestyles project, which was an initiative of the Minnesota American Indian AIDS Task Force in the mid-1990s. In the program, laFavor and Yako Myers (Mohawk/Ojibwe) worked with a group of Native women at the Shakopee women's prison. For more, see Helgeland, "Healthy Talking Circle."

95. Million, *Therapeutic Nations*, 46.

96. Lorde, *Sister Outsider*, 54.

97. MacKinnon and Dworkin, *In Harm's Way*, 148.

98. Momaday, *House Made of Dawn*. See Chadwick Allen's *Blood Narrative* for a nuanced analysis of this trope.

99. Warrior, "Your Skin Is the Map," 350.

100. Warrior, 348.

101. Brant, *Writing as Witness*, 17.

102. Jolivette, *Indian Blood*, 29.

6. An Erotics of Responsibility

1. See Tatonetti, *The Queerness of Native American Literature* and "Tales of Burning Love."

2. Halberstam, *The Queer Art of Failure*, 88.

3. Halberstam, 88.

4. Driskill, *Asegi Stories*, 85.

5. Driskill, 85.

6. Morgensen, "Cutting to the Roots," 43.

7. See, for example, Warren, *Gendercide*; Kristof and WuDunn, *Half the Sky*; and Gerhardt, *The Cross and Gendercide* among many other books on the subject.

8. Warren, *Gendercide*, 22.

9. Miranda, "Extermination of the *Joyas*," 259.

10. McKegney, *Masculindians,* 4; Klopotek, "'I Guess Your Warrior Look Doesn't Work Every Time,'" 251.

11. Miranda, *Bad Indians,* 32.

12. Cuthand's artistic talent runs in the family, as their mother, Ruth Cuthand, is a prominent artist who likewise critiques settler politics and draws attention to the activism and histories of Aboriginal people in Canada.

13. Nixon, "'I Wonder Where They Went,'" 50.

14. Film critic Michelle La Flamme situates Cuthand, who is a member of Canada's Indigenous Media Arts Group (IMAG), as part of "a new First Nations cinema in British Columbia, with Native women at the forefront, [that] has begun to unsettle the West" ("Unsettle the West," 404). La Flamme contends that IMAG "challenges the temporality of Western cinema's geographical and historical constructs by placing the margins at the centre" and that these Indigenous artists reshape "the notion of a frontier by supporting the creation of films and videos that have the ability ... to express [the] unconquered territories of First Nation peoples' imaginative spaces" (404–5).

15. McKegney, *Masculindians,* 2; emphasis added.

16. Tengan, *Native Men Remade,* 16; emphasis added.

17. Halberstam, *Female Masculinity,* 1.

18. Halberstam, 15.

19. My reading of the affective circuit relies on a Deleuzian sense of becoming, which recognizes, and in fact requires, a sense of multiplicity. According to Deleuze and Guattari, such evolving multiplicities have "neither subject nor object, only determinations, magnitudes, and dimensions that cannot increase in number without the multiplicity changing in nature. . . . [Thus] the dimensions of a multiplicity . . . necessarily [change] in nature as it expands its connections" (*A Thousand Plateaus,* 8). Feeling, seeing, and/or knowing are ongoing, interrelated processes rather than discrete, singular events.

20. Muñoz, *Cruising Utopia.*

21. Knoblauch, "Bodies of Knowledge," 52.

22. Knoblauch, 51.

23. Hardt, Foreword, ix–xiii; emphasis added.

24. Ahmed, *The Cultural Politics of Emotion,* 145.

25. Knoblauch, "Bodies of Knowledge," 56.

26. Hardt, Foreword, xiii; emphasis added.

27. Jay Prosser engages these narrative expectations in *Second Skins,* contending that the medical community constructed the first expectations for and readings of trans narratives: "Although transsexuality concerns the deliberate transformation of the material body," he comments, "the diagnosis required for this transformation must instead derive from the patient's

narrative: narrativization as a transsexual necessarily precedes one's diagnosis as a transsexual; autobiography is transsexuality's proffered symptom" (103–4).

28. Knoblauch, "Bodies of Knowledge," 52.

29. Knoblauch, 62; emphasis added.

30. Knoblauch, 62.

31. In an influential essay that circulated for years as a conference paper before being printed in *Two-Spirit People*, Medicine explains: "Among the Lakota (Teton Sioux) there is evidence that other facets of action were bounded within the *winkte* gloss—ritualist, artist, specialist in women's craft production, herbalist, seer, namer of children, rejector of the rigorous warrior role, 'mama's boy,' . . . and the designation [of male homosexual] commonly stated in anthropology books" ("Changing Native American Roles," 150).

32. Knoblauch, "Bodies of Knowledge," 52.

33. McKegney, "Into the Full Grace," 4–5; emphasis added.

34. Whitehead, "Why I'm Withdrawing."

35. Whitehead.

36. See Tatonetti, *The Queerness of Native American Literature*. The Introduction and chapter 1 chart a history of queer Indigenous literatures and theories in what are currently the United States and Canada.

37. For more on the term's etymology see de Vries, "Berdache (Two-Spirit)." Morgensen notes that "this Orientalist term arose first to condemn Middle Eastern and Muslim men as racial enemies of Christian civilization, by linking them to the creation of berdache (in translation) as 'kept boys' or 'male slaves' whose sex was said to have been altered by immoral male desire" (*Spaces between Us*, 36).

38. Miranda, "Extermination of the *Joyas*," 258.

39. Hokowhitu, "Taxonomies of Indigeneity," 84.

40. Spelling of *náadleehí* varies. Here, I follow spelling used by the Navajo Nation Human Rights Commission.

41. For further discussion of *náadleehí* see Thomas, "Navajo Cultural Constructions of Gender and Sexuality." There are Two-Spirit/queer Diné folks who claim and live within these categories today, hence my use of present tense—queer Indigenous people are not artifacts of the past. However, as I discuss later in this chapter, it would be disingenuous not to also acknowledge that there are Diné people who reject the current and/or historical existence of such identity categories or define them narrowly. See Denetdale, "Carving Navajo National Boundaries"; and Navajo Nation Human Rights Commission [hereafter NNHRC], *The Status of Navajo Women and Gender Violence* for more.

42. Thomas qtd. in Lang, "Native American Men-Women," 311.

43. Whitehead, "Why I'm Withdrawing."

44. Lang, "Native American Men-Women," 309.

45. Whitehead, *Jonny Appleseed*, 7. All subsequent citations in text.

46. "NDN" is a term Indigenous peoples in Canada and the United States sometimes use as a shorthand for "Indian."

47. Hardt, Foreword, ix–xiii.

48. Million, *Therapeutic Nations*, 56.

49. Million, "Felt Theory," 54.

50. Innes and Anderson, Introduction, 11.

51. Innes and Anderson, 4.

52. McKegney, "Into the Full Grace," 8.

53. Whitehead, "Why I'm Withdrawing."

54. Ogg, "You Always Come First with Me."

55. Million, "Intense Dreaming," 315.

56. Brant, *Writing as Witness*, 17.

57. Danforth, "Our Bodies, Our Nations," 121.

58. Million, "Felt Theory," 55.

59. I gesture to Muñoz's theory of queer utopias here.

60. I move between Diné and Navajo in this section and the book as a whole, following the lead of Diné scholars in the field.

61. Estrada, "Ojibwe Lesbian Visual AIDS," 400.

62. C. House, "Blessed by the Holy People," 324. All subsequent citations in text.

63. Y. Begay, "Historic and Demographic Changes," 105.

64. While Miranda deploys the term *gendercide* in relation to Spanish attacks on California Indian ways of knowing and being, the settler-colonial legacies at work in such assaults on multiple gender traditions and non-cis people in Dinétah is coeval.

65. C. House, "Navajo Warrior Women," 225.

66. Werito, "Understanding Hózhó," 25. Diné scholar Lloyd Lee too shares such a story of his interactions with his father: "I thought about my father's teachings and conduct. Initially I did not dwell upon cultural knowledges of Diné masculinities, but after further reflection, I realized my father taught me much of what it means to be a Diné man" (*Diné Masculinities*, 2).

67. While it was previously mentioned, I want to emphasize that while House's father married a Navajo woman and lived and worked on Navajo lands, he was Oneida. House's emphasis on Diné masculinity is tied to stories of his entire family—his father and mother as well as other relatives. He notes, for example, "I liked planting corn seeds [with] my uncle, Francis Taliman," and also that "Uncle Guy, Herbert Lee (mother's half-brother), possessed excellent carpentry skills. He also sang beautiful Diné songs, brought

my family local fruits and vegetables, and showed me roping skills" ("Blessed by the Holy People," 327).

68. Lee, *Diné Masculinities*, 24.

69. Lee, 33.

70. He also comments: "Through my mother, her mother, and extension of mothers and grandmothers, our family has inherited Oak Springs and Pine Springs farming, grazing areas, and wildlife habitats" ("Blessed by the Holy People," 332).

71. M. K. Yazzie, "Narrating Ordinary Power," 96.

72. Million, "Felt Theory," 54.

73. Y. Begay, "Historic and Demographic Changes," 122–23.

74. Denetdale, "The Value of Oral History," 76.

75. On a related note, Lee comments that in Diné culture, "gender difference is not based on a gender order or on power relations between groups, but rather by name, relationships, and life cycle, which connects . . . men, women, relatives, and family" (*Diné Masculinities*, 9).

76. Knoblauch, "Bodies of Knowledge," 52.

77. C. House, "Kid," 180–81.

78. Or at least in occupations House depicts as masculine.

79. Lang, "Native American Men-Women," 313.

80. Tatonetti, *The Queerness of Native American Literature*, 152.

81. C. House, "Sweet Grass," 126.

82. M. K. Yazzie, "Narrating Ordinary Power," 85.

83. "An Opening Preface Statement from Commissioner Chairman Steven A. Darden," NNHRC, *The Status of Navajo Women and Gender Violence*.

84. "An Opening Preface Statement."

85. "An Opening Preface Statement." Diné anthropologist Wesley Thomas explains how language relates to sex, gender, and occupation: "Navajo sex-based gender categories are reflected in the language uses to designate people at various stages of their life-cycles. . . . Using the criteria of sex, terms are assigned to females and males according to age. There are also words used for females and males when sex is either irrelevant or unknown. The traditional social gender system, although based initially on biological sex, divides people into categories based on several criteria: sex-linked occupation, behavior and roles" ("Navajo Cultural Constructions," 157).

86. "An Opening Preface Statement."

87. Vice Chair Valerie Kelly, for instance, commented: "The story of how the true náadleehíí originated and how they reunited the Navajo men and women was very interesting. I've heard different versions before but not as

detailed as how it was introduced to us by the medicine people. This brought the issue of same sex marriage to our attention and why, according to the stories told by the medicine people, it cannot be performed in tradition *[sic]* marriage ceremonies" ("Preface Statement from Vice-Chairwoman Valerie Kelly," NNHRC, *The Status of Navajo Women and Gender Violence*).

88. NNHRC, *The Status of Navajo Women and Gender Violence*, 15.

89. House also briefly references these meetings in "Blessed by the Holy People" when detailing his work with and for nádleehi and LGBTIQ/Two-Spirit populations: "I also spoke, per invitation, at the Navajo Nation Human Rights Commission's symposium 'The Status of Navajo Women, Gender Violence, and the Rights of Indigenous People,' but I am not sure if my voice and other voices made an impact" (335).

90. The introduction to the commission's report notes Denetdale's centrality to the inception of the hearings and subsequent report: "In 2012, Commissioner Jennifer Denetdale, associate professor at the University of New Mexico, brought a proposal to the Commission that they undertake an investigation of the status of Navajo women and Navajo Lesbian, Gay, Bi-sexual, Transgender, Queer, and Intersex (LGBTQI) community and violence against them on the Navajo Nation and border towns. Under the direction of then chair Duane 'Chili' Yazzie, the Commission held an initial meeting. . . . The day-long meeting revealed that Navajo women experience violence in the form of domestic violence, assaults, rape, and gender inequalities disproportionately in comparison to other citizens of the Navajo Nation and within the United States ('U.S.'). Further, the meeting revealed that the Navajo LGBTQI community experiences violence that is invisible and unacknowledged by the larger society. Based upon the testimony provided during this meeting, the Commission decided to investigate further into the status of violence against Navajo women and Navajo LGBTQI" (NNHRC, *The Status of Navajo Women and Gender Violence*, 1).

91. Denetdale, "Carving Navajo National Boundaries," 293.

92. Denetdale, 294.

93. Halberstam, *Female Masculinity*, 29.

94. Anderson, Innes, and Swift, "Indigenous Masculinities," 271.

95. Lee, *Diné Masculinities*, 114.

Coda

1. A. Wilson and Laing, "Queering Indigenous Education," 135.

2. L. B. Simpson, *As We Have Always Done*, 35.

3. "Jolene Nenibah Yazzie."

4. Personal conversation, February 15, 2021. See also J. N. Yazzie, "Native Feminisms Artist Interview"; and "Native Feminisms Virtual Tour."

5. Nixon, "#MeToo and the Secrets Indigenous Women Keep."

6. For more on this concept see Belcourt and Nixon, "What Do We Mean by Queer Indigenous Ethics?"

7. Nixon, "#MeToo and the Secrets Indigenous Women Keep."

8. Nixon.

BIBLIOGRAPHY

Ahmed, Sara. *The Cultural Politics of Emotion.* New York: Routledge, 2004.

"AIDS Changes Woman's View of Life." *Sho-ban News,* May 5, 1988, 10.

Akiwenzie-Damm, Kateri. "Erotica, Indigenous Style." In *(Ad)dressing Our Words: Aboriginal Perspectives on Aboriginal Literatures,* edited by Armand Ruffo, 143–51. Penticton, B.C.: Theytus, 2001.

Albers, Patricia C. "Sioux Women in Transition: A Study of Their Changing Status in Domestic and Capitalist Sectors of Production." In *The Hidden Half: Studies of Plains Indian Women,* edited by Patricia Albers and Beatrice Medicine, 123–40. Washington, D.C.: University Press of America, 1983.

Alexie, Sherman. "For Immediate Release." FallsApart Productions LLC. February 28, 2018. nativenewsonline.net.

———. *Reservation Blues.* New York: Warner, 1995.

Allen, Chadwick. *Blood Narrative: Indigenous Identity in American Indian and Maori Literary and Activists Texts.* Durham: Duke University Press, 2002.

———. *Trans-Indigenous.* Minneapolis: University of Minnesota Press, 2012.

Allen, Paula Gunn. *The Sacred Hoop: Recovering the Feminine in American Indian Traditions.* Boston: Beacon, 1986.

———. "The Warriors" (section introduction). In *Spider Woman's Granddaughters: Traditional and Contemporary Writing by Native American Women,* edited by Allen, 29–30. New York: Fawcett, 1989.

———. *The Woman Who Owned the Shadows.* San Francisco: Aunt Lute, 1983.

American Indian Law Resource Center. "Ending Violence against Native Women." indianlaw.org.

American Indians against HIV/AIDS Leadership Project: Presentation by Carole laFavor. Videocassette. University of North Dakota Department of Family Medicine, 1991.

Anderson, Kim. *A Recognition of Being: Reconstructing Native Womanhood.* Toronto: Sumach Press, 2000.

Anderson, Kim, Robert Alexander Innes, and John Swift. "Indigenous Masculinities: Carrying the Bones of Our Ancestors." In *Canadian Men and Masculinities: Historical and Contemporary Perspectives,* edited by Christopher J. Greig and Wayne J. Martino, 266–84. Toronto: Canadian Scholars' Press, 2012.

Anderson, Kim, John Swift, and Robert Alexander Innes. "'To Arrive Speaking': Voices from the Bidewewidan Indigenous Masculinities Project." In *Indigenous Men and Masculinities: Legacies, Identities, Regeneration,* edited by Robert Alexander Innes and Kim Anderson, 283–307. Winnipeg: University of Manitoba Press, 2015.

Anderson-Minshall, Jacob. "Changing Sex, Changing Mind." *Women's Review of Books* 24, no. 4 (2007).

Andrews, Scott. "A New Road and a Dead End in Sherman Alexie's *Reservation Blues.*" *Arizona Quarterly: A Journal of American Literature, Culture, and Theory* 63, no. 2 (2007): 137–52.

Apache 8 Viewer Discussion Guide. Developed by Jamie Lee. Lincoln, Neb.: Vision Maker Media. Native American Public Telecommunications, 2011. visionmakermedia.org.

Associated Press. "Woman Gives AIDS a Face." *Wilmington Morning Star,* August 15, 1988, 6D.

Ball, Eve, and James Kaywaykla. *In the Days of Victorio: Recollections of a Warm Springs Apache.* Tucson: University of Arizona Press, 1970.

Ball, Eve, and Lynda Sánchez. "Legendary Apache Women." *Frontier Times,* October–November 1980, 8–12.

Begay, Sararesa. "Piestewa Renamed 'Lady Warrior.'" *Navajo Times,* April 10, 2003, A1.

Begay, Yolynda. "Historic and Demographic Changes That Impact the Future of the Diné and the Development of Community-Based Policy." In *Diné Perspectives: Revitalizing and Reclaiming Navajo Thought,* edited by Lloyd L. Lee, 105–28. Tucson: University of Arizona Press, 2014.

Belcourt, Billy-Ray. "Can the Other of Native Studies Speak?" *Decolonization: Indigeneity, Education & Society,* February 1, 2016. decolonization.wordpress.com.

———. "Meditations on Reserve Life, Biosociality, and the Taste of Non-sovereignty." *Settler Colonial Studies* 8 (2018): 1–15.

———. "A Poltergeist Manifesto." *Feral Feminisms: An Open Access Feminist Online Journal* 6 (2016): 22–32.

Belcourt, Billy-Ray, and Lindsay Nixon. "What Do We Mean by Queer Indigenous Ethics?" *Canadian Art,* May 23, 2018. canadianart.ca.

Bender, Margaret. "Glimpses of Local Masculinities: Learning from Interviews with Kiowa, Comanche, Apache, and Chickasaw Men." *Southern Anthropologist* 31, no. 1/2 (2005): 1–17.

Bennett, Amanda, and Anita Sharpe. "Medicine: AIDS Fight Is Skewed by Federal Campaign Exaggerating Risks." *Wall Street Journal,* May 1, 1996. pulitzer.org.

Bennett, Cosay. "Fort Apache Hotshots: Home of the Elite Firefighting Crew." *Fort Apache Scout,* August 23, 2002, 1.

Berlant, Lauren. "Nearly Utopian, Nearly Normal: Post-Fordist Affect in *La Promesse* and *Rosetta.*" *Public Culture* 19, no. 2 (2007): 273–301.

Bernardin, Susan K. "On the Meeting Grounds of Sentiment: S. Alice Callahan's *Wynema: A Child of the Forest.*" *ATQ: The American Transcendental Quarterly* 15, no. 3 (2001): 209–24.

Bird, Gloria. "The Exaggeration of Despair in Sherman Alexie's *Reservation Blues.*" *Wicazo Sa Review* 11, no. 2 (1995): 47–52.

Blackman, Lisa, and Couze Venn. "Affect." *Body & Society* 16, no. 1 (2010): 7–28.

Bonnin, Gertrude Simmons. *Oklahoma's Poor Rich Indians: An Orgy of Graft and Exploitation of the Five Civilized Tribes—Legalized Robbery.* Philadelphia: Office of the Indian Rights Association, 1924.

Brant, Beth, ed. *A Gathering of Spirit: A Collection by North American Indian Women.* 1984. Reprint, New York: Firebrand Books, 1988.

———. *Mohawk Trail.* Ithaca, N.Y.: Firebrand Books, 1985.

———. *Writing as Witness: Essay and Talk.* Toronto: Women's Press, 1994.

Bronson, Ruth Muskrat. *Indians Are People, Too.* New York: Friendship Press, 1944.

Brooks, James F. *Captives and Cousins: Slavery, Kinship, and Community in the Southwest Borderlands.* Chapel Hill: University of North Carolina Press, 2002.

———, ed. *Confounding the Color Line: The Indian-Black Experience in North America.* Lincoln: University of Nebraska Press, 2002.

Buffalohead, Priscilla K. "Farmers, Warriors, Traders: A Fresh Look at Ojibway Women." *Minnesota History* 48, no. 6 (1983): 236–44.

Burhansstipanov, Linda, Carole laFavor, Shirley Hoskins, Gloria Bellymule, and Ron Rowell. "Native Women Living beyond HIV/AIDS Infection." In *The Gender Politics of HIV/AIDS in Women: Perspectives on the Pandemic in the United States,* edited by Nancy Goldstein and Jennifer L. Manlowe, 337–56. New York: New York University Press, 1997.

Butler, Judith. *Bodies That Matter: On the Discursive Limits of Sex.* New York: Routledge, 1993.

Byrd, Jodi A. *The Transit of Empire: Indigenous Critiques of Colonialism*. Minneapolis: University of Minnesota Press, 2011.

Callahan, S. Alice. *Wynema: A Child of the Forest*. Edited by A. Lavonne Brown Ruoff. 1891. Lincoln: University of Nebraska Press, 1997.

Carole laFavor Talking on AIDS. Videocassette. Duluth, Minn.: Northcountry Women's Coffeehouse, 1990. Kathryn A. Martin Archives and Special Collections, University of Minnesota Duluth.

Carroll, Al. *Medicine Bags and Dog Tags: American Indian Veterans from Colonial Times to the Second Iraq War*. Edited by William A. Starna. Lincoln: University of Nebraska Press, 2008.

CDC. "Perspectives in Disease Prevention and Health Promotion." *Morbidity and Mortality Weekly Report* 37, no. 17 (1988): 261–68.

Child, Brenda J. "When Art Is Medicine." *New York Times,* May 28, 2020. nytimes.com.

Coulthard, Glen Sean. *Red Skins, White Masks: Rejecting the Colonial Politics of Recognition*. Minneapolis: University of Minnesota Press, 2014.

Cox, James H. *The Political Arrays of American Indian Literary History*. Minneapolis: University of Minnesota Press, 2019.

Csordas, Thomas J. "Ritual Healing and the Politics of Identity in Contemporary Navajo Society." *American Ethnologist* 26, no. 1 (1999): 3–23.

Cummings, Ronald. "Jamaican Female Masculinities: Nanny of the Maroons and the Genealogy of the Man-Royal." *Journal of West Indian Literature* 21, nos. 1–2 (2012): 129–54.

Cuthand, Thirza, dir. *Boi Oh Boi*. Saskatchewan: A Fit of Pique Production, 2012.

———, dir. *Helpless Maiden Makes an "I" Statement*. 2000.

———, dir. *Thirza Cuthand through the Looking Glass*. 1999.

———. "Welcome! Tawaw!" *Thirza Cuthand: Filmmaker, Performance Artist, General Troublemaker*. thirzacuthand.com.

Danforth, Jessica. "Our Bodies, Our Nations: A Conversation with Jessica Danforth." In *Masculindians: Conversations about Indigenous Manhood,* edited by Sam McKegney, 118–24. East Lansing: Michigan State University Press, 2014.

Davis, Jenny L. "More than Just 'Gay' Indians: Intersecting Articulations of Two-Spirit Gender, Sexuality, and Indigenousness." In *Queer Excursions: Retheorizing Binaries in Language, Gender, and Sexuality,* edited by Lal Zimman, Jenny L. Davis, and Joshua Raclaw, 72–80. Oxford: Oxford University Press, 2014.

Deleuze, Gilles, and Félix Guattari. *A Thousand Plateaus: Capitalism and Schizophrenia*. Translated by Brian Massumi. Minneapolis: University of Minnesota Press, 1988.

Deloria, Ella Cara. *Waterlily*. Lincoln: University of Nebraska Press, 1988.

Deloria, Phillip. J. *Indians in Unexpected Places*. Lawrence: University Press of Kansas, 2004.

Denetdale, Jennifer. "Carving Navajo National Boundaries: Patriotism, Tradition, and the Diné Marriage Act of 2005." *American Quarterly* 60, no. 2 (2008): 289–94.

———. "The Value of Oral History and the Path to Diné/Navajo Sovereignty." In *Diné Perspectives: Revitalizing and Reclaiming Navajo Thought*, edited by Lloyd L. Lee, 68–82. Tucson: University of Arizona Press, 2014.

Denial, Catherine J. "'Mother of All the Living': Motherhood, Religion, and Political Culture at the Ojibwe Village of Fond du Lac, 1835–1839." *Early American Studies* 17, no. 4 (2019): 443–73.

Denig, Edwin Thompson. *Indian Tribes of the Upper Midwest*. Circa 1854. Edited with notes and biographical sketch by J. N. B. Hewitt. Project Gutenberg eBook, 2015.

———. *Of the Crow Nation*. Smithsonian Institution Bureau of American Ethnology Bulletin, vol. 151, no. 33. Edited by John C. Ewers. Washington, D.C.: Government Printing Office, 1953.

Denny, Ruby. "Carole LaFavor: An American Indian Woman Talks about Life." *Seminole Tribune*, April 25, 1990, 4.

Desseilles, Martin, Thien Thanh Dang-Vu, Virginie Sterpenich, and Sophie Schwartz. "Cognitive and Emotional Processes during Dreaming: A Neuroimaging View." *Consciousness and Cognition* 20, no. 4 (2011): 998–1008.

de Vries, Kylan Mattias. "Berdache (Two-Spirit)." In *Encyclopedia of Gender and Society*, edited by Jodi O'Brien, 64. Los Angeles: Sage, 2015.

Dias, Brian G., and Kerry J. Ressler. "Parental Olfactory Experience Influences Behavior and Neural Structure in Subsequent Generations." *Nature Neuroscience* 17, no. 1 (2014): 89–96.

Dillon, Grace L. "Introduction: Imagining Indigenous Futurisms." In *Walking the Clouds: An Anthology of Indigenous Science Fiction*, edited by Grace Dillon, 1–14. Tucson: University of Arizona Press, 2012.

Driskill, Qwo-Li. *Asegi Stories: Cherokee Queer and Two-Spirit Memory*. Tucson: University of Arizona Press, 2016.

———. "Stolen from Our Bodies: First Nations Two-Spirits/Queers and the Journey to a Sovereign Erotic." *Studies in American Indian Literatures* 16, no. 2 (2004): 50–64.

Du Bois, W. E. B. *The Souls of Black Folk*. 1903. New York: Penguin Books, 2018.

Eastman, Charles Alexander. "Rain-in-the-Face: The Story of a Sioux Warrior." *Outlook,* October 27, 1906, 507–12.

Ellison, Ralph. "Richard Wright's Blues." *Antioch Review* 57, no. 3 (1999): 263–76. Originally published in *Antioch Review* 5, no. 2 (1945): 198–211.

Ellmann, Maud. *The Hunger Artists: Starving, Writing, and Imprisonment.* Cambridge, Mass.: Harvard University Press, 1993.

Enke, A. "Locating Feminist Activism: Women's Movement and Public Geographies, Minneapolis–St. Paul, 1968–1980." PhD diss., University of Minnesota, 1999.

Erdrich, Louise. *The Beet Queen.* New York: Bantam, 1986.

———. *The Birchbark House.* New York: Hyperion, 1999.

———. *The Porcupine Year.* New York: Harper Collins, 2008.

Estrada, Gabriel. "Ojibwe Lesbian Visual AIDS: On the Red Road with Carole laFavor, *Her Giveaway,* and Native LGBTQ2 Film History." *Journal of Lesbian Studies* 20, nos. 3–4 (2016): 388–407.

Fees, Paul. "Wild West Shows: Buffalo Bill's Wild West." *Buffalo Bill's Center of the West,* February 19, 2015. centerofthewest.org.

Filice, Michelle. "The Journey of Nishiyuu (The Journey of the People)." *Canadian Encyclopedia,* December 2, 2015. thecanadianencyclopedia.ca.

Fisher, Dexter. "Zitkala-Ša: The Evolution of a Writer." In *American Indian Stories,* by Zitkala-Ša, v–xx. Lincoln: University of Nebraska Press, 1985. Rpt. of "Zitkala-Ša: The Evolution of a Writer." *American Indian Quarterly* 5, no. 3 (1979): 229–38.

Ford, Douglas. "Sherman Alexie's Indigenous Blues." *MELUS* 27, no. 3 (2002): 197–215.

Gallagher, James. "Memories Pass between Generations." *BBC News,* December 1, 2013. bbc.com.

Gamsen, Joshua. "Messages of Exclusion: Gender, Movements, and Symbolic Boundaries." *Gender & Society* 11, no. 2 (1997): 178–99.

Gardiner, Judith Kegan. "Female Masculinity and Phallic Women—Unruly Concepts." *Feminist Studies* 38, no. 3 (2012): 597–624.

Gerhardt, Elizabeth. *The Cross and Gendercide: A Theological Response to Global Violence against Women and Girls.* Downers Grove, Ill.: IVP Academic, 2014.

Gilley, Brian Joseph. *Becoming Two-Spirit: Gay Identity and Social Acceptance in Indian Country.* Lincoln: University of Nebraska Press, 2006.

Godfrey, Audrey M. "The Other Magpie." In *Native American Women: A Biographical Dictionary,* edited by Gretchen M. Bataille and Laurie Lisa, 312–13. New York: Routledge, 2001.

Gopinath, Gayatri. *Impossible Desires: Queer Diasporas and South Asian Public Cultures.* Durham: Duke University Press, 2005.

Gravier, J. *Relation ou Journal du voyage du Pere Gravier de la Compagnie de Jesus en 1700.* Reprinted in and edited by R. G. Thwaites, *The Jesuit Relations and Allied Documents,* 65:100–179. New York: Pageant Book Company, 1959.

Gray, Richard. "Phobias May Be Memories Passed Down in the Genes from Ancestors." *The Telegraph,* December 1, 2013. telegraph.co.uk.

Grinnell, George Bird. *The Cheyenne Indians: Their History and Ways of Life.* New Haven: Yale University Press, 1923.

———. *The Fighting Cheyennes.* New York: Scribner, 1915.

Grumet, Robert S. "Sunksquaws, Shamans, and Tradeswomen: Middle Atlantic Coastal Algonkian Women during the 17th and 18th Centuries." In *Women and Colonization: Anthropological Perspectives,* edited by Mona Etienne and Eleanor Leacock, 43–62. New York: Praeger, 1980.

Hafen, P. Jane, ed. *Dreams and Thunder: Stories, Poems, and the Sun Dance Opera by Zitkala-Ša.* Lincoln: University of Nebraska Press, 2001.

Halberstam, Jack. *Female Masculinity.* Durham: Duke University Press, 1998.

———. *The Queer Art of Failure.* Durham: Duke University Press, 2011.

Hardt, Michael. "Foreword: What Affects Are Good For." In *The Affective Turn: Theorizing the Social,* edited by Patricia Ticineto Clough with Jean Halley, ix–xiii. Durham: Duke University Press, 2007.

Hearne, Joanna. *Native Recognitions: Indigenous Cinema and the Western.* New York: SUNY Press, 2012.

Helgeland, A. "Healthy Talking Circle." *The Circle: News from an American Indian Perspective,* April 30, 1988, 17.

Hemmilä, Anita. "Ancestors of Two-Spirits: Historical Depictions of Native North American Gender-Crossing Women through Critical Discourse Analysis." *Journal of Lesbian Studies* 20, nos. 3–4 (2016): 408–26.

Hemmings, Clare. "Invoking Affect: Cultural Theory and the Ontological Turn." *Cultural Studies* 19, no. 5 (2005): 548–67.

Henry, Michele. "Canonizing Craig Womack: Finding Native Literature's Place in Indian Country." *American Indian Quarterly* 28, no. 1/2 (2004): 30–51.

Himmelstein, Drew. "Children's Publishing Reckons with Sexual Harassment in Its Ranks." *School Library Journal,* January 4, 2018. slj.com.

Hokowhitu, Brendan. "Taxonomies of Indigeneity: Indigenous, Heterosexual, Patriarchal Masculinity." In *Indigenous Men and Masculinities: Legacies, Identities, Regeneration,* edited by Robert Alexander Innes and Kim Anderson, 80–95. Winnipeg: University of Manitoba Press, 2015.

Hollrah, Patrice E. M. *The Old Lady Trill, the Victory Yell: The Power of Women in Native American Literature.* New York: Routledge, 2004.

House, Billy, and Mark Shafer. "Mom, Hopi, Hero: Piestewa an Icon." *Arizona Republic*, April 10, 2003. senaawest.org.

House, Carrie. "Blessed by the Holy People." In "Native American Men–Women, Lesbians, Two-Spirits: Contemporary and Historical Perspectives." Special issue, *Journal of Lesbian Studies* 20, nos. 3–4 (2016): 324–41.

———. *I Am*. Balancing Factors, NativeOUT. nativeout.com.

———. "Kid." In *Sovereign Erotics: A Collection of Two-Spirit Literature*, edited by Qwo-Li Driskill, Daniel Heath Justice, Deborah Miranda, and Lisa Tatonetti, 180–81. Tucson: University of Arizona Press, 2011.

———. "Navajo Warrior Women: An Ancient Tradition in a Modern World." In *Two-Spirit People: Native American Gender Identity, Sexuality, and Spirituality*, edited by Sue-Ellen Jacobs, Wesley Thomas, and Sabine Lang, 223–27. Urbana: University of Illinois Press, 1997.

———, dir. *Shi' Life*. 2013. vimeo.com.

———. "Sweet Grass." In *Sovereign Erotics: A Collection of Two-Spirit Literature*, edited by Qwo-Li Driskill, Daniel Heath Justice, Deborah Miranda, and Lisa Tatonetti, 126. Tucson: University of Arizona Press, 2011.

Hunt, Dallas. "'In Search of Our Better Selves': Totem Transfer Narratives and Indigenous Futurities." *American Indian Culture and Research Journal* 42, no. 1 (2018): 71–90.

Innes, Robert Alexander, and Kim Anderson, eds. *Indigenous Men and Masculinities: Legacies, Identities, Regeneration*. Winnipeg: University of Manitoba Press, 2015.

———. "Introduction: Who's Walking with Our Brothers?" In *Indigenous Men and Masculinities: Legacies, Identities, Regeneration*, edited by Innes and Anderson, 3–17. Winnipeg: University of Manitoba Press, 2015.

"An Interruption of the Journey." News and Announcements. *Seasons: The National Native American AIDS Prevention Center Quarterly*, Spring/Summer 1993.

Jahnke, Sara A., Christopher K. Haddock, Nattinee Jitnarin, Christopher M. Kaipust, Brittany S. Hollerbach, and Walker S. C. Poston. "The Prevalence and Health Impacts of Frequent Work Discrimination and Harassment among Women Firefighters in the US Fire Service." *BioMed Research International*, 2019. https://doi.org/10.1155/2019/6740207.

Johnson, E. Pauline. *The Moccasin Maker*. 1913. Tucson: University of Arizona Press, 1987.

Johnston, Basil H. "Young Men of Good Will: A Conversation with Basil H. Johnston." In *Masculindians: Conversations about Indigenous Manhood*, edited by Sam McKegney, 41–47. East Lansing: Michigan State University Press, 2014.

"Jolene Nenibah Yazzie." *Beat Nation: Hip Hop as Indigenous Culture.* Beat nation.org.

Jolivette, Andrew J. *Indian Blood: HIV and Colonial Trauma in San Francisco's Two-Spirit Community.* Seattle: University of Washington Press, 2016.

Jorgensen, Karen. "The Use of Doppelgangers in Sherman Alexie's *Reservation Blues.*" *Studies in American Indian Literatures* 9, no. 4 (1997): 19–25.

Justice, Daniel Heath. "Ander's Awakening." In *Sovereign Erotics: A Collection of Two-Spirit Literature,* edited by Qwo-Li Driskill, Daniel Heath Justice, Deborah Miranda, and Lisa Tatonetti, 150–77. Tucson: University of Arizona Press, 2011.

———. *Dreyd: The Way of Thorn and Thunder, Book 3.* Owen Sound, Ontario: Kegedonce Press, 2007.

———. "Fighting Shame through Love." In *Masculindians: Conversations about Indigenous Manhood,* edited by Sam McKegney, 134–45. East Lansing: Michigan State University Press, 2014.

———. *Kynship: The Way of Thorn and Thunder.* Owen Sound, Ontario: Kegedonce Press, 2005.

———. "Notes toward a Theory of Anomaly." *GLQ: A Journal of Gay and Lesbian Studies* 16, nos. 1–2 (2010): 207–42.

———. *The Way of Thorn and Thunder: The Kynship Chronicles.* Albuquerque: University of New Mexico Press, 2011.

———. *Why Indigenous Literatures Matter.* Waterloo, Ontario: Wilfrid Laurier University Press, 2018.

———. *Wyrwood: The Way of Thorn and Thunder, Book 2.* Owen Sound, Ontario: Kegedonce Press, 2006.

Keene, Adrienne. "The Native Harvey Weinsteins." Native Appropriations blog, October 10, 2017. nativeappropriations.com.

Keiser, N. H. "Strategies of Media Marketing for 'America Responds to AIDS' and Applying Lessons Learned." *Public Health Reports* 106, no. 6 (1991): 623–27.

Kellogg, Laura Cornelius. *Our Democracy and the American Indian: A Comprehensive Presentation of the Indian Situation as It Is Today.* Kansas City, Mo.: Burton, 1920.

Kidston, Martin J. "Northern Cheyenne Break Vow of Silence." *Helena Independent Record,* June 27, 2005.

Kiley, Brendan, and Nina Shapiro. "Sherman Alexie Addresses the Sexual-Misconduct Allegations That Have Led to Fallout." *Seattle Times,* February 28, 2018. seattletimes.com.

King, Frank J., III. "Honoring, Remembering, and Praying for Our Warriors: An Exclusive Interview with the Parents of Pfc. Lori Piestewa." *The Native Voice,* November 5, 2004, 1.

The Kino-nda-niimi Collective, ed. *The Winter We Danced: Voices from the Past, the Future, and the Idle No More Movement.* Winnipeg: Arp Books, 2014.

Kleinman, Arthur, and Joan Kleinman. "How Bodies Remember: Social Memory and Bodily Experience of Criticism, Resistance, and Delegitimation following China's Cultural Revolution." *New Literary History* 25, no. 3 (1994): 707–23.

Klopotek, Brian. "'I Guess Your Warrior Look Doesn't Work Every Time': Challenging Indian Masculinity in the Cinema." In *Across the Great Divide: Cultures of Manhood in the American West,* edited by Matthew Basso, Laura McCall, and Dee Garceau, 251–73. New York: Routledge, 2001.

Knoblauch, A. Abby. "Bodies of Knowledge: Definitions, Delineations, and Implications of Embodied Writing in the Academy." *Composition Studies* 40, no. 2 (2012): 50–65.

Kraker, Daniel. "The Tangled Message of a Servicewoman Killed in Combat." *High Country News* 35, no. 10 (2003): 5.

Kristof, Nicholas D., and Sheryl WuDunn. *Half the Sky: Turning Oppression into Opportunities for Women Worldwide.* New York: Knopf, 2009.

laFavor, Carole. *Along the Journey River: A Mystery.* Ithaca, N.Y.: Firebrand Books, 1996.

———. *Evil Dead Center: A Mystery.* Ithaca, N.Y.: Firebrand Books, 1997.

———. "Face to Face: Native Americans Living with AIDS." *News from Indian Country,* May 1, 1991, 25.

———. "Walking the Red Road." In *Positive Women: Voices of Women Living with AIDS,* edited by Andrea Rudd and Darien Taylor, 262–66. Toronto: Sumach Press, 1992.

Lafitau, Joseph-François. *Customs of the American Indians Compared with the Customs of the Primitive Times.* 1724. Edited and translated by William N. Fenton and Elizabeth L. Moore. Toronto: The Champlain Society, 1977.

La Flamme, Michelle M. "Unsettling the West: First Nations Films in British Columbia." In *Women Filmmakers: Refocusing,* edited by Jacqueline Levitin, Judith Plessis, and Valerie Raoul, 403–18. Vancouver: UBC Press, 2002.

Landes, Ruth. "Dakota Warfare." *Journal of Anthropological Research* 42, no. 3 (1986): 239–48.

Lang, Sabine. "Native American Men-Women, Lesbians, Two-Spirits: Contemporary and Historical Perspectives." *Journal of Lesbian Studies* 20, nos. 3–4 (2016): 299–323.

Latham, Don. "'Manly-Hearted Women': Gender Variants in Louise Erdrich's Birchbark House Books." *Children's Literature* 40, no. 1 (2012): 131–50.

Lavender, Isiah, III. "Ethnoscapes: Environment and Language in Ishmael Reed's *Mumbo Jumbo,* Colson Whitehead's *The Intuitionist,* and Samuel R. Delany's *Babel-17.*" *Science Fiction Studies* 34, no. 2 (2007): 187–200.

Lee, Lloyd L. *Diné Masculinities: Conceptualizations and Reflections.* North Charleston, S.C.: Createspace Independent Publishing, 2013.

Leiby, Mike. "*Apache 8* Debuts Sunday at Native Film Festival in New York." *White Mountain Independent,* April 1, 2011. wmicentral.com.

Lethabo-King, Tiffany. *The Black Shoals: Offshore Formations of Black and Native Studies.* Durham: Duke University Press, 2019.

"A Living Thing: Ericka Hinton on the Sacred Act of Firefighting." *Border Lore: Heritage and Culture of the U.S. Southwest and Northern New Mexico,* August 26, 2018. https://borderlore.org/a-living-thing-ericka-hinton -on-the-sacred-act-of-firefighting/.

Lorde, Audre. *Sister Outsider: Essays and Speeches.* Freedom, Calif.: Crossing Press, 1984.

"Lori Piestewa: The Story of a Brave Soldier." *American Indians in the U.S. Army.* army.mil/americanindians/piestewa.html.

Lowry, Bryan. "Republicans Use Sharice Davids' Own Words against Her as They Push 'Radical' Label." *McClatchy,* September 26, 2018. mcclatchydc.com.

MacDonald, M. L. "Two-Spirit Identity in the Twin Cities Region." In *Queer Twin Cities: Twin Cities GLBT Oral History Project,* 151–65. Minneapolis: University of Minnesota, 2010.

Machiorlatti, Jennifer A. "Indigenous Women in Film and Video: Three Generations of Storytellers and an Interview with Emerging Filmmaker Sally Kewayosh." *Post Script: Essays in Film and the Humanities* 29, no. 3 (2010): 13–26.

———. "Video as Community Ally and Dakota Sense of Place: An Interview with Mona Smith." In *Native Americans on Film: Conversations, Teaching, and Theory,* edited by M. Elise Marubbio and Eric L. Buffalohead, 322–36. Lexington: University Press of Kentucky, 2013.

MacKinnon, Catharine A., and Andrea Dworkin, eds. *In Harm's Way: The Pornography Civil Rights Hearings.* Cambridge, Mass.: Harvard University Press, 1998.

Martino-Trutor, Gina M. "'As Potent a Prince as Any Round about Her': Rethinking Weetamoo of the Pocasset and Native Female Leadership in Early America." *Journal of Women's History* 27, no. 3 (2015): 37–60.

Massumi, Brian. *Parables for the Virtual: Movement, Affect, Sensation.* Durham: Duke University Press, 2002.

————. *Politics of Affect.* Cambridge: Polity Press, 2015.

Mathes, Valerie Sherer. "Native American Women in Medicine and the Military." *Journal of the West* 21 (1982): 41–48.

Mbembe, Achille. *On the Postcolony.* San Francisco: University of California Press, 2001.

McCartney, Martha W. "Cockacoeske, Queen of Pamunkey: Diplomat and Suzeraine." In *Powhatan's Mantle: Indians in the Colonial Southeast,* edited by Peter H. Wood, Gregory A. Waselkov, and H. Thomas Hatley, 173–95. Lincoln: University of Nebraska Press, 1989.

McKegney, Sam. *Carrying the Burden of Peace: Reimagining Indigenous Masculinities through Story.* Saskatoon: University of Regina Press, 2021.

————. "Into the Full Grace of the Blood in Men: An Introduction." In *Masculindians: Conversations about Indigenous Manhood,* edited by McKegney, 1–11. East Lansing: Michigan State University Press, 2014.

————, ed. *Masculindians: Conversations about Indigenous Manhood.* East Lansing: Michigan State University Press, 2014.

————. "Pain, Pleasure, Shame. Shame: Masculine Embodiment, Kinship, and Indigenous Reterritorialization." *Canadian Literature* 216 (2013): 12–33.

McKegney, Sam, with Richard Van Camp, Warren Cariou, Gregory Scofield, and Daniel Heath Justice. "Strong Men Stories: A Roundtable on Indigenous Masculinities." In *Indigenous Men and Masculinities: Legacies, Identities, Regeneration,* edited by Robert Alexander Innes and Kim Anderson, 241–65. Winnipeg: University of Manitoba Press, 2015.

McLeod, Neal. *Cree Narrative Memory: From Treaties to Contemporary Times.* Chicago: University of Chicago Press, 2007.

————. "Tending the Fire: A Conversation with Neal McLeod." In *Masculindians: Conversations about Indigenous Manhood,* edited by Sam McKegney, 203–12. Winnipeg: University of Manitoba Press, 2014.

Medicine, Beatrice. "Changing Native American Roles in an Urban Context and Changing Native American Sex Roles in an Urban Context." In *Two-Spirit People,* edited by Sue-Ellen Jacobs, Wesley Thomas, and Sabine Lang, 145–55. Urbana–Champaign: University of Illinois Press, 1997.

————. "Indian Women: Tribal Identity as Status Quo." In *Women's Nature Rationalizations of Inequality,* edited by Marion Lowe and Ruth Hubbard, 63–73. New York: Pergamon Press, 1983.

————. "'Warrior Women': Sex Role Alternatives for Plains Indian Women." In *The Hidden Half: Studies of Plains Indian Women,* edited by Patricia Albers and Beatrice Medicine, 267–80. Washington, D.C.: University Press of America, 1983.

Miles, Tiya. *The House on Diamond Hill: A Cherokee Plantation Story*. Chapel Hill: University of North Carolina Press, 2010.

———. *Ties That Bind: The Story of an Afro-Cherokee Family in Slavery and Freedom*. Berkeley: University of California Press, 2005.

Miles, Tiya, and Sharon P. Holland, eds. *Crossing Waters, Crossing Worlds: The African Diaspora in Indian Country*. Durham: Duke University Press, 2006.

Miller, Wendy. "Native Eyes Film Festival: Film Showcases Native American Lady Firefighters." *The Explorer*, November 30, 2011. tucsonlocalmedia.com.

Million, Dian. "Felt Theory: An Indigenous Feminist Approach to Affect and History." *Wicazo Sa Review* 24, no. 2 (2009): 53–76.

———. "Intense Dreaming: Theories, Narratives, and Our Search for Home." *American Indian Quarterly* 35, no. 3 (2011): 313–33.

———. *Therapeutic Nations: Healing in an Age of Indigenous Human Rights*. Tucson: University of Arizona Press, 2013.

———. "There Is a River in Me: Theory from Life." In *Theorizing Native Studies*, edited by Audra Simpson and Andrea Smith, 31–42. Durham: Duke University Press, 2014.

Miranda, Deborah A. *Bad Indians: A Tribal Memoir*. Berkeley, Calif.: Heyday Press, 2013.

———. "Dildos, Hummingbirds, and Driving Her Crazy: Searching for American Indian Women's Love Poetry and Erotics." *Frontiers* 23, no. 2 (2002): 135–49.

———. "Extermination of the *Joyas*: Gendercide in Spanish California." *GLQ: A Journal of Lesbian and Gay Studies* 16, nos. 1–2 (2010): 253–84.

———. *The Zen of La Llorona*. Cambridge, UK: Salt Press, 2005.

Momaday, N. Scott. *House Made of Dawn*. New York: Harper & Row, 1968.

Moore, Laura. "Lozen: An Apache Woman Warrior." In *Sifters: Native American Women's Lives*, edited by Theda Purdue, 92–107. New York: Oxford University Press, 2001.

Morgensen, Scott L. "Cutting to the Roots of Colonial Masculinity." In *Indigenous Men and Masculinities: Legacies, Identities, Regeneration*, edited by Robert Alexander Innes and Kim Anderson, 38–61. Winnipeg: University of Manitoba Press, 2015.

———. *Spaces between Us: Queer Settler Colonialism and Indigenous Decolonization*. Minneapolis: University of Minnesota Press, 2011.

Mott, Frank L. "Everybody's Magazine." In *A History of American Magazines*, Volume 5: *Sketches of 21 Magazines, 1905–1930*, edited by Mildred Mott Wedel, 72–87. Cambridge, Mass.: Harvard University Press, 1968.

Mourning Dove [Christine Quintasket]. 1927. *Cogewea the Half Blood: A Depiction of the Great Montana Cattle Range*. Edited by Dexter Fisher. Lincoln: University of Nebraska Press, 1981.

Muñoz, José Estaban. *Cruising Utopia: The Then and There of Queer Futurity*. New York: New York University Press, 2009.

Murrock, Carolyn J., and Patricia A. Higgins. "The Theory of Music, Mood, and Movement to Improve Health Outcomes." *Journal of Advanced Nursing* 65, no. 10 (2009): 2249–57.

"Native Feminisms Virtual Tour with Curator Elizabeth S. Hawley." *Apexart*. apexart.org.

Navajo Nation Human Rights Commission. *The Status of Navajo Women and Gender Violence: Conversations with Diné Traditional Medicine People and a Dialogue with the People*. Navajo Nation (Arizona), July 26, 2016. nnhrc.navajo-nsn.gov.

Navajo Women Warriors: Sani Dez-Bah. DVD. Albuquerque: University of New Mexico Center for Regional Studies, 2005.

Neary, Lynn. "'It Just Felt Very Wrong': Sherman Alexie's Accusers Go on the Record." NPR, *All Things Considered*, March 5, 2018. npr.org.

Nguyen, Athena. "Patriarchy, Power, and Female Masculinity." *Journal of Homosexuality* 55, no. 4 (2008): 665–83.

Niethammer, Carolyn. *Daughters of the Earth: The Lives and Legends of American Indian Women*. New York: Simon & Schuster, 1977.

Nixon, Lindsay. "'I Wonder Where They Went': Post-Reality Multiplicities and Counter-Resurgent Narratives in Thirza Cuthand's *Lessons in Baby Dyke Theory*." *Canadian Theatre Review* 175 (2018): 47–51.

———. "Making Space in Indigenous Art for Bull Dykes and Gender Weirdos." *Canadian Art*, April 20, 2017. canadianart.ca.

———. "#MeToo and the Secrets Indigenous Women Keep." *The Walrus*, July 12, 2019. thewalrus.ca.

———. *Nîtisânak*. Montreal: Metonymy Press, 2018.

Noble, J. Bobby. *Masculinities without Men: Female Masculinity in Twentieth-Century Fictions*. Vancouver: University of British Columbia Press, 2004.

Norrell, Brenda. "Fort Apache Hotshots Battling Blazes: Apaches Like to Be 'Where the Action Is.'" *Indian Country Today*, August 9, 2000, A2.

Obomsawin, Alanis, dir. *Trick or Treaty?* Montreal: National Film Board of Canada, 2014.

Ogg, Arden. "You Always Come First with Me: Kisâkihitin and 'Order of Persons' in Cree." *Cree Literacy Network*, February 12, 2016. creeliteracy.org.

Peterson, Jodi. "Who Is an Indian?" *High Country News* 41, no. 1 (2009): 2.

Pettit, Stefanie. "Slaughter of Horses Leaves Lasting Mark." *Spokesman-Review,* October 1, 2009. spokesman.com.

Porges, Stephen W., and Andrew Rosetti. "Music, Music Therapy, and Trauma." *Music and Medicine* 10, no. 3 (2018): 117–20.

Porter, Kenneth W. *The Black Seminoles: History of a Freedom-Seeking People.* Gainesville: University of Florida Press, 2013.

Powell, Peter J. *People of the Sacred Mountain: A History of the Northern Cheyenne Chiefs and Warrior Societies, 1830–1879, with an Epilogue, 1969–1974.* New York: Harper & Row, 1981.

Powers, Marla N. *Oglala Women: Myth, Ritual, Reality.* Chicago: University of Chicago Press, 1986.

Pretty-shield, and Frank Bird Lindeman. *Pretty-shield, Medicine Woman of the Crows.* 1932. Lincoln: University of Nebraska Press, 2003.

Price-Waldman, Sam. "Video: The Apache Firefighters Who Stop America's Biggest Wildfires." *Atlantic,* November, 11, 2014. theatlantic.com.

Prosser, Jay. *Second Skins: The Body Narratives of Transsexuality.* New York: Columbia University Press, 1998.

Pruden, Harlan. "Celebrating Two Spirit: Interview with Allison Devereaux." CBC, January 12, 2015. soundcloud.com.

Pyle, Kai Minosh. "The Creation Story Is a Spaceship." *Anomaly* #27. anmly .org.

———. "Ozaawindib, the Ojibwe Trans Woman the U.S. Declared a Chief." *The Activist History Review,* June 13, 2019. activisthistory.com.

Quintero, Nita. "Coming of Age the Apache Way." *National Geographic* 157 (1980): 262–71.

Raheja, Michelle H. *Reservation Reelism: Redfacing, Visual Sovereignty, and Representations of Native Americans in Film.* Lincoln: University of Nebraska Press, 2010.

Rasch, Björn, and Jan Born. "Reactivation and Consolidation of Memory during Sleep." *Current Directions in Psychological Science* 17, no. 3 (2008): 188–92.

Reclaiming Power and Place: The Final Report of the National Inquiry into Missing and Murdered Indigenous Women and Girls. National Inquiry into Missing and Murdered Indigenous Women and Girls. Volume 1a (2019). mmiwg-ffada.ca.

Rendon, Marcie. "Mystery Activist." *The Circle: News from an American Indian Perspective,* February 28, 1998, 12.

———. "Native People with HIV Disease and Traditional Healing." *Seasons: The National Native American Aids Prevention Center Quarterly,* Autumn 1993, 36–42.

Richardson, Janine. "Magic and Memory in Sherman Alexie's *Reservation Blues.*" *Studies in American Indian Literatures* 9, no. 4 (1997): 39–51.

Rickard, Jolene. "Diversifying Sovereignty and the Reception of Indigenous Art." *Art Journal* 76, no. 2 (2017): 81–84.

Rifkin, Mark. *The Erotics of Sovereignty: Queer Native Writing in the Era of Self-Determination.* Minneapolis: University of Minnesota Press, 2012.

———. *When Did Indians Become Straight? Kinship, the History of Sexuality, and Native Sovereignty.* New York: Oxford University Press, 2011.

Roanhorse, Rebecca. "Postcards from the Apocalypse." *Uncanny: A Magazine of Science Fiction and Fantasy* 20 (2018). uncannymagazine.com.

Roberts, David. *Once They Moved Like the Wind: Cochise, Geronimo, and the Apache Wars.* New York: Touchstone, 1994.

Robinson, Dylan, and Keavy Martin. "The Body Is a Resonant Chamber." In *Arts of Engagement: Taking Aesthetic Action in and beyond the Truth and Reconciliation Commission of Canada,* edited by Robinson and Martin, 1–20. Waterloo, Ontario: Wilfrid Laurier University Press, 2016.

Robinson, Sherry. *Apache Voices: Their Stories of Survival as Told to Eve Ball.* Albuquerque: University of New Mexico Press, 2000.

———. "Lozen: Apache Woman Warrior, American Shaman." *Wild West* 10, no. 1 (1997): 52–59.

Roscoe, Will. "'That Is My Road': The Life and Times of a Crow Berdache." *Montana: The Magazine of Western History* 40, no. 1 (1990): 46–55.

Roy, Susan, and Ruth Taylor. "'We Were Real Skookum Women': The Shishálh Economy and the Logging Industry." In *Indigenous Women and Work: From Labor to Activism,* edited by Carol Williams, 104–19. Urbana: University of Illinois Press, 2012.

Ruby, Robert H., and John A. Brown. *The Spokane Indians: Children of the Sun.* Norman: University of Oklahoma Press, 1970.

Ruoff, A. Lavonne Brown. "Editor's Introduction." *Wynema: A Child of the Forest,* edited by Ruoff, xiii–xlviii. Lincoln: University of Nebraska Press, 1997.

Rustin, Nichole T. "'Mary Lou Plays Like a Man!' Gender, Genius, and Difference in Black Music Discourse." *South Atlantic Quarterly* 104, no. 3 (2005): 445–62.

Schmidt, Ethan A. "Cockacoeske, Weroansqua of the Pamunkeys, and Indian Resistance in Seventeenth-Century Virginia." *American Indian Quarterly* 36, no. 3 (2012): 288–317.

Scudeler, June. "'This Show Won't Mean Anything Unless It Comes from the People': Wâhkôtowin in Tomson Highway's *Kiss of the Fur Queen* Movie Treatment." *Canadian Literature* 230–31 (2016): 108–22.

Secretary of Health and Human Services. *Charter Presidential Advisory*

Council on HIV/AIDS. January 15, 2020. https://files.hiv.gov/s3fs -public/pacha-charter-2020.pdf.

Sedgwick, Eve Kosofsky. *Touching Feeling: Affect, Pedagogy, Performativity.* Durham: Duke University Press, 2003.

Sedgwick, Eve Kosofsky, and Adam Frank, eds. *Shame and Its Sisters: A Silvan Tomkins Reader.* Durham: Duke University Press, 1995.

Seigworth, Gregory J., and Melissa Gregg. "An Inventory of Shimmers." In *The Affect Theory Reader,* edited by Gregg and Seigworth, 1–25. Durham: Duke University Press, 2010.

Senier, Siobhan. "Rehabilitation Reservations: Native Narrations of Disability and Community." *Disability Studies Quarterly* 32, no. 4 (2012). https://dsq-sds.org/article/view/1641.

Simpson, Audra. "The State Is a Man: Theresa Spence, Loretta Saunders, and the Gender of Settler Sovereignty." *Theory & Event* 19, no. 4 (2016). muse. jhu.edu/article/633280.

Simpson, Leanne Betasamosake. *As We Have Always Done: Indigenous Freedom through Radical Resistance.* Minneapolis: University of Minnesota Press, 2017.

———. *Dancing on Our Turtle's Back: Stories of Nishnaabeg Re-creation, Resurgence, and a New Emergence.* Winnipeg: Arp, 2011.

———. "Fish Broth and Fasting." In *The Winter We Danced: Voices from the Past, the Future, and the Idle No More Movement,* edited by The Kino-nda-niimi Collective, 154–57. Winnipeg: Arp Books, 2014.

Sinclair, Niigaanwewidam James, and Sam McKegney. "After and Towards: A Dialogue on the Future of Indigenous Masculinity Studies." In *Masculindians: Conversations about Indigenous Manhood,* edited by Sam McKegney, 223–37. East Lansing: Michigan State University Press, 2014.

Skånland, Marie Strand. "Music, Health, and Well-being." *International Journal of Qualitative Studies in Health and Well-being* 8, no. 1 (2013). ncbi. nlm.gov.

Smith, Marian W. "The War Complex of the Plains Indian." *Proceedings of the American Philosophical Society* 78, no. 3 (1938): 425–64.

Smith, Mona, dir. *Her Giveaway: A Spiritual Journey with AIDS.* Videocassette. New York: Women Make Movies, 1988.

———, dir. *An Interruption in the Journey.* Videocassette. Minneapolis: Minnesota AIDS Consortium, 1991.

Snyder, Christina. "Conquered Enemies, Adopted Kin, and Owned People: The Creek Indians and Their Captives." *Journal of Southern History* 73, no. 2 (2007): 255–88.

Soliz, Andrew. "Every Step That I Take Becomes a Prayer." September 29, 2006. npr.org.

Spack, Ruth. "Dis/engagement: Zitkala-Ša's Letters to Carlos Montezuma, 1901–1902." *MELUS* 26, no. 1 (2001): 173–204.

Spinoza, Benedictine de (Baruch). *Ethic Demonstrated in Geometrical Order and Divided into Five Parts.* 1894. 2nd ed. Translated by W. Hale White. Revised translation by Amelia Hutchinson. New York: Macmillan; Forgotten Books, 2012.

Steinberg, Marc. "Myth, Folk Tale and Ritual in Anna Lee Walters's 'The Warriors.'" *Studies in Short Fiction* 34 (1997): 55–60.

Stimson, Adrian, and Terrance Houle. "Deeper than a Blood Tie: A Conversation with Adrian Stimson and Terrance Houle." In *Masculindians: Conversations about Indigenous Manhood,* edited by Sam McKegney, 142–59. East Lansing: Michigan State University Press, 2014.

Stockel, H. Henrietta. *Women of the Apache Nation: Voices of Truth.* Reno: University of Nevada Press, 1991.

Stoler, Ann Laura. *Race and the Education of Desire: Foucault's History of Sexuality and the Colonial Order of Things.* Durham: Duke University Press, 1995.

Stoller, Robert. *Splitting: A Case of Female Masculinity.* 1973. New Haven: Yale University Press, 1997.

St-Onge, Nicole. "'He Was Neither a Soldier nor a Slave: He Was under the Control of No Man': Kahnawake Mohawks in the Northwest Fur Trade, 1790–1850." *Canadian Journal of History/Annales Canadiennes d'Histoire* 51, no. 1 (2016): 1–32.

Tatonetti, Lisa. "Affect, Female Masculinity, and the Embodied Space Between: Two-Spirit Traces in Thirza Cuthand's Experimental Film." In *Sexual Rhetorics: Methods, Identities, Publics,* edited by Jonathan Alexander and Jacqueline Rhodes, 211–33. New York: Routledge, 2016.

———. "Dancing That Way, Things Began to Change: The Ghost Dance as Pantribal Metaphor in Sherman Alexie's Writing." In *Sherman Alexie: A Collection of Critical Essays,* edited by Jeff Berglund and Jan Roush, 1–24. Salt Lake City: University of Utah Press, 2010.

———. "Detecting Two-Spirit Erotics: The Fiction of Carole laFavor." *Journal of Lesbian Studies* 20, nos. 3–4 (2016): 372–87.

———. "Indigenous Fantasies and Sovereign Erotics: Outland Cherokees Write Two-Spirit Nations." In *Queer Indigenous Studies: Critical Interventions in Theory, Politics, and Literature,* edited by Qwo-Li Driskill, Chris Finley, Brian Joseph Gilley, and Scott Lauria Morgensen, 155–71. Tucson: University of Arizona Press, 2011.

———. *The Queerness of Native American Literature.* Minneapolis: University of Minnesota Press, 2014.

———. "Tales of Burning Love: Female Masculinity in Contemporary Native Literature." In *Indigenous Men and Masculinities: Legacies, Identities, Regeneration,* edited by Robert Alexander Innes and Kim Anderson, 130–44. Winnipeg: University of Manitoba Press, 2015.

Teaiwa, Teresia. "The Ancestors We Get to Choose: White Influences I Won't Deny." In *Theorizing Native Studies,* edited by Audra Simpson and Andrea Smith, 43–55. Durham: Duke University Press, 2014.

Tengan, Ty P. Kāwika. *Native Men Remade: Gender and Nation in Contemporary Hawai'i.* Durham: Duke University Press, 2008.

———. "Re-membering Panalāʻau: Masculinities, Nation, and Empire in Hawaiʻi and the Pacific." *Contemporary Pacific* 20, no. 1 (2008): 27–53.

Thomas, Rodney G. "Daughters of the Lance: Native American Woman Warriors." *Journal of the Indian Wars* 1, no. 3 (2000): 147–54.

Thomas, Wesley. "Navajo Cultural Constructions of Gender and Sexuality." In *Two-Spirit People,* edited by Sue-Ellen Jacobs, Wesley Thomas, and Sabine Lang, 156–73. Urbana–Champaign: University of Illinois Press, 1997.

Tomkins, Silvan. *Shame and Its Sisters: A Silvan Tomkins Reader.* Edited by Eve Kosofsky Sedgwick and Adam Frank. Durham: Duke University Press, 1995.

Vandervort, Bruce. *Indian Wars of Canada, Mexico and the United States, 1812–1900.* New York: Routledge, 2006.

Vernon, Irene. "AIDS: The New Smallpox among Native Americans." *Wicazo Sa Review* 14, no. 1 (1999): 235–49.

———. *Killing Us Quietly: Native Americans and HIV/AIDS.* Lincoln: University of Nebraska Press, 2001.

Vizenor, Gerald. *Manifest Manners: Narratives on Postindian Survivance.* Lincoln: University of Nebraska Press, 1999.

Vowel, Chelsea. "Attawapiskat: You Want to Be Shown the Money? Here It Is." *Huffington Post,* December 6, 2011.

Waggoner, Josephine. "Itéomagáżu: Rain in the Face." In *Witness: A Húŋkpapȟa Historian's Strong-Heart Song of the Lakotas,* edited by Emily Levine, 435–38. Lincoln: University of Nebraska Press, 2013.

Walters, Anna Lee. *The Sun Is Not Merciful.* Ithaca, N.Y.: Firebrand, 1985.

———. "The Warriors." In *Spider Woman's Granddaughters: Traditional Tales and Contemporary Writing by Native American Women,* edited by Paula Gunn Allen, 111–24. New York: Fawcett Columbine, 1989.

Warren, Mary Anne. *Gendercide: The Implications of Sex Selection.* Totowa, N.J.: Rowman & Allanheld, 1985.

Warrior, Robert. "Your Skin Is the Map: The Theoretical Challenge of Joy

Harjo's Erotic Poetry." In *Reasoning Together: The Native Critics Collective*, edited by Craig Womack, Daniel Heath Justice, and Christopher Teuton, 340–52. Norman: University of Oklahoma Press, 2008.

Wayne, Taylor, Jr. "Lori Died a True Hopi Warrior." *Indian Country Today*, April 27, 2005, A3.

Werito, Vincent. "Understanding Hózhó to Achieve Critical Consciousness: A Contemporary Diné Interpretation of the Philosophical Principles of Hózhó." In *Diné Perspectives: Revitalizing and Reclaiming Navajo Thought*, edited by Lloyd L. Lee, 25–38. Tucson: University of Arizona Press, 2014.

Whitehead, Joshua. Introduction. In *Love after the End*, edited by Whitehead, 5–10. Manitoba: Bedside Press, 2019.

———. *Jonny Appleseed*. Vancouver: Arsenal Pulp Press, 2018.

———. "Why I'm Withdrawing from My Lambda Literary Award Nomination." *The Insurgent Architects' House for Creative Writing*, March 14, 2018. tiahouse.ca.

Wilkinson, Andy. "Wild Horses: Palo Duro Canyon Tragedy." *Wild Horses*. netnebraska.org.

Williams, Raymond. *Marxism and Literature*. Oxford: Oxford University Press, 1977.

Williams, Walter L. *The Spirit and the Flesh: Sexual Diversity in American Indian Culture*. Boston: Beacon, 1986.

Wilson, Alex, with Marie Laing. "Queering Indigenous Education." In *Indigenous and Decolonizing Studies in Education: Mapping the Long View*, edited by Linda Tuhiwai Smith, Eve Tuck, and K. Wayne Yang, 131–45. New York: Routledge, 2018.

Wilson, Pamela. "Indigenous Documentary Media." In *Contemporary Documentary*, edited by Daniel Marcus and Selmin Kara, 87–104. New York: Routledge, 2015.

Womack, Craig. *Drowning in Fire*. Tucson: University of Arizona Press, 2001.

———. *Red on Red: Native American Literary Separatism*. Lincoln: University of Nebraska Press, 1999.

Wood, D. R., D. Davis, and B. J. Westover. "'America Responds to AIDS': Its Content, Development Process, and Outcome." *Public Health Reports* 106, no. 6 (1991): 616–22.

Yazzie, Jolene Nenibah. "Native Feminisms Artist Interview." *Apexart*. apexart.org.

Yazzie, Melanie K. "Narrating Ordinary Power: Hózhóójí, Violence, and Critical Diné Studies." In *Diné Perspectives: Revitalizing and Reclaiming Navajo Thought*, edited by Lloyd L. Lee, 83–99. Tucson: University of Arizona Press, 2014.

Zeig, Sande, dir. *Apache 8: Facing Fire Is Just the Beginning.* Produced by Heather Rae, Dolly Hall, Sande Zeig, and Victoria Westover. Lincoln, Neb.: Vision Maker Media, 2011.

——. "Producer's Notes." *Apache 8 Viewer Discussion Guide.* Vision Maker Media, 2017. visionmakermedia.org.

Zitkala-Ša. *American Indian Stories.* Lincoln: University of Nebraska Press, 1985.

——. "The Indian Woman." *The Suffragist* 6, no. 23 (1918): 7. *Nineteenth Century Collections Online.*

——. *Old Indian Legends: Retold by Zitkala-Ša.* 1901. Lincoln: University of Nebraska Press, 1985.

——. "A Warrior's Daughter." In *American Indian Stories,* 137–53. Lincoln: University of Nebraska Press, 1985.

INDEX

LISA TATONETTI is professor of English at Kansas State University. She is the author of *The Queerness of Native American Literature* (Minnesota, 2014) and coeditor of *Sovereign Erotics: A Collection of Two-Spirit Literature*.